Power and the Division of Labour

Power and the Division of Labour

Dietrich Rueschemeyer

Stanford University Press
Stanford, California
1986

Stanford University Press
Stanford, California
© 1986 Dietrich Rueschemeyer
Originating publisher: Polity Press, Cambridge,
   in association with Basil Blackwell, Oxford
First published in the U.S.A. by
   Stanford University Press, 1986
Printed in Great Britain
Cloth ISBN 0-8047-1324-3
Paper ISBN 0-8047-1325-1
LC 85-51798

Contents

Preface

This is an essay in social theory. It asks fundamental questions about division of labour and thus joins one of the longest-sustained dialogues in the history of social thought. In particular, it explores the role of power in shaping division of labour. Focusing on the conditions that are decisive for the advance, stagnation and decline of division of labour, as well as for the directions and forms it takes, the discussion enters into problems that are central to all social theory – issues concerning human needs and wants, their aggregation through markets and through collective action, social consensus and social conflict, power and organized domination. Yet these issues are not treated in the abstract, responding to philosophical questions of theory construction; they are considered as it becomes necessary in the course of the argument, and that deals throughout the volume with the relationship between power and division of labour.

The thesis that power must be a critical element in any explanation of division of labour is first developed analytically and set off against alternative conceptions. If is then explored and tested for its explanatory power in several different areas of investigation, all related to the rapid transformations of modern societies under the impact of capitalism – the division of authority in public and private organizations of rule, the changing division of labour in industry, professionalization and the expanding use of knowledge as well as various processes of 'dedifferentiation' that are important in themselves but also throw a light on the conditions of advancing division of labour and increasing social differentiation.

The ideas of this book have long been in gestation. Reading, more than thirty years ago, Gunnar Myrdal's *The Political Element in the Development of Economic Theory* gave me an impetus that never really lost its momentum. The knowledgeable reader will easily identify different and perhaps not easily reconcilable influences – of Durkheim and Marx, of Talcott Parsons, Gerhard Lenski and Mancur Olson, and of course of Max Weber, whose ideas (with all their complexities and unresolved problems) are perhaps closest to the positions taken here.

Many people have helped me to develop and revise the arguments of this book. Graduate students at Brown University responded to my ideas in their most tentative form. Mark Elchardus, Josef Gugler and Marty Martel commented on drafts of papers that first set out the basic argument. Jeffrey Alexander initiated a stimulating correspondence upon publication of one of these papers. He, as well as Peter Evans, Gian Poggi and Mark Shields, gave me their detailed and incisive reactions to the larger part of the manuscript, and John Stephens did the same for a draft of the whole book. Gavin Mackenzie and Tony Giddens encouraged me to complete what they had seen. I am profoundly grateful to all of them for their critical and yet supporting intellectual company. I am grateful to Wolfson College and the Centre for Socio-Legal Studies at Oxford University for their hospitality in the Spring of 1982, and I thank Debbie Grenier, Alice McManus, Judith Quattrucci and Carol Walker for typing and retyping a long succession of chapter drafts.

Books used to be dedicated to powerful patrons who enabled authors to do their work by providing them with a livelihood. Modifying this tradition slightly, I dedicate this book to those who sustained me in specialized pursuits by being closest to me as human beings, transcending even the most elementary separations of division of labour. . .
to Philipp, Eufemia, Marilyn, Julia and Simone.

Permission was granted to use ideas and text from two papers of the author: Structural differentiation, efficiency and power. *American Journal of Sociology*, 83, 1–25, University of Chicago Press, 1977; and Professional autonomy and the social control of experts. In R. Dingwall and P. Lewis (eds), *The Sociology of the Professions*. London: Macmillan, 1983, 38–58.

1

Power and Division of Labour
Introduction to the Problem

If one takes a large view of human history, the contrast between very simple societies and vastly extended complex social structures springs to the eye. Hunting and gathering bands were the only form of human society until about ten thousand years ago. They were small, ranging from less than fifty to a hundred members or in rare cases a few dozen more. They were also simple in structure, with few organizational forms aside from the household and the band as a whole and little role specialization beyond a division of labour by sex and age. It is only since neolithic times that human social life has slowly taken on the complexity which we know from recorded history and the study of contemporary society. There was no straight progression towards ever-greater complexity. Simpler forms of human social life have not been displaced completely; the 'development' of modern social forms (if that wording can be used) shows long periods of remission as well as reversals; cumulative change proceeds along more than one or two lines; and it is by no means the most complex social structures of a given time in human history that experienced the next major advances in complexity.

Division of labour and social differentiation are the social processes that underlie shifts towards more complex social structures. Yet while they are far more advanced in agrarian and especially in industrial societies than in the earliest and simplest forms of human society, *some* patterns of specialization are found in all human social life. In the simplest societies they follow to a large extent differences in age and sex; however, division of labour is rarely altogether confined to these two dimensions. More important, patterns of specialization are not biologically determined even where they coincide with divisions of age and sex. While biological differences between men and women have some relation to the division of labour by sex, the content of men's and women's work, the structure of their relations to each other and even their roles in the upbringing of children vary widely – even between societies that are otherwise quite similar in economic level, in overall social complexity or in such cultural characteristics as literacy or type of religion. The same is true of age differences in relation to division of labour and social differentiation.

Division of labour, then, is a universal characteristic of human social life. Yet even in its most elementary forms it is more than a biological phenomenon: it is a human creation and peculiarly social in character. Division of labour advanced immensely during the past ten millennia; but it took a quantum jump during the past two or three centuries. It is on the tremendous advance in division of labour brought about by the capitalist transformation of the world that our analysis will focus.

Division of labour and its more generalized conceptual extension, the 'structural differentiation of functions', though recognized much earlier in Plato's dialogues, became central concepts in the attempts of nineteenth- and twentieth-century social theorists to understand the long-term 'evolution' of human social life as well as the much more rapid and therefore more dramatic social transformations which came with industrialization. These concepts had a crucial place in the theories of social thinkers as different as Auguste Comte and Adam Smith, Karl Marx and Herbert Spencer, Emile Durkheim and Max Weber. Often concerned with a diagnosis of their time and its future, they typically paid more attention to the consequences of division of labour than to its causes; and if they sought to give an explanation of the overall increase of social complexity in human history, such evolutionary theorems tended to be closely connected to – in fact, were often an extension of – their analysis of the more recent transformation of European social life.

This book does not review the classical theories of evolution and the modern transformation, nor is it a treatise on industrialization or a theory of world history. Rather, it seeks to contribute to the causal analysis of division of labour. The thesis of this book is that the role of power is crucial for any understanding of division of labour. The interests of the powerful and the conflicts among groups with different power resources critically shape the processes that advance division of labour or block it, and that determine the forms it takes. The role of power has been greatly neglected throughout the long history of thought about division of labour. Considerations of power variously took second place to such other factors as the pursuit of productivity, the extent of the market, even the avoidance of conflict and competition. In exploring the role of power we will keep close company with the classic theorists and their arguments. While we will choose topics for analysis from a wide range of times and places, we will, as they did, pay special attention to the transformations of economy, society and politics in the course of capitalist development.

'Structural differentiation is a process whereby one social role or organization . . . differentiates into two or more roles or organizations . . . The new social units are structurally distinct from each other, but taken together are functionally equivalent to the original unit.' Smelser's definition (1959: 2; 1963: 34) is a useful point of departure. It establishes a concept that is more inclusive than the older 'division of labour'. This book will deal with both division of labour *and* structural differentiation. Division of labour is often understood as limited to the economic sphere; but since it is only in modern social patterns that the economic sphere is recognizably separate from others and that 'labour' is sharply set off from consumption, political activity, social and religious ritual or the upbringing of children, I will often use the term in a meaning not confined to economic activities. The concept of structural differentiation also deals with more complex structural units than elementary work roles – with organizations and, on occasion, with even broader and less tangible phenomena such as institutions, values and cultural complexes. It is useful to have such a broader concept, which goes back to Herbert Spencer; but we must be ready to reintroduce finer distinctions wherever the analysis requires it. The diverse components included in the broader concept may respond in opposite ways to similar causal constellations. For instance, the growth of the modern state demonstrates that a specialization of work roles may go hand in hand with an agglomeration of functions at the level of organizations and institutional complexes.

If division of labour, then, technically refers to specialization of work roles where they are socially distinguished, while structural differentiation of functions is more inclusive – extending beyond 'work' and encompassing organizations and broader social institutions as well as roles – there will be occasions when I use division of labour and structural differentiation interchangeably, trusting that the context will make the usage sufficiently clear and unambiguous.

DIVISION OF LABOUR AND MARKET EXCHANGE

Specialization requires exchange. The producers of a specialized product must be able to receive in return what they need to satisfy their wants and desires. In the simplest forms of division of labour this exchange may be quite limited. It may take place within the household or, going beyond that, it may be barter: a direct exchange of goods and services one for the other. Higher degrees of division of labour require much more flexible forms of exchange, of which the prototypical instrument is money. What plainly is needed to make more complex forms of exchange possible is a *medium of exchange* which is widely acceptable, so that it becomes unnecessary to match specific buyers and sellers, each interested in what the other has to offer. Money is such a medium of exchange. Even in its rudimentary forms – precious objects like shells of ornamental and ritual significance, silver, gold or useful animals – money serves to open up vast new possibilities of exchange. At the same time, money becomes a means to express in a single measure the value of very different things or activities, and it constitutes a highly generalized way of storing economic assets.

Monetary market exchange, then, is a social 'invention' which significantly broadens the possibilities for division of labour. It does not only do that, however. Where it is used widely it radically transforms social and economic relations. These changes became a major preoccupation of nineteenth-century social theorists. In his disturbing essays 'On the Jewish Question', the young Marx speaks in romantic blasphemy of the new 'monotheism' in which money becomes the measure of all things: 'Money abases all the gods of mankind and changes them into commodities. Money is the universal and self-sufficient *value* of all things. It has, therefore, deprived the whole world, both the human world and nature, of their own proper value' (1843/1964: 37).

Exchanging in contractual market transactions things and services for money enables buyer and seller to disregard broader ties and obligations and to reduce their relationship to the 'cash nexus'. The economic exchange relationship becomes specialized, structurally differentiated from other mutual concerns, claims and duties of the parties. This separation of economic exchange from other social relations makes possible and encourages conscious and precise calculation of advantage and disadvantage'. It thus makes possible and encourages that increase in economic rationality which is constitutive of capitalism and modern economic forms in general.

There are further ramifications of these changes, and their moral ambiguities and contradictions have provided the cloth from which the grand ideologies of the nineteenth century tailored their garb. Loss of community was as much a major theme as freedom from the confinements of tradition, poverty and social oppression. Emancipation of the individual personality stood in tension with the use of others as a mere means for one's goals. Theories glorified but also sought to show the domestication of greed and egotism.

All major theories contained some of these tensions *within* them, often more so than their reputation today indicates. Yet there were important contrasts in analysis *and* evaluation between the conservative and the radical critics of the emerging capitalist order and between these critics and those who saw the same developments as the incarnation of reason – however imperfect and open to improvement. At the end of the nineteenth century we find fascinating syntheses of these divergent strands of social thought in the work of theorists such as Emile Durkheim and Max Weber.

THE ROLE OF POWER

Why should power be a major factor in processes of division of labour and social differentiation? There are several strong reasons. The first takes off from the same insight as the market argument. Any kind of specialization requires a steady demand for the specialized product – a demand backed up by appropriate resources. Adam Smith expressed this in his famous theorem 'that the division of labour is limited by the extent of the market' (1776/1937: 17). Yet in simpler societies it is not market exchange that accumulates the necessary capital and concentrates demand sufficiently, but rather political power. Gerhard Lenski (1966: 151–2) describes the growth of political power and its consequences in the 'advanced horticultural

societies' of sub-Saharan Africa and of Central America before the
Spanish conquest, contrasting them with their technically and
economically less advanced cousins:

> Clearly the most important single factor in the growth of occupa-
> tional specialization has been the growth of state power. All the larger
> and more powerful kingdoms required complex governmental
> systems with numerous officials and soldiers...Each of these
> officials, especially those at the higher levels, was surrounded by
> his court, which included a great variety of specialists – magicians
> of various types, priests, tax collectors, advisers, military men,
> common soldiers, wives and concubines usually by the hundreds,
> eunuchs to guard them, entertainers of many kinds, and artisans
> of unusual skill and talent. In some societies full-time craftsmen were
> found only at the king's court and the various tools, weapons, and
> other things the common people needed were made either by the
> people themselves or by part-time specialists...Contrasted with
> politically advanced groups such as the Incas, Aztecs, Dahomeans,
> and Ganda are other groups such as the Plateau Tonga of Northern
> Rhodesia...Among these people specialization was, till recently,
> limited to part-time work in a few fields of activity.

In evolutionary terms there is good support for the hypothesis that
the emergence of organized domination was a necessary condition
for developments that go beyond the most elementary division of
labour built on differences of age and sex, on the organization of
family and kinship, and on the occasional recognition of differences
in individual aptitude in the form of part-time specialization. In
the emergence of more complex social structures, then, power plays
a role similar to that of monetary market exchange. It mobilizes
economic resources and makes them available for more specialized
pursuits. If monetary market exchange attracted the lion's share
of analytic attention in theories about the emergence of the modern
world and the development of capitalism, concentration of power
was a more important factor at least in earlier advances of the
division of labour.

It is worth noting that on this point Talcott Parsons (1964: 342),
in his essay on 'evolutionary universals', comes to a very similar
conclusion:

> Two evolutionary universals are closely interrelated in the process
> of 'breaking out' of what may be called the 'primitive' stage of social

evolution. These are the development of a well-marked system of stratification, and that of a system of explicit cultural legitimation of differentiated functions, preeminently the political function.

These two developments are crucial because they free economic resources as well as the political will of the dominant groups from the restraints and rigidities of the web of kinship.

With the latter argument we step beyond the thesis that organized domination furthers division of labour because it is one mode of concentrating economic resources. Once organized domination is to some extent removed and freed from the wishes of the governed, it can *impose* division of labour. It can allocate people to disagreeable work – to dirty work, in the literal and in the figurative sense, or to work subject to tough discipline – and it can make people work on disadvantageous terms. Division of labour can now be arranged more single-mindedly and with a new ruthlessness, because those who are the driving force and the main beneficiaries of a new organization of work are not any longer identical to those whose work is given a new shape. The emergence of strong concentrations of political power thus opened distinctly new possibilities for division of labour and social differentiation. At the same time this disjunction between actual work in production and reaping the benefits of innovation may in many areas lead to stagnation because it withholds rewards and incentives from those who best understand production problems.

The most important patterns of division of labour in antiquity and in the Middle Ages (as indeed in most of recorded history) have been associated with extreme distances between ruler and ruled – with the roles played by slaves and serfs and with the relations between conquerors and subject populations and, in subsequent developments, between dominant and subordinate ethnic groups. Ludwik Gumplowicz, the Jewish sociologist who grew up and first worked in Poland and then taught in Austria, reflects in his work the multi-ethnic composition and the often raw power relations of nineteenth-century Eastern and Central Europe. Indeed he saw division of labour primarily as created and maintained by coercion and only secondarily as a spontaneous differentiation process (Gumplowicz, 1885/1963).

It is against this background of previous history that we have to understand why the hopes of Western intellectuals from Saint-Simon

and the Scottish moralists to John Stuart Mill and Herbert Spencer
were invested in an emerging new form of society which would be
shaped by trade and industry rather than by power and war.
Spencer (1876–97/1975: I, 544–63) contrasted two social types with
each other, the militant and the industrial. In the first, division
of labour and cooperation are based on coercion; in the second,
they result from free choice, and the whole society (including the
necessary regulating apparatus) is 'characterized throughout by that
same individual freedom which every commercial transaction
implies' (Spencer, 1876/97/1975: I, 557).

The very conditions, however, that made the new order of capitalism possible were the result of major shifts in power and extended
conflicts. The institution of serfdom did not crumble because of
a thrust towards progress inherent in history; yet free labour is
essential to the capitalist organization of production. Population
decline in the fourteenth century made labour more scarce and
threatened the power of lords over serfs. Other power resources,
however, were equally important. Peasants gained their freedom
in Western Europe but not without struggle; and in Eastern Europe
– in particular Pomerania, Brandenburg, East Prussia and Poland –
decline in population from the late fourteenth century was accompanied by an ultimately successful movement toward imposing
extra-economic controls, that is serfdom, over what had been, until
then, one of Europe's freest peasantries (Brenner, 1976: 41).
Freedom of labour from personal and hereditary subservience, then,
was even under favourable conditions the outcome of prolonged
struggle. Or as Brenner (1976: 44) puts it: 'Serfdom was a relationship of power which could be reversed, as it were, only on its own
terms, through a change in the balance of class forces.'

Are we then to conclude that power is indeed very important for
those changes in the division of labour that preceded and led up to
the emergence of industrial society, but that in the latter it is not
power and coercion but the peaceful search for individual gain and
the invisible hand of the market that steer and promote the processes
of division of labour and structural differentiation? The utilitarian
tradition of the enlightenment has often been read this way. Such
a reading underlies in fact much of recent 'modernization theory'
– an ironic turn of intellectul events considering that this theory
had its roots in a conception of sociology as the corrective counter-
tradition to individualist utilitarian social theory (Parsons, 1937).

It is a major contention of this book that power was indeed a crucial element among the causal conditions that shaped division of labour and social differentiation even in the civil society of early competitive capitalism. If the bourgeois vision of peaceful commerce and industry, fair deals and voluntary cooperation among equals, the rule of law and decentralized self-government acquired a social reality – which undoubtedly it did, as many accounts of its civilizing influence in the late eighteenth and early nineteenth century testify – this change took place primarily among the new urban middle classes, transforming the old elite in the process and affecting many other groups as well. It certainly did *not* transform in the same way relations between dominant and subordinate classes, new or old. Nor did it reach universalistically beyond all boundaries of confined moral communities, beyond the boundaries that separate nation from nation or beyond the boundaries that set ethnic groups and races apart from and against each other, and that establish the right of imperial powers to rule over colonial populations.

That power remained a major element in the division of labour under capitalist conditions was recognized partially even in the writings of the liberal–utilitarian tradition, though it was most forcefully argued by Karl Marx. There is, first, the structure of contract and property which is protected by legal coercion. Though formally available to all in equal measure, this seemingly neutral legal structure is in social reality anything but neutral. Adam Smith's account (1776/1937: 670) was not yet as much tainted by ideological piety as we have come to take for granted.

> Wherever there is great property, there is great inequality. For one rich man, there must be at least five hundred poor, and the affluence of the few supposes the indigence of the many. The affluence of the rich excites the indignation of the poor, who are often both driven by want, and prompted by envy, to invade his possessions. It is only under the shelter of the civil magistrate that the owner of that valuable property, which is acquired by the labour of many years, or perhaps of many successive generations, can sleep a single night in security. He is at all times surrounded by unknown enemies, whom, though he never provoked, he can never appease, and from whose injustice he can be protected only by the powerful arm of the civil magistrate continually held up to chastise it. The acquisition of valuable and extensive property, therefore, necessarily requires the establishment of civil government. Where there is no property,

or at least none that exceeds the value of two or three days labour,
civil government is not so necessary.

Protection of property gained crucial importance for division of
labour as accumulated capital acquired an even greater role in the
organization of production. This development alone, in Smith's
view, shifts the balance of advantage favouring the property owners
against the workers.[1]

The unequal results of equal protection of property are paralleled
and complemented by legal guarantees for contracts and their social
effects. The more contract law *assumes* equality between parties and
grants them freedom as to the terms of contract, the more it per-
petuates and reinforces actual inequalities. Adam Smith, no less
than Karl Marx, was well aware that masters and legally free
workers contract with each other under conditions in which the
masters have the greater bargaining power. Though both need each
other, the workers' need is more immediate while the masters can
hold out. Fewer in number and favoured by the law, as well as
by their place in the community, the masters can also far more
easily form combinations and come to agreements which eliminate
the pressure of competition among them. While very difficult among
workers, such combinations of masters are 'the usual, and one may
say, the natural state of things' (Smith, 1776/1937: 66).

Marx, however, drew from very similar insights a conclusion
that Smith did not draw: there is a fundamental difference between
division of labour among autonomous parties and a division of
labour that takes place under the authority, and in the interest,
of one dominant party, between 'division of labour in society' and
'division of labour in manufacture'. It was, of course, the latter which
became ever more important as capitalism developed.

> Division of labor within the workshop implies the undisputed
> authority of the capitalist over men, that are but parts of a
> mechanism that belongs to him. The division of labor within the
> society brings into contact independent commodity-producers, who
> acknowledge no other authority but that of competition, of the
> coercion exerted by the pressure of their mutual interests.

This distinction highlights the role of power in capitalist division
of labour. For the same reason, Marx argues, it is neglected and
obscured by liberal analysts:

The same bourgeois mind which praises division of labour in the workshop, life-long annexation of the labourer to a partial operation, and his complete subjection to capital, as being an organization of labour that increases its productiveness – that same bourgeois mind denounces with equal vigour every conscious attempt to socially control and regulate the process of production as an inroad upon such sacred things as the rights of property, freedom and unrestricted play for the bent of the individual capitalist. It is very characteristic that the enthusiastic apologists of the factory system have nothing more damning to urge against a general organization of the labour of society, than that it would turn all society into one immense factory.

The asymmetry of power embodied in the coexistence of different forms of division of labour in society and in the workshop is an essential feature of capitalism: '. . . anarchy in the social division of labour and despotism in that of the workshop are mutual conditions the one of the other' (Marx, 1867/1959: 356 for all three quotes). Marx's distinction represents a theoretical breakthrough of the first order in the study of division of labour, one that was lost again in later analytic approaches – most notably in Durkheim's theory of division of labour (Durkheim, 1893/1964; cf. Rueschemeyer, 1982) and, at least as far as emphasis and theoretical focus are concerned, in later functionalist theories of modernization and development. The distinction is a cornerstone of my own analysis of the role of power in advancing and shaping the division of labour.

CONCEPTUAL ISSUES

What do we mean by 'power'? To answer with Max Weber's definition – 'the probability that one actor within a social relationship will be in a position to carry out his will despite resistance, regardless of the basis on which this probability rests' (Weber, 1922/68: I, 53) – clears the ground, but leaves many difficult conceptual questions open. Though this is not the place to discuss these issues in any detail, they cannot be brushed aside either. From a theoretical point of view there are two conceptual problems that above all need attention. The first concerns the usefulness of the concept of power in this broad form. The concept is, as Weber put it, 'sociologically amorphous', since power can be based on an infinite variety of conditions.

The second conceptual difficulty emerged from more recent discussions about the very substance of power. If one party dominates the premises of the common social life so much that its potential oppponents cannot even make the injury to their interests a social issue, the dominant group certainly has vast power. It controls the 'agenda' of what is up for public and possibly contested decision. Yet this power is hard to identify if one looks for a contest of wills as Weber's definition suggests. Ultimately, the resolution of this issue involves assumptions about the different parties' *objective* interests and about the relations of opposition, overlap and harmony among these interests (Schattschneider, 1960; Bachrach and Baratz, 1970; and Lukes, 1974).

Neither problem is in principle beyond solution, although the second requires an interlinking of philosophical and sociological analysis which goes against the grain of many contemporary social scientists, as their avoidance or redefinition of concepts such as exploitation and alienation shows.[2] Weber's response to the first issue was to focus his analysis on the more distinctive concept of domination, the likelihood of finding obedience to one's commands in a social relationship. We can accept this emphasis to some extent, but other forms of power *are* important and thus crucial for our inquiry. Even in this introductory discussion we have encountered relevant differences in power based on the availability of economic resources, on the ease of collective organization with others in a similar situation and on legally backed supports, obstacles and neutral spaces for different interests. Later, some of these issues will have to be taken up in more detail so as to avoid contradiction and ambiguity.

Though this book focuses on the role of power in the causation of division of labour and the differentiation of social structure, it must be made clear from the outset that power, even in its greatest concentration, is never identical with social causation. Power is not the ultimate mover of history, and power conglomerations are often quite limited in their capacity to transform social reality. Other, less dramatically visible factors, such as population change, environmental conditions, cultural presuppositions, and technological developments, are not denied their part in explaining the division of labour if we emphasize the role of power.

Power and organized domination rest, furthermore, on a wide range of causal conditions. In a broader perspective both may well be considered merely as proximate causes which mediate the impact of other factors. Proximate causes are, however, crucially important if we want to come to an understanding of historical processes of differentiation and division of labour. Much past theory has focused on broad evolutionary trends. Durkheim (1893/1964: 233) put his explanatory programme thus:

> If one takes away the various forms the division of labor assumes according to conditions of time and place, there remains the fact that it advances regularly in history. This fact certainly depends upon equally constant causes which we are going to seek.

Had Durkheim simply meant to say that he was looking for regularities which transcend the concreteness of each and any particular historical instance, we could certainly follow him. But if we read him (more accurately I think) as proposing to look directly at broad evolutionary patterns, both in order to identify what must be explained and to pin down factors useful in explanation, his programme is more problematic. Broad evolutionary trends towards greater structural complexity are indeed of interest, especially if they are identified with greater care than is typical in simplistic theories of social evolution – but their explanation ultimately must be founded on a theoretical understanding of the specific processual mechanisms that underlie division of labour and structural differentiation. An important premise of our analytic strategy is that such a process analysis will profit as much from analysing blockages to division of labour and processes of dedifferentiation as from studying positive instances. Ultimately, the part played by power in these processes may only be that of a proximate cause, but understanding this role is crucial for a process analysis of division of labour.

THE PLAN OF THE BOOK

In the following chapter we review ideas and claims about the consequences of increasing division of labour and its ramifications in the wider social structure. This establishes the pivotal role of division of labour in shaping whole social formations and the quality of life in them. At the same time it prepares the critique of prevailing explanations of structural differentiation in the third chapter –

functionalist explanations which take off from the productivity gains attributed to specialization. The next four chapters explore the role of power in advancing, blocking and shaping processes of division of labour in different contexts. Following Marx's emphasis on the particular character of 'division of labour in manufacture', chapters 4 and 5 deal with division of labour within a system of domination, while chapter 6 discusses 'professionalization' – the development of new institutional forms for the increases in the use of knowledge that have marked modern societies. In chapter 7 we turn to dedifferentiation and the fusion of functions in certain social structures, and seek to draw lessons for understanding the processes of differentiation from negative instances. The final chapter reviews the argument and places these process analyses of division of labour and differentiation into a broader context. This chapter also returns to certain persistent issues encountered in the course of the argument, among them the relations between empirical–theoretical analysis and evaluative assessment, as well as the problems of social choice and historical inevitability.

2

The Results of Increasing Division of Labour

Social theorists since the eighteenth century have focused their attention more on the consequences of division of labour than on its causes. The radical transformation of social and economic life that we know as the rise of capitalism and the industrial revolution posed large intellectual questions. Which changes were of historical importance? How did they relate to each other? Which developments were irreversible and lasting, which open to political intervention? How were they to be evaluated? Did they represent progress or destruction? The division of labour played a central role in these discussions from the beginning, and the interest in moral diagnosis concentrated attention on its results rather than its causes.

Although this book seeks to contribute to a causal analysis of division of labour and social differentiation, an overview of ideas and claims about their consequences is useful because some tenets about the results of specialization are at the heart of certain explanations of division of labour. In addition, looking at the effects of increasing division of labour gives us a sense of its significance – its determining influence on those large social structures which are beyond everyday experience and yet constitute its institutional framework, as well as its immediate impact on the quality of life of people variously located in these wider social formations.

The earliest theme was the link between specialization and productivity. Adam Smith's famous analysis in the opening chapters of his *An Inquiry into the Nature and Causes of the Wealth of Nations* (1776) already built on a tradition of modern economic thought. As capitalist industrialization gathered momentum, and as its impact on social life and institutions became more evident, other themes were added. First came questions about the human quality of factory work. Closely related were the relations between masters and workers and the issue of exploitation. This led to inquiries about how division of labour shapes social inequality and the class structure of a society. Finally, the fundamental tensions and conflicts, as well as the nature of social cohesion – in short the basic character of society – came to be viewed as rooted in the division of labour. Taking my cue from this sequence of problem formulations, I shall first discuss productivity effects of division of labour, then its impact on the human quality of work and those broader ramifications to which Marx gave the name of 'alienation', and finally social inequality and the nature of social order as shaped by division of labour.

The far-reaching effects of changes in the division of labour are not peculiar to industrial societies; after all, even Plato's dialogues contained ideas about specialization that became a springboard for modern analyses. Yet the issues came to a head and assumed a radically new salience with the rise of capitalism and industrialization; so our discussion will be primarily concerned with modern developments and problems.

PRODUCTIVITY

The relation between specialization and efficiency is not a simple matter, even though it has often been treated as self-evident ever since the classical economists advanced their arguments. In fact, Adam Smith's list of reasons is both rather incomplete and misleading in its emphasis. Taking off from the example of pin-making, he attributed the greater productivity of specialized labour to three circumstances: improved dexterity; saving of time (which is commonly lost in passing from one sort of work to another); and application of machinery invented by workmen (Smith, 1776/1937: 7–10). Of these, the third argument seems the weakest. Smith himself concedes in the immediately following section: 'All the improvements in machinery, however, have by no means been the invention of those who had occasion to use the machines. Many improvements have been made by the ingenuity of the makers of the machines when to make them became the business of a peculiar trade (Smith, 1776/1937: 10). And in a later passage – one of great interest for other effects of division of labour – he turns the original proposition virtually into its opposite: 'The man whose whole life is spent in performing a few simple operations. . .has no occasion to exert his understanding, or to exercise his invention in finding out expedients for removing difficulties which never occur' (Smith, 1776/1937: 734).

We can let Smith's first two arguments stand, though the increase in competence is easily overrated if the tasks in questions are already composed of simple operations. Yet these theorems are far from giving a full account of the relation between division of labour and efficiency.[1]

A more comprehensive account can be stated in several propositions. These begin with two fundamental separations, which were highlighted in the work of such nineteenth-century social theorists as Marx, Spencer, Bucher, Durkheim and Weber, and continue with specifications that emerge in contemporary sociological analyses.

1 Separating instrumental tasks and interests – those where getting things done has priority – from other human concerns makes it possible to arrange matters more single-mindedly for a rational pursuit of chosen ends. This is of fundamental importance because social roles, relationships and organizations best suited for 'getting things done' are by no means optimal for other abiding human concerns which are, at least in the long run, equally urgent – for instance, enjoying the fruits of one's labour, getting along with each other, bringing up children and coming to terms with fundamental problems of meaning and motivation. In turn, social arrangements most consonant with these other concerns tend to detract from rationally going about instrumental goals and activities, if for no other reason than that they allow for and encourage many different preoccupations at once.[2] The separation of occupational work from family and household is the most obvious, but by no means the only, example of this differentiation. In reality, the separation of instrumental from other concerns can never be pure and radical. Even the most rational and task-oriented work groups have to deal with issues of group cohesion and of getting along with each other, and they have to find ways of coexisting with other social forms in which their

members can fulfill other 'expressive' needs and wants. Saying that work organizations 'have to deal with such issues' does not of course mean that these problems are solved; they often are not, as we know from common experience as well as from poignant studies in contemporary sociology.

2   The second major separation of similar significance is the division of dominant from subordinate roles. Taken for granted and left unanalysed by Smith, it was stressed by Marx in his distinction between division of labour in manufacture and division of labour in society (see chapter 1), and it clearly will occupy us at length later. Specialized authority roles commanding sufficient resources make it possible to impose further specialization, to bring the specialized parts together into a coherent operation, to plan organizational change and to exert continuous social control at work.

3   Delimiting tasks narrowly and clearly facilitates evaluation of performance. This, in turn, allows rewards as well as deprivation to be tied more closely to differences in work performance. It also helps in assessing who *will* do different kinds of work well in the future and thus aids in more rational hiring and assignment of work.

4   Separating simple from complex tasks permits economies in training and recruitment. 'The modern system,' asserts William Goode (1967: 17), 'is more productive because its social structures *utilize the inept more efficiently* rather than because it gives greater opportunities to the more able.'

5   Dividing instrumental tasks further and further – whether in complex organizations or in self-employed work – makes concentration on a few activities possible, an advantage that seems greater (as argued above) in the more demanding kinds of work.

6   Specialization of work – and even minute specialization – also diminishes the time used for switching from one activity to another, as Smith already pointed out.

7   Dividing tasks to their most elementary level also opens the opportunity to replace human labour with the operation of machines, although this is not the only way in which technological innovation is related to division of labour. Perhaps the most important link is a quite general one – the principle of rationalization of instrumental activities which is embodied in, and facilitated by, various features of increasing division of labour.

However great the contribution of technical innovation to the growth of productivity is estimated to be, much of it is contingent on prior advances in division of labour and is shaped by the forms the division of labour has taken.

8   Finally, once the pattern of division of labour is fully established, it becomes possible to conceive of work roles and organizational units as building blocks of an intentional social architecture – components which can be arranged and rearranged as rational adaptation to changing circumstances, technological innovations and new goals requires. The principle of rationalization also becomes powerfully operative in the overall social organization of production. Needless to argue (though perhaps useful to note) this tendency also can never be realized in pure and radical form, though its exact limits are not easily pinpointed.

While these propositions are plausible, they are not at all the established last word on the relation between division of labour and efficiency. 'Parkinson's law', according to which bureaucratic organizations subdivide and multiply without reason, shows by caricature the folly of believing that every form of specialization contributes to productivity. The popular images of red tape and impractical planning by bureaucracies equally insist that these paragons of specialization may not always be models of rationality.

At this juncture we may point to the discipline of the market, to the effects of competition and the selection mechanisms of profit, loss and bankruptcy. While, indeed, not all forms of specialization increase productivity under given conditions, those that do will be rewarded with profits, and those that make for waste will be punished with losses. Over a long period of time, this argument runs, competitive pressures result in the survival and spread of the most productive forms of division of labour and in the extinction of wasteful ones.

This is a powerful argument. It adds to the potential productivity advantages discussed so far a screening and selection device in the form of competitive market pressures.[3] However, the argument can easily be overextended. The steering it points to is a quite loose one wherever, and to the extent that, competition is less than perfect or where ideas depicting the current mode of production as the best are so firmly entrenched that they become a given for all competitors. The latter qualification is especially consequential if the organizational changes that might lead to greater productivity are both costly and uncertain in outcome: the risks inherent in high costs and uncertainty would powerfully add to the stability of the status quo. All these points apply with even greater force to specialized work which is not exposed in any direct and literal sense to market pressures – work in government organizations, for example, or in universities – although competitive pressures and selective survival play a not insignificant role here as well.

Wherever the competitive situation deviates substantially from the model of perfect competition, the participants have a monopolistic leeway for less than maximally efficient arrangements. While those who reap the advantages of efficient work should still have an interest in pushing for the most productive organization of work, they may also have other interests, which counterbalance the drive towards efficiency. Beyond that we must not take for granted that even managers single-mindedly concerned with productivity are certain what to aim for and know how best to achieve their goals. This brings us back to our sketch of propositions about the efficiency advantages of increased specialization.[4]

For each of the features of division of labour discussed above as contributing to greater efficiency, we can ask at least three questions the answers to which are far from clear. First, under what conditions and for what specific purposes does a given feature of division of labour yield efficiency advantages? Even if, for instance, the proposition that 'subordination and discipline are indispensable in economic enterprises' were defensible in its general sweep, there are surely differences between creative and routine tasks, agreeable and repugnant kinds of work, or antagonism and harmony in the interests of workers and executives that make the imposition of authority more or less important for purposes of maintaining and improving productivity.

The second question to be asked of each factor is: how much of a difference does it make? This is more than a matter of tidying up the picture. If one wanted to bring values to bear on the social organization of work which are at odds with the pursuit of productivity – if one wanted to make work less impersonal for instance, render it less monotonous and boring or subject workers to fewer commands and less supervision – it would be of great interest to know whether the reduction in productivity (if any) is minor or quite substantial.

The third question, finally, asks whether particular features of division of labour engender side-effects that significantly diminish efficiency and thus detract from the overall productivity advantage. What counts, of course, is the net outcome in productivity, and that is an open question if there are counteracting side-effects of specialization.

Virtually all aspects of division of labour have such side-effects. Any specialization creates some need for coordination, which is not without cost. Much modern division of labour under-utilizes workers' intelligence and has to make up for that with an expansion of the white-collar work force. The disjunction of instrumental and expressive activities, the reduction of security by a system of reward by merit, as well as the more or less radical simplification of tasks, are among the factors that have often been held responsible for problems of motivation and morale. Compensating measures of supervision and control are not only costly in themselves, but may provoke worker resistance, engender apathy and lead to a further decline of workers' goodwill and initiative.

The critical issue, then, concerns whether and under what circumstances these other effects of increasing division of labour outweigh its positive contributions to productivity. The answer is by no means a forgone conclusion. Nor can we take for granted that rational planning, with or without the spur of market competition, will find the optimal balance. Recent experiments with 'humanizing' work in Europe and America seek to correct inefficiencies created by 'scientific management' since the late nineteenth century.

While there is little doubt about the fundamental insight of Karl Marx that the social engine of capitalism pushed for and made possible a vast expansion of production, and that specialization – in particular, specialization under the control of owners and managers interested in profit – is a most important part of this capitalist organization of production, the details of how and under what conditions division of labour increases productivity are largely unknown. These are not just 'empirical questions', as a common phrase has it, but unresolved theoretical problems.

ALIENATION

Productivity gains are not the only significant outcome of increases in the division of labour. In particular the advances of specialization

associated with the emergence of capitalism and its further development have from the beginning been evaluated in terms of other
criteria which pertain to the human quality of work and the effects
of work on the quality of human life. As Smith (1776/1937: 734–5)
observed:

> In the progress of the division of labour, the employment of the far
> greater part of those who live by labour, that is, of the great body
> of the people, comes to be confined to a very few simple operations;
> frequently to one or two. But the understandings of the greater part
> of men are necessarily formed by their ordinary employment. The
> man whose whole life is spent in performing a few simple opera-
> tions, of which the effects too are, perhaps, always the same, has
> no occasion to exert his understanding... He naturally loses,
> therefore, the habit of such exertion and becomes as stupid as it is
> possible for a human creature to become. The torpor of his mind
> renders him not only incapable of relishing or bearing part in any
> rational conversation, but of conceiving any generous, noble, or
> tender sentiment, and consequently of forming any just judgment
> concerning many even of the ordinary duties of private life. Of the
> great and extensive interests of his country he is altogether incapable
> of judging... His dexterity at his own particular trade seems, in this
> manner, to be acquired at the expense of his intellectual, social, and
> martial virtues. But in every improved and civilized society this is
> the state into which the labouring poor, that is, the great body of
> the people, must necessarily fall, unless government takes some pains
> to prevent it.

True, Adam Smith makes these astounding remarks in a very
circumscribed context – in answer to the question whether the state
should give attention to the education of the people; and he implies,
though one can hardly say that he argues convincingly, that an
elementary education of the common people can counteract these
effects of division of labour. Yet whatever the remedy, he leaves
no doubt that these results of division of labour affect the very
essence of human life. To begin with an issue at first glance obscure
to us – the extinction of a 'martial spirit' – Smith argues that this
is not merely relevant for the defence of country:

> A coward, a man incapable either of defending or of revenging
> himself, evidently wants one of the most essential parts of a character
> of a man. He is as much mutilated and deformed in his mind as

another is in his body, who is either deprived of some of its most essential members or has lost the use of them. He is evidently the more wretched and miserable of the two; because happiness and misery...must necessarily depend more upon the healthful or unhealthful, the mutilated or entire state of the mind, than upon that of the body (Smith, 1776/1937: 739).

From here the argument is extended to points more familiar to the twentieth-century ear:

The same may be said of the gross ignorance and stupidity which, in a civilized society, seem so frequently to benumb the under- standings of all the inferior ranks of people. A man without the proper use of the intellectual faculties of a man, is, if possible, more contemptible than even a coward and seems to be mutilated and deformed in a still more essential part of the character of human nature (Smith, 1776/1937: 739–40).

The critical theme sounded in these passages from the back pages of the *Wealth of Nations* was not to be muted for the two centuries that separate us from the time of Smith and the beginnings of capitalism. Two generations later, Alexis de Tocqueville advanced an analysis that begins by acknowledging the productivity gains of specializa- tion and production on a large scale, but then focuses on the human and social consequences of division of labour. His main interest is in the impact which the division of labour in manufacture has on the class structure of society, but he also has some striking things to say about its effects on the quality of work and life outside of work.

When a workman is unceasingly and exclusively engaged in the fabrication of one thing, he ultimately does his work with singular dexterity; but at the same time, he loses the general faculty of applying his mind to the direction of work...it may be said of him, that in proportion as the workman improves the man is degraded. What can be expected of a man who has spent twenty years of his life in making heads for pins? , ,When a workman has spent a considerable portion of his existence in this manner, his thoughts are for ever set upon the object of his daily toil;...in a word, he no longer belongs to himself, but to the calling he has chosen. In pro- portion as the principle of the division of labor is more extensively applied, the workman becomes more weak, more narrow-minded and more dependent (de Tocqueville, 1835–40/1966: 168–9).

More than Adam Smith, de Tocqueville fastens his attention on the new patterns of domination and subordination and explores the peculiar new relations between workers and capitalist employers:

> At the very time at which the science of manufacture lowers the class of workmen, it raises the class of masters...This man resembles more and more the administrator of a vast empire – that man, a brute (de Tocqueville, 1835–40/1966: 169)

> The workman is generally dependent on the master, but not on any particular master: these two men meet in the factory, but know not each other elsewhere; and whilst they come into contact on one point, they stand very far apart on all others. The manufacturer asks nothing of the workman but his labor; the workman expects nothing from him but his wages...they are not permanently connected either by habit or by duty. The aristocracy created by business rarely settles in the midst of the manufacturing population which it directs: the object is not to govern that population but to use it (de Tocqueville, 1835–40/1966: 170–1).

Though Tocqueville says of division of labour and the economy of large-scale production, 'I know of nothing in politics which deserves to fix the attention of the legislator more than these two new axioms of the science of manufactures' (168), and though he considers the 'manufacturing aristocracy which is growing up under our eyes...one of the harshest which ever existed in the world' (171), the impact of capitalist division of labour on work and the worker is not his central concern. For him the main question is whether the 'new aristocracy' will threaten freedom and equality in politics.

It was the young Marx who made the human quality of work and the quality of human life under capitalism central issues of his critical analysis. Marx gave earlier observations (of which the comments of Smith and de Tocqueville are merely examples) a conceptual home and a systematic position in a wider framework of analysis through the Hegelian idea of alienation. This concept has since been deformed beyond recognition by the use it found in many very divergent intellectual perspectives, until today the word is often used to point to nothing more than a persistent dissatisfaction or frustration. For Marx, who adapted Hegel's conception for his own purposes, alienation means fundamentally an estrangement of people from their humanity. The detailing of the concept as a tool of critical analysis therefore reveals – at the same time as it criticizes specific features of reality as inhumane – Marx's conception of true human nature.

Alienation, in Marx's view, reaches its extreme form under capitalism. Alienation derives from division of labour, but that concept is now detailed and broadened beyond mere technical specialization of work. Human nature, centrally defined by productive and fulfilling activity, is deformed by a division of labour that develops under the control of capital-owners and is imposed on workers who are formally free yet subject to the pressures of a competitive market. Labour is hired by the owners of the means of production – a commodity like any other. The product of labour is no longer under the worker's control. Owned by another, it becomes a means of further domination. 'The object produced by labour, its product, now stands opposed to it as an *alien being*, as a power *independent* of the producer.' Moreover: 'If the product of labour does not belong to the worker, but confronts him as an alien power, this can only be because it belongs to *a man other than the worker*' (Marx 1844/1964: 122 and 130). Thus, domination and subordination in the organization of production and the appropriation of what is produced are at the very foundation of Marx's analysis of alienation. Exploitation is not something added to a more sublime psychological experience called 'alienation'; rather, it is part of the same phenomenon, and a constitutive part at that.[5]

In the process of production, as distinguished from its product, alienation has several different aspects, all of which derive from division of labour under the domination and in the interest of someone other than the workers. The work itself is arranged and subdivided without regard for the needs and wants of the worker who therefore cannot 'fulfill himself in his work but denies himself, has a feeling of misery rather than wellbeing. . .'. He 'feels himself to be freely active only in his animal functions – eating, drinking and procreating, or at most also in his dwelling and in personal adornment – while in his human functions he is reduced to an animal' (Marx, 1844/1963: 125). He becomes alienated from himself.

The worker is powerless. He can neither direct his own labour nor freely choose his employment; given unfavourable market conditions he virtually has to accept whatever work he can find. His work – albeit formally free – becomes 'forced labour'. Finally, alienation also means estrangement from others. The work process itself is organized without regard for human relations among workers. Beyond that, the experience of alienated work deforms all relations among people. It shapes their standards and double-standards, it deforms what they take for granted and it stunts their wants and ideals. Even the capitalist partakes ultimately in this condition of alienation.

These critiques indicate indirectly the standard they apply – Marx's conception of human nature or, as he called it, the 'species-being of man', which is violated by the conditions analyzed. Human beings find their fulfilment, Marx thought, in active work and creative activity rather than, say, in contemplation or in the enjoyment of consumption. They put something of themselves into what they make and find themselves in their product. This conception of human nature, then, makes work so central that nothing outside of work can counterbalance a dehumanization of the labour process. A labour process and patterns of life as a whole that are consonant with the true nature of the species would give full range to the development of creative faculties, allow for free choice and autonomy, and combine individual freedom with a full realization of the social character of human existence. As Marx and Engels described the future society in the *Communist Manifesto,* 'we shall have an association, in which the free development of each is the condition for the free development of all.'

Marx's critique identifies massive violations of this true nature of man throughout history, and especially under conditions of advancing capitalist division of labour. These violations are at the same time more radically seen as unacceptable *and* viewed as less open to amelioration than they appeared in the observations of Adam Smith and Alexis de Tocqueville. In the long run of history, however, this unrelieved suffering stands for the underlying nature of man and represents a token and a guarantee of the ultimate resolution of contradictions and the full realization of the potential of human beings as a species.

It is an understatement to say that these views have not gone uncontested. To take as an example the response of a scholar not particularly given to political polemic, Reinhard Bendix(1956:xviii) argues that Tocqueville's and Marx's ideas as well as similar views of others

have not been a reflection of experience, but the impassioned outpourings by men of ideas who reacted imaginatively to conditions of factory work with which they were not ultimately familiar. The critique of industry tended, therefore, to project the disquiet and dissatisfactions of intellectuals upon the prototype of 'the' industrial worker, who either longed for the return to the imagined warmth of the 'good old days' or for the creative satisfactions of individual workmanship and collective participation. As in other falsehoods there is a little truth in these perceptions, but it is not enough to outweigh the romantic imagery of the industrial worker as an embodiment of the purely human which has been suppressed by greedy men and by inhuman machinery.

The awkwardness of 'literati calling literati literati' (K. Tucholsky) aside, the main thrust of this critique – that we are dealing here with nothing but illusionary romantic projections of men who were themselves disturbed by the radical transformation of their civilization – is not very convincing in view of the significant, albeit incomplete, convergence of diagnoses by writers as different in temperament as well as political and philosophic outlook as Smith, Tocqueville and Marx. Yet the passage does indicate major areas of critical argument about Marx's alienation thesis.

We can distinguish three main questions. First, are the empirical assertions valid – assertions about the consequences of division of labour for the quality of work and its ramifications beyond work and about worker satisfaction in contrasting work situations? Second, how plausible are the assumptions about fundamental realities of human existence which are the intellectual foundation of Marx's conception of human nature? Finally, how persuasive are the ideals expressed in this conception of human nature, which ultimately guided the empirical critical analysis?[6] I want here to do little more than raise these questions. Even beginning to answer them would require a monograph of its own. It is possible, however, to sketch the outline of some findings in order to bring certain issues to life and to show by example the range of problems raised by any attempt to assess the consequences of division of labour.

There is substantial evidence to suggest that many specific assertions of the alienation thesis do hold. Industrial sociology after World War Two was on the whole certainly not radical, let alone Marxist, in outlook; but it nevertheless documented (on occasion inadvertently) pervasive antagonism between workers and management grounded in contradictory economic interests and unequal power, tensions arising out of relations of subordination and control, problems of trust and communication between supervisors and subordinate workers, and the salience – but also the resilience – of spontaneous and autonomous social relations among workers (cf. Mayo, 1945; Friedmann, 1961; Mann, 1973; Hill, 1981).

Studies of the most fragmented jobs – on car assembly lines for example – showed this work to be devoid of intrinsic satisfaction, tightly regimented and resulting in social isolation. They also found that workers on assembly lines voiced more often than other workers explicit dissatisfaction, and that they experienced symptoms of psychosomatic distress more often (Walker and Guest, 1952; Chinoy, 1955; Blauner, 1964; Kornhauser, 1965; *Work in America*, 1973). Historically, workers often resisted advances in the division of labour. For instance, the minute specialization, detailed supervision and reduction of intelligence and initiative required of workers which were brought about by Taylor's 'scientific management' around the turn of the century met with strikes and violent resistance stretching over two decades in America (see chapter 5).

These findings cannot, however, be interpreted as a straightforward confirmation of the alienation thesis. First, the features of industrial work denounced in nineteenth-century critiques and assembled by Marx into the conception of alienation are far from universal. While the antagonism of economic interests between workers and management is indeed virtually ubiquitous in industrial societies – recognized no less by the exhortations and the remedial proposals of the 'human relations' school of thought (Mayo, 1945) than by the more realistic and more radical analyses which prevail in the social science literature today – there are vast differences between different kinds of work in regard to job complexity, worker autonomy and leeway for social relations at work.

Second, if higher rates of dissatisfaction with, and prolonged worker resistance against, job fragmentation are taken as evidence for the inherently noxious character of minutely specialized employment, it must be pointed out that even most assembly line workers actually declare themselves satisfied with their work, and that the unions in Western industrial countries have focused their energies far more on pay and job security than on the quality of work. Such apparent contentment with work arrangements is not in itself decisive. It can and has been argued that the priority of pay and job security simply reflects necessity and says little about acceptance of work conditions as humane, and that expressions of satisfaction in opinion surveys represent an adjustment to a situation beyond one's control – a situation which confines wants and, perhaps, stunts the imagination. Indeed, such submissive adaptation may be taken as a symptom of a deeper deformation by inhumane work conditions than resentment and conflict indicate.

Third, alienation in the Marxian sense is a concept that transcends the immediate work situation; it is a characteristic of the whole ensemble of institutional arrangements shaping the relations of production. The transition from competitive capitalism to the monopolistic and oligopolistic corporate economy of today raises complex questions in this regard. Unionization, state regulation and expanding public employment have modified (though in varying degrees) the character of labour as just another commodity traded on competitive markets. Production relations within large firms in favourable market positions are very different from the early capitalist organization of work (see chapter 5). There is no doubt that antagonism over control and economic interests has by no means been eliminated, but it is not easy to specify for these new conditions clear standards by which alienation in this comprehensive sense can be identified.

While careful investigation can help to clarify the issues of human satisfaction at work as well as the implications of larger institutional changes for the organization of work, these arguments ultimately lead us back to questions of what Marx called the 'species nature' of human existence. His model of man is not uncontradicted. Steven Lukes (1967) has shown that Emile Durkheim's view of human nature, embodied in his conception of anomie, stands in fundamental opposition to that of Marx even though it rejects *some* of the same things as inhumane that Marx did. Both are, moreover, heirs to divergent strands of modern social philosophy with Rousseau and later romantic views on one side, Hobbes and, say, Freud on the other.

> Whereas anomic man is, for Durkheim, the unregulated man who needs rules to live by, limits to his desires, 'circumscribed tasks' to perform and 'limited horizons' for his thoughts, alienated man is, for Marx, a man in the grip of a system, who 'cannot escape' from a 'particular exclusive sphere of activity which is forced upon him'.
>
> Where Marx valued a life in which in community with others 'the individual' has the means of 'cultivating his gifts in all directions',

and where the relations between men are no longer defined by externally imposed categories and roles – by class and occupation – and men freely come together in freely-chosen activities and participate in controlling the conditions of their social life, Durkheim held that 'we must contract our horizon, choose a definite task and immerse ourselves in it completely, instead of trying to make ourselves a sort of creative masterpiece', and hoped to see men performing useful functions in a rationally organized society, in accordance with clearly defined roles, firmly attached to relevant groups and under the protective discipline of rules of conduct at home, at work and in politics. They both sought liberty, equality, democracy and community, but the content which they gave these notions was utterly different (Lukes, 1967: 141 and 149).

Such contrasting views of human possibilities transcend the constraints of specific historical formations. They rest on arguments of what is possible in principle, and at the same time they embody – fused with notions of what is and is not humanly possible – conceptions of what is ultimately desirable. Though one can, and should, reason about such conceptions, in the end they involve moral and political choice and personal commitment. Historically, these choices and commitments are themselves fundamentally shaped by division of labour, relations of power, and cultural hegemony.

INEQUALITY, CONFLICT AND THE NATURE OF SOCIAL ORDER

The advances of division of labour that came with industrialization increased production *and* led to problematic conditions of work. Though both of these outcomes were neither uniform nor brought about by specialization alone, the conditions which heightened the likelihood of each were quite similar. We can conclude from our discussion so far, then, that the consequences of increased division of labour are complex and multidimensional, contradictory in nature when evaluated by plausible standards of desirability, and uneven in their impact on different parts of the population.

If we have so far painted a picture of the more immediate outcomes of division of labour with rough strokes indeed, filling in the consequences for the wider social structure can and must remain still less detailed – even a mere review of macrosociology is clearly beyond our reach here. What is to be demonstrated at the same time prevents a full discussion: that the division of labour is one of the most important determinants of social structure at large.

Structured inequality in society grows directly out of division of labour, though additional factors are needed to arrive at a full explanation. Most theories of stratification and social class agree on this proposition. Both material and non-material advantages tend to be associated with contrasting locations in the pattern of positions created by division of labour. There is also wide agreement on the kinds of differentiation that are crucial for understanding different historical systems of inequality. Among them are the division of labour by sex and age in household and family as well as in the wider society; the difference between roles lived out within the context of family and kinship, and those structurally differentiated from the matrix of kin relations; the division of dominant and coordinating positions from subordinate and executing ones; and the differentiation of roles according to knowledge and skill.

Different theories of stratification and social class, however, stand in sharp contrast to each other when it comes to identifying the most significant features of stratification in a society, particularly in the most advanced capitalist countries. Equally stark contrasts are found in the causal detailing of how division of labour and inequality are linked, and in analyses of the consequences of structured inequality. Not unexpectedly, these differences are related to contrasting fundamental questions which the theories pursue and, again, to conceptions of what is ultimately possible and desirable in human social life.

Marx's analysis of class and class conflict was primarily interested in understanding long-run historical change, especially in uncovering the 'laws' of change that would transform the social and economic order of capitalism. This led to a focus on the two classes whose nature and antagonism revealed the fundamental character as well as the inherent tensions of capitalism: the bourgeoisie whose capital became the dominant element in the new organization of economic production and the proletariat that owned nothing but a labour power which could no longer be effectively employed except in the service of capital. Marx's writings refer to other classes, but these two occupy most of his attention; there is little concern with giving a complete picture of the whole complement of classes since the distribution of advantage and deprivation is not, as such, the central issue.

The same perspective leads Marx to conceive of classes as (potential) collective actors rather than merely as aggregations of people in similar conditions and with similar life chances. The transition from one to the other is made problematic in several places which deal with the development of class consciousness, class solidarity and class organization for political action. But in most discussions of long-term developments this transition from classes as defined by objective conditions – 'classes in themselves' in the jargon of the Hegelian tradition – to classes that have acquired a collective identity and the capacity for collective action – 'classes in and for themselves' – is taken for granted.

The emergence of the two classes of bourgeoisie and proletariat is rooted in the advancing division of labour in capitalist manufacture and modern industry. It takes place in an institutional framework of private property and contractual market exchange – both unencumbered by the broader obligations of an earlier time – which is guaranteed and nurtured by modern state structures. These latter have become differentiated from the organization of economic production, yet they serve the interests of the capitalist order. Eventually, due to a growing concentration of capital and a tremendous growth and impoverishment of the proletariat, the proletarian revoution will destroy capitalism and transform it into the future society of autonomy, affluence and free association.

A completely different account of the relation between division of labour and structured social inequality is given by functionalist stratification theory which dominated sociology in the first two decades after World War Two (see Parsons, 1940 and 1953; Davis and Moore, 1945; Barber, 1957; and, with certain variations and a narrower problem formulation, Treiman, 1977). Here the central intellectual interest, informed largely by Durkheim's vision of human social life and modern society, is the question: What makes the cohesion and functioning of societies as social 'systems' possible? Functionalist stratification theory focuses on distributional issues with special emphasis on differential evaluation – the distribution of prestige. Its fundamental theorem is that division of labour, conceived as occupational specialization whether autonomous or under the control of others, inevitably leads to differential evaluation of occupational positions in terms of more or less shared value standards.[7] This prestige differentiation, in turn, is closely related to differences in material advantage, though the latter have also a dynamic of their own.

The unequal distribution of material and non-material advantage contributes in two major ways to the functioning of society. It is, first, an incentive system which promotes instrumental efficiency by matching talent and task as well as by motivating people in their work. The functionally most important tasks carry the highest rewards, and therefore are accomplished by the best-prepared people with the greatest care. Secondly, because – and to the extent that – the distribution of advantage and deprivation reflects shared values and common ideals, it represents a material embodiment of the *conscience collective*: merit is rewarded and lesser accomplishments find comparatively meagre compensation. By thus reinforcing common standards and ideals, social inequality contributes to social cohesion and the integration of society. In the more naively function-alist versions of the theory, not only are these positively functionalist consequences attributed to structured inequality, but stratification exists – indeed is inevitable – because it thus serves the functioning of society.

Stratification theory aims primarily at an understanding of structured inequality in its relation to functional problems of society in general. This universalizing thrust often gives its arguments an abstract and ahistorical character. Even when stratification in con-temporary industrial society is the subject, much structural detail – about corporations for instance, their interrelations through indirect ownership and interlocking directorates or the scope of their operations and the issues of economic and political power entailed by that scope – is omitted or flattened into generalized features of 'economic institutions'. Perhaps we find here also the explana-tion for the peculiar fact that most stratification theorists treat the division of labour simply as occupational specialization, neglecting the insight of Tocqueville and Marx that it makes a decisive difference for the structure of inequality whether this specialization takes place under the dominance of capitalist entrepreneurs or represents a differentiation of autonomous actors.

Durkheim, none of whose major works deals primarily with stratification and social class, laid the foundation for an understand-ing of industrial society that complements functional stratification theory. The 'higher societies' (*sociétés supérieures*) of the modern world are, according to him, developing an 'organic' form of cohesion which rests, in contrast to the 'mechanical' coherence of simpler societies, on the complex interdependencies created by advancing division of labour. Correspondingly, new values and fundamental understandings emerge which consensually represent the new order in cognitive as well as moral terms (*conscience collective*). Among the major elements both of the emerging new social order and of this new 'religion' of industrial societies are life chances based on equal opportunity and merit, just regulation of cooperation and exchange, a balance of obligation and duty defined and secured for all by autonomous associations that emerge from the division of labour, and an individual life at once more personal and more solidary than in any previous society.

Did Durkheim overlook or directly deny what Marx and others saw as major outcomes of the industrial transformation of the world: inequalities and misery based on power and defeat rather than on merit and fault, increasing conflict between classes, destruction of community and a peculiarly precarious individual existence? No; he explicitly acknowledged these and other developments in modern history. However, he saw them as transitory 'pathologies' that would disappear once the new type of society had fully worked itself out and found its equilibrium.

When it comes, then, to the ultimate consequences of the rapid advance in division of labour that defines the emergence of modern social life, both Marx and Durkheim resort to a vision of a future society that reflects their theory of human nature as well as their ultimate ideal commitments. To this we can respond in a variety of ways.

We can search for systematic evidence in support of the different assertions which led Marx and Durkheim, as well as the representatives of similar ideas, to their contrasting views. This will not resolve all differences, but can clarify them and settle some. We can also take each view as a guide to more or less powerful sociological problem formulations. Taken in this way, these views are not judged as valid or invalid, but as more or less fruitful; a one-sided, even an ultimately implausible, view may well be more intellectually fertile than a well-balanced one.

Building on both of these responses we may consider the ultimate premises about human nature and a humane existence expressed in such theories and take a stand – with reason and conviction. Yet we may also – and this is how I see Max Weber's position – reject such all-inclusive visions and stoically face the incomprehensibility of the horizons of our social existence and its future, and at the same time assert reason, individual freedom and human solidarity, however limited their realizable scope.

Whichever response we choose, the analyses of Marx and Durkheim agree on the persuasive contention that the significance of division of labour goes far beyond issues of efficiency of production and the human quality of work; it is ultimately of paramount importance for the fundamental character of modern society and its future.

3

The Role of Efficiency and Power in Explanations of Division of Labour

We now turn to our main concern – the explanation of division of labour and the role power plays in its development. The preceding discussion of the results of division of labour has, paradoxically, already introduced us to major notions of causal explanation. This is due to the particular prevailing mode of analyzing division of labour.

The most common explanation of division of labour is its efficiency. The overall advances of division of labour, as well as the specific forms it takes, are seen as coming about because the more differentiated roles and organizations 'function more effectively in the new historical circumstances' (Smelser, 1963: 34; see also 1959: 2). This is a functionalist explanation: division of labour occurs, advances and takes specific forms because its consequences are 'functional' for a broader system.

This explanation is pervasive in current sociology and current social thought in general, even though it is rarely stated in fully developed form. In fact, it is perhaps more accurate to say that this explanation is rarely made explicit *because* it is so much taken for granted. The formulation just quoted, for instance, is part of Smelser's *definition* of structural differentiation; technically, then, any assertion about more specialized roles being more efficient becomes a tautology since greater efficiency has been made part of the very concept of structural differentiation. In recent structural–functional theories of evolution and modernization (Parsons, 1966 and 1971; Smelser, 1959 and 1963), structural differentiation holds a central place, but it is often not directly explained. It mainly serves merely to identify the social changes studied, while the analysis focuses on the interrelations between different components of these processes (between differentiation and integration, for example) and on some of their consequences, rather than on their own explanation. However, structural differentiation is in these theories so closely associated with higher productivity, improved efficiency and greater 'adaptive capacity' that an efficiency explanation suggests itself – is, in fact, implied.

In his attempt to construct a theory of occupational prestige Donald Treiman (1977: 6) flatly states this implication: 'The basic factor promoting the division of labor is its efficiency. Relative to unspecialized labor, specialized labor is far more efficient.' Treiman then proceeds to give some reasons for expecting greater productivity from division of labour, but he does not bother to explain how the latter is caused by the former – how, to put it drastically, the child, greater productivity, gives birth to its mother, specialization.

THE FUNCTIONALIST MODE OF ANALYSIS

The structural–functionalist conception of society is not the only theoretical position that views division of labour as propelled and steered by efficiency gains. Similar ideas are found commonly in classical and neoclassical economics as well as in different varieties of Marxian thought.[1] It will be useful to take a closer look at the logic of functionalist analysis. This provides a counterfoil against which we can give our conception of the role of power in processes of division of labour and differentiation a more sharply defined profile.

Functional explanations do involve intricate problems, though these are not as insurmountable as the simile of child and mother, used above, suggests. Functional analysis takes off from the observation that, under varying circumstances and in spite of apparent obstacles, a social goal is repeatedly realized, a social formation remains stable, a pattern of change keeps its direction. It then asks which mechanisms are responsible for these persistent outcomes – even under adverse conditions. It asks how the political economy of capitalism gains its astounding staying power, why the upbringing of the young is a success in the overwhelming number of cases or in what way conflicts are kept from escalating into a violence that ruptures the social fabric. So far there is nothing specially problematic about this approach. It identifies important issues for investigation.

The problems begin when the existence and social reproduction of the functional patterns themselves are explained by the 'function they serve' – when stratification is explained by the part it plays in insuring that the work of society gets done, the incest taboo by its role in the protection of parental authority, division of labour by its contribution to greater productivity. It plainly will not do just to make the *assumption* that what is functionally important will, therefore, somehow come into existence and continue to play an active part under varied and adverse conditions – whether the functional 'need' is that of a society or of a dominant class. 'If wishes were horses, beggars would ride.' Rather what is necessary, if the functionalist approach is to be extended from a fruitful problem formulation to a comprehensive explanation, is an account of how the development and maintenance of the functional mechanisms come about and how their own causation and reproduction are linked to their functional contributions.

A functional analysis that is also able to provide a comprehensive causal explanation, then, consists of a set of interlinked causal propositions. To return to the efficiency explanation of division of labour, it has to theoretically specify and empirically demonstrate that division of labour makes for greater efficiency and how mechanisms related to this outcome activate processes which, in turn, bring about division of labour, its general advance, and the specific forms it takes. Each component of this agenda is problematic. The efficiency outcomes of specialization cannot be taken for granted; the 'feedback mechanisms' tying effects of division of labour back to its conditions are far from clear; and, as we shall see, even the very meaning of efficiency becomes, on closer examination, a Pandora's box of unresolved questions.

Although it has been taken as established beyond doubt since the beginnings of modern economic and social thought, the proposition that specialization makes for greater efficiency cannot (as we have seen in the last chapter) be taken for granted.[2] It does rest on a number of plausible hypotheses, yet for each of these there are variable conditions favouring or inhibiting the predicted outcome that are not at all well understood. Furthermore, the relative importance of the different factors remains rather obscure. Finally, and most important, division of labour has effects other than those listed in the typical discussion of its productivity advantages – effects which counterbalance those commonly singled out. Such 'costs' of differentiation arise, for instance, from the need to coordinate and integrate the specialized parts, or from problems of morale and motivation created by job fragmentation. The balance of costs and gains in regard to efficiency may be positive or negative, depending on the specific patterns of specialization and on complex social and cultural conditions. What ultimately counts, of course, is the net effect; it is not a forgone conclusion that it will be positive.

The question of how new forms of specialization come about *because* of their positive results for productivity may seem at first sight simpler. If a convincing answer can be found to that question, it promises to solve with the same stroke the knotty problem just discussed, because it would be only the positively functional forms of division of labour that would be so encouraged, that is, those which enhance productivity. The selective advance of functional forms of division of labour is intuitively plausible on two grounds. First, with something as desirable and important as getting work done efficiently people will, so it seems, know or eventually learn about cause and effect and act accordingly. Second, this plausible subjective response would be reinforced and complemented by objective constraints. Social selection would, in analogy to natural selection, eliminate inefficient forms. Parasites with a precarious life cycle involving different host organisms 'need' to produce masses of eggs for the species to survive in a given environment. The varieties which did not develop this or an equivalent adaptation did not survive. Similarly, the forms of division of labour are exposed to constant selective pressures; in comparison to others, those which are wasteful are shown up as impossibly costly by these pressures. This similarity would seem no less relevant, if the variety of forms on which this selective pressure works does not come about by random variation, as do genetic mutations, but also involves rational anticipation and evaluative assessment of events after the fact.

Both of these ideas have been used in the analysis of division of labour, though different theories give more weight to one or the other.[3] I shall briefly describe and comment on two theoretical accounts – those of Neil Smelser and Talcott Parsons – before

I turn to a closer analysis of the concepts of efficiency and productivity, which will bring out radical problems for a functionalist
understanding of social differentiation.

TWO FUNCTIONALIST ACCOUNTS OF DIVISION OF LABOUR

Neil Smelser (1959) applies a theoretical paradigm of structural
differentiation to changes in the Lancashire cotton industry from
1770 to 1840. In his theoretical scheme – and it, rather than the
details of its application to the historical data, is of interest here
– he posits seven phases of change. These begin with dissatisfaction
about the status quo, which may give rise to disturbances and
utopian schemes; these then are subjected to social control; experi-
mental attempts at solutions follow, which are assessed in terms
of reasserted societal values; eventually, selected new forms of social
organization are established and routinized (Smelser, 1959: 15f.
and 404). Not all phases occur necessarily in each instance of social
change, says Smelser, nor are the phases neatly separated from each
other in the flow of historical events. There also can be a return
to earlier phases. Yet the end result is a more differentiated organization of production, and of working-class family life, that is also more
productive. The overall process represents a collective response to
felt problems and dissatisfactions which is steered by common
values. Shot through with irrational disturbances and groping trial
and error, differentiation is seen as a fundamentally rational adaptation of collective organization to changed circumstances.

Smelser's approach interestingly combines rational and non-
rational moments in social change and yet it can, by using collective
values as a reference point, see the final outcome as collectively
rational after turbulences are subdued. Smelser offers little argument
as to why we should expect exactly this combination of moments
in the process of differentiation – why non-rational responses should
subside or be subdued; why more productive and more specialized
arrangements should be the final outcome. These questions point
to important unresolved theoretical problems. Foremost is one
mentioned earlier. The outcome of increased division of labour is
never really in question because improved efficiency is made part
of the concept of differentiation, and because differentiation is
conceived as an overall process within which different specific causal

factors find their place rather than as a phenomenon which itself needs explanation. Dedifferentiation, different forms of division of labour that are not necessarily more specialized or even the maintenance of the status quo, however tension-ridden, are not even contemplated as potential outcomes. Nor is it asked whether such alternatives are possibly of similar or perhaps greater efficiency. Here I take issue not so much with Smelser's historical interpretation, but with an analytic paradigm that does not even raise these questions.

In view of twentieth-century functionalism's debts to Durkheim it is ironic that Smelser's approach, with its focus on an ultimately rational pursuit of productivity gains, is also open to the criticism Durkheim leveled against the utilitarian analysis of division of labour (provided Smelser's approach is extended to that long-term advance of division of labour which primarily interested Durkheim). Needs and wants, as well as common values, change historically. Hence, Durkheim argued, they cannot provide a long-term reference point for changes in a division of labour steered by efficiency gains:

> If [our ancestors] were so greatly tormented by the desire to increase the productive power of work, it was not to achieve goods without value to them. To appreciate these goods, they would have had to contract tastes and habits they did not have, which is to say, to change their nature. That is indeed what they have done, as the history of the transformations through which humanity has passed shows. For the need of greater happiness to account for the development of the division of labor, it would then be necessary for it also to be the cause of the changes progressively wrought in human nature, and for men to have changed in order to become happier (Durkheim, 1893/1964: 240).

I should repeat that Durkheim's criticism does not directly apply to Smelser's argument since Smelser begins his analysis with felt dissatisfaction. It does, however, raise serious questions about efficiency advantages as the reference point for a long-term functional explanation of differentiation. In particular, Durkheim's argument also seems to be at odds with any conception of functional requisites of societal life determinate enough to allow clear-cut explanations of social differentiation. All societies have to deal with problems of scarcity; all have to educate the young; all have to contain conflicts; all have to keep the motivation of sufficient numbers of people sufficiently alive; and all have to bring these various concerns under 'one roof' – arrange for coping with them more or less simultaneously.[4] But the question is whether there are not a very large number of options for doing so. If that is the case, even a definitive list of functional requirements of human social life would not be determinate enough to constitute a satisfactory reference point for a functional explanation of division of labour. Human needs and wants and social values would *variably* give more specific meaning to such bare-bone 'functional requisites' in different cultures and societies.

Needs, wants, values and the functional requirements for realizing or approximating them are, in the conception of human history which this interpretation ascribes to Durkheim, shaped by social and cultural forces. Among other factors, the very pattern of division of labour whose explanation is to be furthered by references to these culturally variable needs, wants and values is responsible for changes in the latter. We will take up these ideas of Durkheim again when we look more closely below at the meaning of 'efficiency' and 'productivity'.

In *Societies: evolutionary and comparative perspectives* (1966), Talcott Parsons develops his 'paradigm of evolutionary change', a conceptual framework for tracing the ramifications of specific 'developmental breakthroughs' throughout the functional subsystems of a society.[5] Parsons' discussion is even less concerned than Smelser's with a causal explanation of social differentiation. There are fewer directly explanatory ideas and Parsons's paradigm is more open-ended. His arguments, nevertheless, have a number of interesting implications for problems of causation. A first is that evaluative assessment of past experience and rational anticipation move into the background as we turn from families and economic enterprises to whole societies as units of analysis. In Parsons's account of societal evolution the main 'feedback mechanism' linking the outcomes of evolutionary advances to their conditions is competitive pressure, though imitation and borrowing also play a role. However, the outcomes of competitive pressure have a far from clear-cut relationship to specific 'developmental breakthroughs'. They do not simply give a premium to developments that are, other things equal, an enhancement of efficient functioning in dealing with one aspect of a given environment. One reason for this is that competitive advantage results from a balance of many factors and a given innovation may be outweighed by other factors. Certain societies 'may, indeed, be so beset with internal conflicts or other handicaps that they can hardly maintain themselves, or will even deteriorate. But among these may be . . . some of the most creative societies from the viewpoint of originating components of great long-run importance' (Parsons, 1966: 23).

The creative decadence of what Parsons calls 'seedbed societies' is not the only element that blurs the correspondence between competitive advantage and innovations that enhance efficiency. The following broad statement by Parsons (1966: 23–4) indicates quite a few alternatives to selective survival of the most efficient forms of social organization – and only of those:

> A [developmental] breakthrough endows its society with a new level of adaptive capacity in some vital respect, thereby changing the terms of its competitive relations with other societies in the system. Broadly, this kind of situation opens four possibilities for societies not immediately sharing the innovation. The innovation can simply be destroyed by more powerful, even if less advanced rivals. If the innovation is cultural, though, it is difficult to destroy completely, and may assume great importance even after its society of origin has been destroyed. Second, the terms of competition may be evened through adoption of the innovations. The present drive to 'modern-ization' among underdeveloped societies is an obvious and important case in point. A third alternative is the establishment of an insulated niche in which a society can continue to maintain its old structure, relatively undisturbed. The final possibility is the loss of societal identity through disintegration or absorption by some larger societal system. These posibilities are type concepts, and many complex combinations and shadings of them may occur.

The 'feedback' from efficiency outcomes of social differentiation to the conditions which account for its advances – the link of crucial importance in the explanatory chain of a functional efficiency explanation of division of labour – is thus beset by many problems and ambiguities. Rational assessment and understanding, differen-tial survival of competing arrangements, and diffusion from one organization or society to another are all relevant and important here; but they are all subject to severe qualifications, which vary in unknown ways with changing circumstances. Evaluative assess-ment and anticipatory planning are never fully rational; they are the more limited the larger the social unit in question and the more complex its functioniong. Competitive pressures may select against important innovations and let ineffective patterns survive in relative isolation. And diffusion, often based on less than thorough understanding, may or may not result in successful transplants and recombinations of elements in the overall sociocultural pattern of the host society. The circumstances under which these 'feedback' mechanisms work with different degrees of imprecision, and the ways in which they influence each other, are problems that remain rather obscure.

THE CONCEPT OF EFFICIENCY

There is a still more far-reaching problem that stands in the way of successful functionalist explanations of division of labour based on increased efficiency or 'adaptive capacity'. This concerns the meaning of efficiency. Any judgement about efficiency – the economical use of means in the pursuit of specific goals – hinges on a ranking of goals and on an evaluation of the cost of alternative means to reach these goals – cost being equal to the value of goals forgone by using the means chosen. What is an efficient use of means by one preference structure informing such ranking and evaluation may clearly be wasteful in terms of another.

It is at this point that we return to 'Durkheim's problem'. Insisting that people acquire different needs and wants – in effect, change their nature in 'the transformations through which humanity has passed' – Durkheim objected to a utilitarian explanation of division of labour as driven by a search for greater happiness. The same insight, when applied to divisions of experience, interests and values *within* a society at one time, turns into an objection to reasoning in terms of efficiency advantages for a whole society.

Not only different cultures, but lord and serf, entrepreneur and worker, executive and employee, as well as many other groups and social categories, differ fundamentally in their evaluations of the price paid and the advantage gained with a new arrangement of their social relations; and if their preferences and cost–benefit calculi vary, the meaning of efficiency, determined by varied interests and value commitments, also differs. In addition, we have seen in the previous chapter that division of labour has multiple consequences, contradictory in nature even when evaluated by a single set of standards of desirability and uneven in their impact on different groups. Once the formal character of the concept of efficiency is recognized, the question of which – or better, *whose* – preferences and interests are determinant in shaping social processes cannot be avoided. A functional explanation of division of labour in terms of efficiency gains as such becomes meaningless except in the border-line case of a society with virtually complete consensus about needs, wants and values.[6] It is for these reasons that I argue for including power systematically into the explanatory paradigm.

Before I discuss the implications of such a focus on power for explaining division of labour, however, I have to return to an issue briefly touched earlier in chapter 2. Is the problem of contradic-tory preferences not solved by the market? Classical and neoclassical economics argue that the market overcomes the divergence and contradiction among individual preferences by assigning an economy-wide value to all costs and products. Market prices – for materials, capital, labour as well as goods produced and services rendered – aggregate individual patterns of evaluation and represent a collective preference structure. This solution of the problem, it is argued, does not require shared values nor the exercise of power. It relies solely on the autonomous interaction of the participants in economic exchange.

The market represents indeed an instrument of coordination and integration of the greatest significance; one not sufficiently appre-ciated and studied by much of sociological analysis. However, the market does not provide a solution to our problem. Most obviously the market argument does not apply to non-marketed activities, to household work no more than to tax collection. Even for goods and services that are contractually exchanged the proposition that the market's integration of individual choices into a collective preference pattern does not involve power and bypasses issues of value con-sensus and divergence depends on unrealistic assumptions.

It presupposes completely free access to all markets so that market participation itself is not a privilege. It requires perfect competition within markets so that no one of the competitors can influence the price through decisions about supply or demand. It assumes an equal distribution of financial resources with which to turn needs and wants into effective demand. And it has to make the assumption that costs and benefits which do not enter the market calculus – from parental love and public defence to pollution and health hazards – do not give one set of people advantages over another. If these conditions were met, the outcome of the market's operation might still not conform to a particular conception of humane work and just distribution, but it would indeed represent a collective pattern of choice that is independent of shared or contested values and not the result of imposition by power.

Yet each of these assumptions is unrealistic. The very institutional infrastructure needed for the market's functioning, the legal regulation of property, contract, association and incorporation, is never neutral *vis-à-vis* the interests of different economic actors; yet it is guaranteed by the coercion machinery of the state.[7] Access to markets is often limited by custom and law as well as by capital and skill requirements. Perfect competition exists, in a literal sense, only in the economists' imagination; though it is true that many of its effects (such as the spur to pursue one's advantage assiduously) are retained in less than perfectly competitive markets, any deviation from the model implies power inequalities among the competitors and between those who buy and those who supply a particular good or service. Income is always unevenly distributed; so much so in most societies that the needs and wants of the poor, however urgent, do not affect the market choices as much as even superficial whims of the wealthy. Finally which resources – from roads and aircraft carriers to education and health maintenance – are made available outside the market and which are left to the play of supply and demand is to a large extent a matter of politics and of the role of the state in the political economy; so is the issue of whether dirty air becomes a priced cost of industrial production. Each of these qualifications underscores the role of power even in market exchange. Rather than representing an alternative to a power solution of the problem of divergent preferences, the market is in fact one of the mechanisms through which power is acquired and imposed.[8]

FOCUSING ON POWER

How does a focus on power help us deal with the problem of multiple and divergent interests? Disproportionate power, power concentrated in the hands of individuals and groups with similar interests and preferences, means that a certain type of cost–benefit calculus gains a disproportionate influence. The interests and reactions of the most powerful are thus a point of great leverage for any analysis of division of labour. In fact they actually are treated in such a manner in many studies, but the strategy typically remains implicit and does not receive adequate theoretical recognition. As we have seen, Smelser (1959) makes 'dissatisfaction' the first of several phases in a development of structural differentiation, but he does not specify theoretically whose dissatisfaction is relevant. In the empirical application of the theoretical framework this turns out to be the dissatisfaction of the early entrepreneurs and shop-owners. Eisenstadt, in his comparative analysis of pre-modern bureaucratization (1963), comes close to the position advocated here. He emphasizes in his explanation the interests of the ruler and, secondarily, those of the aristocracy and of urban groups, who gain importance and power with the advance of market exchange and bureaucratic rule.

If we focus on the interests of the powerful, the structure of theoretical reasoning may very well, though not necessarily, remain functional in character, taking off from efficiency gains and other consequences of division of labour and then seeking to identify links between these consequences and conditions favourable or unfavourable for processes of differentiation. The points of reference in the analysis, however, are strategically altered by focusing on the powerful. The preference structures relative to which the consequences of division of labour are analysed become more amenable to investigation. The unmanageable complexity of an endless variety of preference structures is reduced to a few. Furthermore, the behaviour and even the attitudes and sentiments of the more powerful are better documented in the historical record than the behaviour and attitudes of common people, an obvious advantage for any investigation of long-term social change (which almost by necessity must make use of historical sources).

Of similar if not greater theoretical interest is the fact that it appears possible to predict some of the interests pursued by the powerful. Clearly, this would very much increase the explanatory power of the analysis. It seems reasonable to assume (though this need not remain an untested assumption) that those in positions of power will seek to maintain their advantage and under certain conditions even attempt to increase it. It has been argued against this proposition that the assumed tendency depends on the total balance of benefits and costs experienced by incumbents of power positions as compared to their life chances when out of power, and that this balance varies with different circumstances in ways not easily predictable.[9] No doubt the proposition can and must be further refined and specified as to varying conditions. Yet as a rough generalization it seems established that greater power is not only often attractive in itself but tends to be associated with privilege and advantages of many kinds, even though these prizes need not always be so great as to invite fratricidal succession fights as they did, to cite one of the more famous examples, after the death of King David (1 Kings, chapters 1 and 2).

In addition, those in power will often think and act in terms of positional – in contrast to, and in addition to, personal – interests, strengthening a concern with maintaining their power resources. The interest in power is then transformed from a personal inclination into something owed to one's lineage, corporation or public office. Finally, for analyses involving large numbers of powerful individuals and groups one can advance the statistical argument that the proportion of those who seek to maintain and extend their advantage will be increased by virtue of the fact that they have a better chance of remaining in power positions than those who make no such efforts. This argument merely presupposes that power can vanish if it is not safeguarded, and that attempts to husband and extend power resources have some effect in the intended direction. Clearly, the powerful will pursue other interests as well; concern with maintaining their power resources is inevitably only one of several interests. However, to identify even one substantive interest that is relatively stable and relevant for policy and large-scale change is an important theoretical gain. We may speak, then, of a *raison du pouvoir* as an orientation of action that will typically be found among the powerful in all but the least complex societies.

The study of the 'causal loops' or 'feedback mechanisms' linking the consequences of division of labour to its conditions is also aided by a focus on power. Not only are the intentional reactions to perceived consequences stronger if they are those of the powerful; we can also exclude a number of effects from the analysis because in many instances the powerful will not suffer, and thus count as 'costs' some of the consequences of their policies. Increased monotony of work or heightened job insecurity, for instance, have been of little concern to entrepreneurs unless worker morale or the politics of labour relations seemed affected. Moreover, one can at least speculate that there is a correlation between holding positions of power and tending towards rational action – that is, action based on a review of goals and means in the light of one's basic preferences and the best information available about the consequences of alternative courses. Rational action in this sense is not independent of privilege; in fact it could be considered part of the standard package of social advantage except that privilege on occasion removes the spurs of ambition and necessity and dulls the urgency of goal-seeking. Rational action represents a causal loop linking consequences and conditions of division of labour to each other that is probably the more important the more we focus on power elites in command of a staff of domination.

It is not only the power of the most powerful – of political elites, of dominant classes, of the owners or executives controlling economic enterprises – that needs attention. Their counterparts, even if subordinate, also wield some power. The impact of interests and values different from those of the most powerful groups on processes of division of labour depends similarly on its backing by countervailing power of varying strength, and on similar issues concerning the translation of interests into assiduously pursued goals. For most subordinate groups the problem of how disparate actors can be brought together for collective action is especially grave. The problem is not absent in the case of aggregates of separately powerful actors with similar interests, but the many have greater difficulty to join forces for concerted action than the few; 'the masters,' as Adam Smith observed, 'being fewer in number, can combine much more easily' than workers or countrymen (Smith, 1776/1937: 66). Still, subordinate groups do not completely lack power, even without inclusive organization; and under favourable conditions they can also acquire the advantages that derive from attaining a capacity for effective collective action (Marx, 1847/n.d.: 145–6; Dahrendorf, 1959; Olson, 1965). Not only dominant power concentrations, but also the countervailing strength of subordinate groups, as well as the ensuing conflicts and their outcomes, must be taken into account in analyses of division of labour.

Formally, this can be represented in a simple model of a modified functional analysis, which Arthur Stinchcombe (1968: 93–8) has called 'Marxian functionalism'. The consequences of a given structural arrangement for different interests elicit responses in terms of these interests which are backed up by different amounts of power. The resulting balance of forces determines the maintenance of, or change in, the social structure in question, be it the institutions of representative democracy, the factory organization of work or a certain degree of job fragmentation. This model neglects a great many theoretical issues, including the problems of rational assessment and anticipation of facts and options, the difficulties of organizing for collective action, and the fact that even overwhelming power is not equivalent to social causation. It does, however, identify an important part of the agenda for an explanation of division of labour that focuses on power and retains the functional format of analysis.

Thus, focusing on phenomena of power in the study of division of labour and social differentiation leads out of the impasse that results for the prevailing functionalist efficiency explanations from the formal character of the concept of efficiency. It identifies more clearly the reference points for a modified functional analysis; it spells out more plausible 'causal loops' linking outcomes of division of labour to factors which, in turn, modify the patterns of specialization and differentiation; and it simplifies the empirical investigations required.

We can push the contrasting analysis of a functional explanation of division of labour, which uses shared values in a society as the ultimate reference point, and an explanation focusing on power one step further. Durkheim insisted that division of labour always presupposes a unity of the social whole within which division of labour takes place:

> The division of labor can. . . be produced only in the midst of a pre-existing society. By that we do not mean simply that individuals must adhere materially, but it is still necessary that there be moral links between them.

This insistence is related to his critique of utilitarian social theory (as he understood it), especially of Herbert Spencer's theory:

> If this important truth has been disregarded by the utilitarians, it is an error rooted in the manner in which they conceive of the genesis of society. They suppose originally isolated and independent individuals, who, consequently, enter into relationships only to cooperate, for they have no other reason to clear the space between them and to associate. But this theory, so widely held, postulates a veritable *creatio ex nibilo*.

...Collective life is not born from individual life, but it is, on the contrary, the second which is born from the first (Durkheim, 1893/1964: 276–7 and 279).

This thesis – that division of labour can take place only within a moral community because collective life has analytic priority over individual life – led Durkheim to crucial insights. It was the foundation of his argument that contract cannot function without non-contractual institutional underpinnings and, more generally, that the institutions necessary for social life of a certain kind cannot be created at will by contracting individuals. At the same time, this thesis can hardly be maintained in a literal sense. Durkheim's own inconclusive discussion of international trade and international division of labour attests to this.[10]

Durkheim's conception of society as an overarching moral community has been of tremendous influence in twentieth-century functionalist social theory. It contains ideas worth preserving, even if one is critical of a consensus model of society which assumes fundamental agreement on values throughout society and which often implies this agreement is spontaneous. We have just seen that an analysis of social power (and of division of labour in terms of power) must be able to understand how mere aggregates of individuals and groups can acquire a broader collective identity that makes collective action possible. Any functional explanation of division of labour involves collective interests as reference points, be they those of an organization, a class, or a society. Thus, any contribution to an 'integration theory' that can help us understand the emergence of collective identities should be welcome to a wide variety of theoretical positions. Such contributions need not assume that individual and group allegiances to a wider collectivity are spontaneous, nor that they explain the integration of whole societies; they may well explain the coherence of classes and class fragments or even only of associations and organizations, rather than that of whole societies.

The exercise of power is one of the most important ways through which the inclination of rational members of large groups to opt for a 'free ride' may be counteracted and through which people can be made to support the common good of a collectivity (cf. Olson, 1965); coercive taxation in support of state action is only the most obvious, if not the least important, example. This is not to deny other bases of collective identity and collective action, including attachments to others, hostility to outgroups, identification with collective symbols and value commitments. A focus on power is, in fact, not in the least excluded by recognizing these factors.

It is important to state with great emphasis (though I will not elaborate it much here) that explanations of division of labour which focus on power *need not* be part of a larger theoretical argument of the functionalist kind. The substance of power interests and the distribution of power resources can more simply be analysed as causal determinants of social changes connected with division of labour and social differentiation. The approach I am proposing is very much concerned with a *process analysis* of division of labour. Power interests, differential power resources and the balance of power among different contestants are likely to be prominent among the causes of specific processes of specialization and differentiation, as well as among the causal conditions of blockages and reversals of differentiation. The promise that power variables hold for a better understanding of *processes* of division of labour is thus another important reason why a focus on power in the study of division of labour recommends itself.

Efficiency, productivity, individual and social welfare – these concepts may be considered 'essentially contested concepts' (Gallie, 1955–6), much like justice or democracy, exploitation or alienation. Insisting on the formal character of the concept of efficiency and arguing that what is good for some people may be bad for others, I have sought to bypass a contest about the substance of efficiency and welfare, individual or collective. Opting for the power approach to the analysis of division of labour and social differentiation means, then, that at this point in the argument empirical–theoretical and moral–evaluative analyses part ways. The powerful interests which steer and promote division of labour need not be good or just, nor must we think of them as unjust and evil merely because they are powerful. The moral–evaluative judgement, even if based on more complex grounds, is suspended. However, if this formulation is permitted, moral–evaluative arguments are merely differentiated from empirical–theoretical analysis (in the usual hope that the latter can be improved by pursing it more single-mindedly); the two modes of analysis are not absolutely and forever severed from each other. Even though their integration is not the main concern of this book, I will comment on some problems relating to this in the final chapter.

In the following chapters the thesis that power is a critical element in any adequate account of division of labour is further explored and put to the test. We will investigate in different contexts to what extent division of labour is shaped by the most powerful interests as well as by the struggle between groups with opposing interests and different power resources, and we will explore how much a focus on power can contribute to a better understanding of the actual processes of change in division of labour. I shall not begin at the most obvious point, the development of division of labour in industrial work, but consider first problems of dividing authority, problems that are of utmost importance in understanding secular change in organizational forms.

4

Division of Authority, Legitimation and Control

Marx's concept of division of labour in the workshop can be generalized beyond economic production. Specialization under a single authority, shaped by one set of powerful interests even if they are counteracted by subordinate forces, is distinguished usefully from the specialization of autonomous units. This distinction cuts across the boundaries of economic life and applies to political, religious and military organization as well. Such social differentiation *within* a system of domination is the subject of this and the next chapter. I will focus, first, on problems of division of labour at the top of the power pyramid, in particular on problems pertaining to relations between the ruler and his immediate agents. The next chapter deals with the imposition of new forms of division of labour at the bottom of the pyramid, with the resistance that often emerges in spite of large disparities of power and with the control of this resistance.

A political ruler building or extending his apparatus of domination and an entrepreneur developing his firm of employed workers are two model cases of powerful actors facing issues of division of labour within their own domain of authority.[1] The insight reached earlier – that division of labour has multiple and contradictory consequences – holds in these instances too. While potential gains in efficiency are a strong incentive to move forward, division of labour does not leave the relation of domination untouched. To be sure, specialization in many ways enhances the power interests of ruler and entrepreneur. As we saw in the chapter 2, specialization makes more precise evaluation of the contribution of a subordinate possible, allows the head to link reward and performance more closely, enables him to impose stricter work discipline, and ultimately turns the aggregate of subordinate roles into the pliable raw material for rational organization-building.

However, substantial advances in division of labour at the same time create radical problems for the maintenance of power – problems which in fact need to be solved before most of the advantages can be reaped. Two issues are of special importance. First, as the subordinate organization becomes more complex, problems of supervision and control multiply and demand a *division of authority* at the top. Second, the changed relations of domination and cooperation, both within the immediate apparatus of power and between the ruler and the body of subordinates as a whole, imply different moral premises – a different ethos and world-view – which require new forms of *legitimation* for the maintenance of authority; these are often difficult to establish. Although, as Max Weber has shown, these two problems are closely intertwined, I will first discuss issues of division of authority separately from questions of legitimation.

Beyond some point of differentiation, increases in the number of specialized roles, as well as the often correlated expansion in the number of people and the scope of operations, require a division and delegation of authority because one person (and even one family or clan) is no longer able to cope with the problem of supervision, discipline and direction. Delegation of authority, however, puts continued central control into question. 'He finds it difficult to delegate' is one of the most common complaints about chief executive officers in today's universities, business firms and government departments. Common sense typically puts the issue in terms of personal disposition rather than structural power relations. This is not altogether mistaken since, as we will see, modern organizational structures provide for both delegation of authority *and* the retention of central control. Here, however, we are interested in the same issues *before* such stable institutional patterns are established; in that case, problems of organizational structure are paramount.

It is not merely the increase in the number of specialized roles and in the scope of operations that causes the problem. Increased division of labour also often entails a subdivision of the whole organization – into departments, divisions, or ministries with their own social identity. This aggravates control problems and potentially puts the power of the ruler into further jeopardy. Moreover, higher levels of organizational and technological complexity require not only specialized skill but expert knowledge, and this development, which historically becomes pervasive as more knowledge is used in the actual operations of governments and economy, has similar consequences. Those in power become dependent on experts who are much harder to control than those whose work, even if specialized, is open to common-sense evaluation.[2]

POWER DILEMMAS AS BLOCKS TO DIVISION OF LABOUR

Historically, the dilemmas of division of authority and delegation of power have had a variety of outcomes. A first, which only in the experience of our own day appears as a minor variant, is negative – a failure to come to terms with the issue. Rulers or entrepreneurs may, because of the problems indicated, shy away from further division of labour and organization or fail in their attempts to cope with these issues and lose much of their power. Since their power was the aggregating force that made further differentiation possible, its splintering would very likely also arrest the process of differentiation. The repeated centrifugal developments in European feudalism may serve as well-known examples of such an arrest of social differentiation. Rather than staying or becoming specialized agents of the ruler, powerful retainers developed and expanded their own power base independent of the centre. They became lords in their own right or were only tenuously subordinated to central control. The result was a continuation of parallel, 'segmented' political organization rather than the emergence of a more centralized and, at the same time, functionally more differentiated form of rule.[3]

This type of outcome is by no means confined to the political sphere. A systematic investigation of the history of business firms with these issues in mind would undoubtedly turn up many examples of an unwillingness to engage in a division of authority, especially in the early phases of modern economies. 'It is perhaps legitimate', says Payne (1978: 192) in a review of entrepreneurship and management in the economic development of Britain,

> to regard the business unit of the industrial revolution, the individual proprietorship or the partnership, as partly the product of risk avoidance. By the unification of ownership and control, the entrepreneur was able to reduce the real or imagined dangers inherent in entrusting his business to a manager... The offsetting disadvantage of owner-management was, of course, the restraint which it imposed

on the scale of operation, a restraint deriving from the difficulties of delegation; but at this stage of Britain's economic evolution, the benefits outweighed this disadvantage.

Business historians often assume that issues of delegation did not pose much of a problem in Europe until the last decades of the nineteenth century because management issues remained rather simple, and that when the need for division of authority became more urgent it was achieved without much ado.[4] There are good theoretical reasons to see this instead as a serious problem for which reliable solutions had to be found before differentiation and institutional growth could proceed further. It is interesting to note that by 1862 a report for the *Zollverein*, the common market which in northern Germany preceded the unified empire, identified issues of control and difficulties with managers as a significant obstacle to further growth of enterprises.[5]

MAKESHIFT SOLUTIONS

Even though it proved insufficient in the long run as organizational growth continued, an important preliminary solution to the control dilemmas of divided authority was to rely on family ties. The role this device has often played in maintaining royal control over expanding domains is well known. It found a similar use as business enterprises expanded both laterally and in organizational complexity. Jürgen Kocka describes his own findings and the results of other German research:

> As in Great Britain fifty years earlier, or in the developing countries today, it was difficult for Germany factory-owners around 1850 to find qualified and reliable officials and office staff to perform those tasks which the entrepreneur could not closely control himself. Under the constant threat of fraud, employers found loyalty and honesty even more important criteria in the selection of staff than training and ability. As far as possible, employers of the time put relatives and close friends into those positions which carried decision-making power and which were hard to control... Often the senior salaried employee of a company was the brother or cousin of the founder, and the first general manager his closest friend from school or military service... Thus family loyalty provided the control – albeit

informal – necessary for the successful decentralization of responsibility and authority . . . The 'nepotism' of early industrialists not only
was a function of their strong family feeling but also facilitated the
growth and success of the enterprise. Of course, such personal
methods of co-ordination achieved only a loose connection between
the various parts of the concern. Much autonomy was left to sub-
divisions, whether organized on functional or geographical lines.
But as long as this level of co-ordination was sufficient, family loyalty
was the outstanding tool – both inexpensive and manageable – for
achieving it.[6]

The level of coordination afforded by family members, trusted
friends and directly interested partners soon becomes insufficient
if division of labour, organizational complexity and the scope of
operations continue to increase significantly. Thus, in a second type
of response to the problems of dividing authority, the ruler responds
to the challenge to his control by deploying complex additional
arrangements of supervision and discipline. Often this involves the
use of the old technique of domination 'divide and rule' – putting
one set of subordinate officers against another in order to shore
up and strengthen the power of the centre.[7] The most dramatic
and best-documented examples come from the political arena, from
the early efforts of political rulers to build bureaucratic machines
of domination.

If we take the government of eighteenth-century Prussia as a case
in point (see for instance Rosenberg, 1958; Smith, 1972), these
measures included the establishment of collegial rather than individual authority at the intermediate level. This made responsibility
diffuse and ambiguous, but it allowed for multiple lines of information to the centre and for mutual control of higher civil servants.
A related device was the construction of organizations paralleling
other bureaucratic offices with the primary task of spying, inspection
and control. The recruitment and promotion of certain officers with
an eye as much to loyalty as to ability and expertise also remained
an important feature. However, it made a decisive difference
whether these officers had or could acquire proprietory rights in
their office, or whether they served at the pleasure of the ruler,
recompensed out of funds under his control. Compared to older
patterns of rule, these were costly arrangements; they could weigh
heavily on the negative side of an efficiency analysis, but they did

answer problems of central direction and control created by increasing organizational complexity and expanding jurisdiction.

BUREAUCRATIZATION

Viewed in retrospect from the vantage point of modern bureaucratic organizations, such complex and often clumsy arrangements appear as transitory patterns. What Max Weber analysed in a broad comparative perspective as the pure type of bureaucratic domination (Weber, 1922/68), and what I count here as the final response to the control dilemmas of divided authority, is a new institutional and cultural form of world-historical significance. Modern bureaucracies are organizational machines which, more than any other form of organization, depersonalize internal relations as well as external operations. Not only are they the most efficient way of arranging large-scale administrative activities but they also, in principle, make it possible at the same time to divide and delegate authority as well as maintain organizational coherence and central control.

Beyond the material resources required to sustain a bureaucratic organization and the pool of competent personnel necessary for its functioning, there is a less tangible but equally critical side to building a bureaucratic apparatus of rule. Any institution-building requires orientations which transcend individual rational-instrumental behaviour. This is one of the fundamental arguments against a simplistic utilitarian social theory, which assumes that institutions can be created *ad hoc*, whenever needed, by agreement between the actors involved. Durkheim (1893/1964) crystallized this critique in ' his formula of the 'non-contractual elements of contract' that underlie the system of market exchange. In exact analogy, we can speak of the *non-bureaucratic elements of bureaucracy*. An effective process of institution-building must reshape the goals, priorities and commitments of at least the core participants and inculcate shared assumptions, attitudes and value commitments on which rational organizational action can be based. In the model case these orientations are stable and reliable without continuous and detailed supervision and control; yet at the same time they are consonant with the wishes of those in the top organizational positions. Bureaucratic loyalty thus has a formal character, separated to a large extent from direct personal attachments as well as from substantive interests and ideals.

Even rough approximations to such a pattern of organization represent a crucial *breakthrough* in the emergence of a modern institutional order. The early developments of this kind were typically uncertain and protracted processes. They involved the emergence of an *esprit de corps* among the higher officials grounded in such foundations as similar origins, shared education, stable career prospects and a common privileged status in society. What was required on the part of the ruler were two dispositions normally at odds with each other: a willingness to delegate and a determination to impose one's will on the administrative apparatus. Success at both required, in turn, a tremendous amount of power based on economic, political, cultural and personal resources. Given these resources, the ruler could provide generous rewards without becoming dependent on his subordinates; he could secure honour and status for them; he could influence and shape the emergent group ethos by invoking old ideals and fostering new ones, as well as by controlling their education and training; he could destroy hostile alliances and forge or support agreeable ones; and he could coerce or threaten to coerce when necessary. The joint impact of such interventions had to be steady over a long period of time, exceeding the generational turnover of rulers and officials, before new orientations were developed and firmly institutionalized – a new cultural amalgam supported by habit and upbringing, group pride and individual commitment, as well as by the material and non-material interests of the core personnel.[8]

While some advantages of furthering such developments may have been quite clear to intelligent rulers and their advisors, the institutional outcome and its overall significance were beyond the horizon of even the most powerful and far-sighted actors. As such, the new institutional and cultural patterns are best regarded as fortuitous developments. But once they came to fruition (even if only partially realized) they could be seized upon – nurtured as they appeared, consciously spread to other parts of an apparatus of rule, and taken as objects of imitation by rivals and allies.

When private business faced similar problems of divided authority, the patterns established in public bureaucracies were of special importance in those countries where the rationalization of public administration had preceded the emergence of large enterprises by a substantial period of time. The clearest case is perhaps Prussia–Germany. Here government bureaucracy did not merely provide a model for private organization; rather, civil servants acting as entrepreneurs and government enterprises were directly involved in the transformation towards a modern economy. The educational system was shaped by the needs of the state and permeated by civil service styles and ideals. While tensions existed between the world of business and of educated classes employed by the government or more indirectly under the tutelage of the state, bourgeois culture as a whole was impregnated by the bureaucratic ethos more than in any other European country (Rueschemeyer, 1973). Business firms initially used the devices of family and friendship ties to cope with the incipient problems of decentralized authority. But when multifunctional enterprises became feasible and desirable (a development which for complex reasons came relatively earlier in Germany than in Britain) bureaucratic modes of management were quickly adopted. Jürgen Kocka (1971, 1969) has described this development in detail for the case of the Siemens and Halske electric manufacturing firm. Siemens and Halske was not an isolated example by any means; in fact, for a time its competitor AEG moved ahead in bureaucratization, while Siemens went through the process of shedding familistic forms of management adopted earlier.

'If bureaucratic organizations had not preceded the rise of the multifunctional firm, they would have, it seems, been developed when it appeared.' Kocka's functionalist assertion (1971: 155) is tempered by his hypothesis that, by the end of the nineteenth century, Germany had a significant economic advantage over Britain and possibly also over American business because of the 'systematic, orderly and efficient overall management' of its large firms. It is instructive to look briefly at the emergence of delegated management in England.

DELEGATION OF AUTHORITY WITHIN A COMMON SUBCULTURE

Public bureaucracies were much less developed than in the larger continental states, and they certainly did not shape social structure to a degree even distantly approaching the case of Prussia. Yet, on occasion public management patterns influenced private business in England as well. The most obvious case was the railroads, which drew heavily on the army for men able to manage large numbers of employees as well as complex and far-flung operations (Pollard,

1965: 134). More important, however, was the autonomous growth of relations of trust between owners and managers within different industries.

Sidney Pollard has described 'the full circle since the days when it was held to be axiomatic that control by salaried managers was the quickest way to ruin', an opinion for instance expressed by Adam Smith, to the time around 1830, when 'the more advanced industries, and the larger firms, had learnt to detach the function of management from the person of the proprietor and to see it as a separate set of activities, sensibly and rationally performed, if necessary by a separate set of individuals' (Pollard, 1965: 270). The new relations of trust were based on similar schooling, master–apprentice relations, family traditions and marriage connections, emergent professional attitudes and associations and – last but not least – the prize of a future partnership. In effect, we see here the emergence of loosely knit *status groups* of owners *and* managers, within which new orientations about merit, human value, reliability and trust could be nurtured, developed into the ethos of a circumscribed milieu, and endorsed with an informal social certification.[9] These networks of owning and salaried managers and entrepreneurs in Britain played a role similar to the status group of higher civil servants in the Prussian state appartus, with their *esprit de corps* and bureaucratic ethos. Yet the new values, attitudes and patterns of behaviour among the British entrepreneurs and managers remained much more amalgamated with older orientations and styles of life, embodied in networks of kinship ties and personal loyalties. Even this more limited development of social relations that owners could rely on took time – possibly as much as twenty to thirty years, in Pollard's estimation (1965: 270). Once crystallized, these patterns had to be broken up and reshaped later when the advantages of vastly more complex companies made bureaucratic organization far more useful.

THE BUREAUCRATIC MODEL QUALIFIED

The pure bureaucratic pattern is nowhere fully realized. This is more than to ritually repeat the caveat that Max Weber's concept is, of course, an 'ideal type' – a pure conceptual construct. The reasons for some of the 'imperfections' commonly found in reality can be located in power interests. The apex of government and business administrations is (variations among different countries and cultures notwithstanding) shot through with family and patronage relations. Access to positions of power may no longer be, as they once were, exclusively reserved for those with close ties of loyalty to those already there. Yet this aspect of recruitment into high office remains an important feature of organizational hierarchies in all modern societies. It is, of course, more important in privately owned business, but still significant even where private property has become formally irrelevant, as in all modern state apparatuses.

Another 'deviation' from Weber's pure model of bureaucracy that is pertinent here can best be understood when we realize that transformations in the ethos of administrative officials (important as they are) tend to be much more limited than the model and certain simplistic formulations about modern administration indicate. The formal readiness of officials to serve loyally in a system of divided authority is put to the test when policies run counter to the interests and established value commitments of the officials themselves, especially if these interests and commitments have become part of the culture of a well-defined status group of civil servants. Beyond a certain measure of such tension between political direction from the top and the policy inclinations of a body of civil servants, the apparatus of power will cease to be the pliable instrument of a coherent central purpose.

The range of policies given unstinting support by a corps of civil servants, then, has limits, even if these may be wide enough to accommodate policy changes from, say, the moderate left to the moderate right in today's capitalist democracies. It is for this reason that we find complex control arrangements – built as much on the 'divide-and-rule' maxim as those of eighteenth-century Prussia – in the National Socialist regime in Germany (Burin, 1952) and the Communist system of post-war Eastern Europe (Fainsod, 1963; Beck, 1963). Dual, and in fact multiple, hierarchies of information flow and command are not, however, confined to such exotic extremes of modern history. The tensions between White House advisors and their staff, on the one hand, and various government departments dealing with the same issues, on the other, make for an almost continuous news coverage of this particular instance of dual bureaucratic organization. Yet without the White House control organization, Washington policies would have even less coherence than they do have. Peter Evans (1975), in an elegant formal derivation, has shown the control advantages of multiple hierarchies and has also indicated how common they are in today's business organizations. It may actually be the case that in many Western countries the normative appeals at the disposal of business executives are so weak that, in comparison to many state organizations and perhaps to business firms in less individualist countries such as Japan, the bureaucratic ethos is diluted and does not suffice to guarantee the proper functioning of divided authority.

In spite of these modifications, however, it remains true that, to a degree which was inconceivable only two hundred years ago, modern institutional patterns do provide for division and delegation of authority as well as for the retention of central control in complex organizations. This does not mean that power and power shifts are no longer objects of contention and conflict, nor that such contention has become irrelevant for issues of division of labour. It does mean that different echelons in the organizational pyramid of authority can gain or lose power, divide authority more or less, and do so along changing lines without the necessity of reinventing the institutional framework for specific new organizational arrangements.

THE POWER INTERESTS OF SUBORDINATES

A brief look at the interrelations between power interests and division of authority at intermediate levels of organizational power will complement the previous analysis. Officials and organizational sections holding some share of power are likely to resist organizational differentiation if their jurisdiction would be subdivided in the process. This resistance will, other things equal, be the stronger the more the contemplated advance in the division of labour infringes on their economic privileges and their social status in society. The resistance will be further reinforced if the officials are committed to certain policies and values for which they claim special responsibility and which they see threatened by the new alignment of jurisdiction. Conversely, a realignment of divided authority and jurisdiction will be favoured by those who thereby gain in privilege, status, or power, which they may or may not exercise with claims to a wider responsibility. The outcome of such contradictions between vested interests will depend largely on the power resources of opposing factions and on the interests and the power resources of higher-level decision-makers.

These common-sense considerations suggest a number of less obvious conclusions. A rather direct first implication is that, once those in authority come to see it as advantageous, division of labour in an organization is likely to proceed more smoothly the lower the rank of those affected because opposition is less likely to be powerful.

Second, if such disputes and conflicts have been negotiated a number of times, the result is quite likely a polarization in terms of privilege and status between those at the bottom of the hierarchy and those whose loyalty and cooperation have to be repeatedly secured. Such a polarization is, in effect, the result of another application of the maxim of divide-and-rule, this time dividing more powerful and privileged subordinates from those with less or no power – one of the most common features of power systems in general. Viewing it as the result of repeated processes reduces the implausibility of considering the structure of organizational power as the outcome of rational foresight and design in the interests of the most powerful. The crucial role of the 'staff of domination' is most clearly recognized in the social and political theory of Max Weber (1922/68 and 1919/58); it is, in fact, at the very centre of his analysis of power. The way relations among staff members and between the chief and his staff are structured and legitimated significantly shapes the character of the whole system of domination. Indeed, differences in legitimation are crucial for Weber's analysis of systems of rule primarily because of the difference they make for the apparatus of power. [10]

The consolidated power of the body of officers in subdominant positions of authority may turn against those originally in control of the organization – against king or capitalist owner. This is not merely a transitional possibility before bureaucratic institutional patterns are established, nor one confined to fairly extreme differences in orientation between staff and ruler. It is a possibility which, in one form, receives support from the very logic of bureaucratization: the principles that underlie the denial of proprietory rights in one's office to subordinates and that mandate substitution of merit and performance as criteria for appointment and tenure can also be turned against the heriditary and proprietory rights of kings and

owners. Private property has virtually become irrelevant as an entitle-
ment to political rule in the twentieth century, and even the control
of private business in capitalist economies has undergone significant
transformations which have limited the role of private property title,
though they did not eliminate it by any means (Berle and Means,
1932; Zeitlin, 1974). It is interesting to note that normative arguments
about private property have shifted from an unquestioned legitimacy
of property rights to various propositions about the efficiency of decentralization and of self-interested modes of motivation. The autonomy
tendencies of a unified staff with a meritocratic ethos are one – though
not, of course, the only – force behind these developments.[11]

One last conclusion suggested by our initial common-sense propositions about the interrelations of power interests and division of
authority at an intermediate level merits brief mention, even though
it points in a quite different direction. Wherever opposition to
division of labour and organizational differentiation from vested
interests is considerable in established organizations, more complex
organizational forms may develop more easily in new organizations
than through the transformation of existing ones. This is at odds
with simplistic conceptions of division of labour and differentiation
according to which more complex social patterns evolve directly
and smoothly out of simpler ones. A stalemate of opposing vested
interests, in conjunction with normative fixations of established
patterns, often makes this impossible. Once new organizational
forms are established next to the old ones, the less efficient old forms
may be gradually eliminated, be it by decree and central funding
decisions or as the result of competitive pressures. However, they
may also succeed in surviving under certain (and not necessarily
rare) conditions. This results in the not unfamiliar picture of a coexistence of several different organizational forms side by side with
each other, the character of each testifying to the conditions that
shaped its early development (see for instance Stinchombe, 1965).
Even in the most advanced countries, market pressures are not sufficient to bring about a homogeneous pattern of business organization.

ISSUES OF LEGITIMATION

In conclusion, I will turn briefly to certain broader problems in
the *legitimation* of rule that are raised by advancing division of

labour. We have already touched on legitimation issues in our discussion of the breakthrough towards a bureaucratic institutional order and some of its consequences. Max Weber saw legitimation beliefs so closely intertwined with the organization of rule that he defined his three ideal types of rules – charismatic, traditional and rational–legal or bureaucratic domination – in terms of distinctive kinds of legitimation. It is not that he saw these justifying beliefs as the main motives for compliance;[12] rather, in his view they concern and shape the organizational forms and the social relations that are constitutive of a system of rule. While the organization of the staff – the apparatus of domination – is most important, the reactions, dispositions and beliefs of the ultimate subjects are not irrelevant. Weber does not maintain that the consent of the governed is required for stability of domination; yet 'experience shows', he argued, 'that in no instance does domination voluntarily limit itself to the appeal to material or affectual or ideal motives as a basis for its continuance. In addition, every such system attempts to establish and to cultivate the belief in its legitimacy' (Weber, 1922/68: I, 213).

Those in control of a system of domination encounter two broad problems as division of labour advances. First, there are problems of transition from older bases of legitimation to new ones that are in line with, and support, high degrees of social differentiation. Second, not only remnants of old legitimation patterns but also new ideological developments may stand against further division of labour and undermine supporting beliefs. For both reasons, those in control may want to slow the advance of division of labour or keep it from spreading to certain spheres of social life. Both issues require brief discussion.

A full transition from the moral and intellectual premises of relatively undifferentiated social life to an 'ethos of divided labour' is an even more fundamental sociocultural development than the emergence of a viable normative framework for divided authority. In fact, the bureaucratic ethos discussed earlier is a special case of a *conscience collective* consonant with the high levels of social differentiation and the related institutional structure of modern societies. The processes involved in this transformation – the decline of tradition and community, the rise of individualism, and a growing rationalization of all spheres of social life – have been major themes of sociological analysis since the nineteenth century, from Toennies' dual conceptions of *Gemeinschaft* and *Gesellschaft* and Durkheim's *solidarité méchanique* and *solidarité organique* to Parsons's 'pattern variables'. We are here concerned only with certain tensions and contradictions that tend to develop in the process of change.

Advanced division of labour derives much of its advantage from the free allocation of people, independent of traditional controls and unencumbered by complex mutual obligations, and from single-minded attention to performance judged by universalistic criteria, which neglect who a person is aside from the business at hand. Rearranging social relations along these lines tends to undermine authority that rests to an important extent on ascriptive fixations and traditional consent. The threats to established authority obtain not only on the ideological level as such; in addition, specialized positions often gain some autonomy from direct control in the process of division of labour, and the related expansion of market exchange has similar results. Furthermore, the increased inter-dependence between specialized units, which is so important a correlate of division of labour, also tends to open new channels for the flow of communication and cultural diffusion. This, too, is often destructive of established, and especially traditional, authority. Perhaps the most dramatic acknowledgement of this effect were the radical isolationist policies with which the rulers of Tokugawa Japan pursued social and political stability from the seventeenth to the nineteenth century.[13]

Rulers whose power in wider society rests to an important extent on the immobility of relatively undifferentiated social relations and on traditional forms of legitimation are particularly vulnerable. They may find that bureaucratizing their apparatus of rule, advancing division of labour in general, and broadening the scope of market exchange may endanger the security of their rule. Eisenstadt (1963) analyzed this as a central dilemma of the ruler who attempts bureau-cratization in a feudal political economy. On the one hand, he needs the support of aristocrats whose interests lie on the side of stability and tradition in order to shore up the old foundations of his own rule; on the other, bureaucratization requires freeing material and human resources from their traditional controls, which entails undercutting aristocratic privilege, expanding market exchange and supporting new urban strata. Successful balancing of these contra-dictory alliances – another application of the 'divide-and-rule' maxim – may lead in the long run to a shift towards new bases of power and legitimation that are more consonant with bureaucratic rule and a highly differentiated social structure.

Yet even after long periods of negotiating such tensions and struggles and building new institutions, the ruler and his more conservative class allies may find it useful to keep division of labour and commercialization from spreading into certain areas of social life. This is one important cause of the phenomenon of 'partial modernization' (Rueschemeyer, 1969), especially common in late-developing countries. An example is the conscious use of agricultural protectionism and other legal measures in late nineteenth-century Germany in attempting to preserve traditional peasant-family farming in a state explicitly contrasted to the figure of the commercial farmer of England and America – a negative symbol in the accompanying propaganda. We can see similar attempts in certain paternalist policies of industrial 'rulers', as when Krupp in Germany and, later, large firms in Japan sought to tie their workers more closely to the enterprise with long-term employment contracts, pension schemes, company-owned housing, and supplementary symbolic gestures.

While certain features of these developments have universal significance, many of the issues encountered here can be seen as transitory in a longer-term perspective. Not only are the principles of authority and legitimation less heterogeneous and contradictory in more modernized societies, but also the modern institutional structure offers – with general legal norms, enacted law and formalized adjudication, and with such legal forms as contract, property and corporation – a firmly established and widely accepted framework in which individuals and collectivities can gain and lose power, or set up organizational forms and recompose them, without in each case having to secure anew the necessary foundation of power and justification in the wider society.

However, even when we consider a 'fully modern' institutional order, with little structural and ideological remnants of what can be reasonably called a 'traditional' social order, there are bound to exist, and develop anew, interests and ideological orientations opposed to continued division of labour and differentiation and to an institutional order that supports them. This comes as little surprise once we see division of labour as determined to a large extent by the structure of power in society and by the interests of the dominant groups.

Max Weber has given us an ideal typical model of early, competitive capitalism in which there exists a perfect functional fit between competitive market exchange, rational conduct of enterprises, formally rational law, bureaucratic rule and widely held appropriate legitimation beliefs. As throughout his work, he did not mistake this functional correspondence for a causal explanation, which he found in complex and conflict-ridden historical processes with multiple roots. The formalism of market, autonomous law, and competent bureaucratic administration appears, and presents itself, as socially neutral precisely because of its near-automatic and formal character. Yet in fact it has consequences, Weber argued, that are in social and economic reality anything but neutral. It confirms existing disparities and favours the powerful and privileged. Weber did not see capitalist development and its future as a 'harmonious rationalization process', as Wright (1978: 217) has charged.

The formalist triad of market, law and bureaucracy affects, in Weber's view, different interests in vastly different fashion, and its effects clash with substantive conceptions of justice held by various groups. While the formal rationality of the market, bureaucratic administration and the formal justice of modern law are peculiarly characteristic of modern Western societies and have tremendous staying power, they do not reign absolute. It is not merely due to historical accident, but to structural reasons inherent in modern social formations that they are counteracted by effective substantive demands and supporting ideological orientations asserted by workers, farmers, professionals and many other groups. As the relative power of different groups and social classes shifts, the formalist social order becomes increasingly shot through with substantive elements at odds with its formal automatism. This means that not only specific instances of division of labour but also the institutional framework undergirding processes of differentiation remain subject to the conflict of social forces with opposing interests and ideologies. I will return to some related issues in chapter 7, where developments of dedifferentiation are discussed.

5

The Organization of Work
in Industry
Imposition and Resistance

What are the forces that determine the division of labour in industrial production, on the shop floor? An answer to this question must be based on the historical record of the transformations of work organization which occurred in the course of capitalist development.[1] This history shows major and recurrent conflicts between workers and employers over the organization of work – whether craft work was undermined by cottage industry, factories brought large numbers of workers under one roof as well as closer control, new technologies changed old work routines, or 'scientific management' displaced craft control of the labour process. By and large, however, these conflicts were unequal contests from which owners and managers tended to emerge as winners; and after shorter or longer transition periods we often find that workers have acquiesced in the new work arrangements and take them for granted as givens of their existence.

Both phenomena, recurrent conflict as well as successful imposition and worker acquiescence, require explanation if a theoretical account is to be adequate. Recurrent conflict may be claimed as evidence for the critical role of power in advancing division of labour and in determining the specific forms it takes; and long periods of worker acquiescence do not necessarily contradict this view if we can show why the power balance was likely to be lopsided. This is indeed the interpretation we will explore further in this chapter.

However, the sheer fact of recurrent conflict and in particular the subsequent acceptance of new arrangements of production are also compatible with a fundamentally different view. Technological and organizational inventions which increase productivity ultimately win, on this by now familiar account, simply because they are more productive. Resistance and conflict at the points of transition can also be accommodated within this consensual productivity explanation (though only at the price of modifications the theoretical import of which is often neglected).

The resistance and conflict which typically accompany changes in the industrial division of labour can be understood as the frictions which occur when the social encrustations of an old order are broken up and discarded. Any socially established form of organization becomes aligned with, and supported by, the norms and values as well as the vested interests of the different groups involved. If such integrated patterns are disturbed, says this argument of Durkheimian provenance, conflict results – not primarily over contradictory interests rationally pursued, but because of non-rational attachments to a given social order. This explanation of intermittent resistance to new arrangements of the labour process can be seen as vaguely akin to Marx's conception that the social relations of production increasingly come to be a constraint for the free development of productive forces, before they are blown away and this contradiction is resolved into a new equilibrium at higher levels of productivity.[2]

The Durkheimian interpretation of industrial conflict is not completely devoid of reason. In principle one can separate it from the productivity explanation of change in the organization of work; and we will explore later to what extent it can be integrated into our framework of analysis which rejects productivity advances as the ultimate and ineluctable moving force of division of labour. Yet we will also see that this explanation alone is insufficient to account for the conflicts that accompany the introduction of new organizational forms of the labour process.

BASIC CONCEPTIONS FROM MARX AND WEBER

Marx and Weber describe the situation of labour in competitive capitalism in ways that are similar in fundamental analytic respects. For both it is critical that labour be 'free labour' – freed not only from involuntary servitude but also from other social attachments, obligations and pre-established claims that limit its use. It is exchanged contractually, for wages, on the market; it is purchased by capitalists who own the means of production without which work is not any more feasible. Labour becomes, in Marx's formulation, a 'commodity'.

At this point Marx introduces a distinction which at first glance may appear abstruse, but which leads to powerful insights into what happens in 'the hidden abode of production, on whose threshold there stares us in the face: "No admittance except on business"' (Marx, 1867/1959: 176), the distinction between labour and labour power. What the capitalist purchases on the job market is labour power, not labour – the capacity for work, not work done; what the capitalist needs, however, is labour, not labour power. It is the organization of the actual labour process that determines how much work is accomplished during the time for which labour power was purchased. On this depends the rationality of the labour process from the point of view of the capitalist. His interest in a rational work organization is more urgent the larger the share of labour costs in the total costs of the product (and by today's standards most industrial production in early capitalism was labour-intensive). Given a competitive product market, the capitalist has little choice but to seek work arrangements which insure the fastest pace of work and the harshest labour discipline compatible with continued employment of the required work force.[3]

The distinction between labour and labour power is, however, double-edged in its implications. At the same time as it explains 'exploitative' work organization, it points to the need to elicit cooperation from the worker and to the chance of resistance. Here is a decisive difference between labour power as a commodity and other commodities – materials, machines and even mules. Labour power becomes a commodity but the labourer does not. Even slaves, legally conceived as so close to things as the idea can be pushed, remain human beings who use discretion in their work, who must be trusted where they cannot be controlled, who can speak and conspire. Orlando Patterson makes the point emphatically in the conclusion of his comprehensive study of slavery (1982: 338–9):

> The slave resisted his desocialization and forced service in countless ways, only one of which, rebellion, was not subtle. Against all odds, he strove for some measure of regularity and predictability in his

social life. . . In all slaveholding societies the existential dignity of
the slave belied the slaveholder's denial of its existence.

Marx, of course, gave a critical role to this ultimately ineradicable
countervailing power of human subjects, albeit in a roundabout
way. Workers under capitalism, he argued, do not so much directly
resist imposed forms of work organization but they will politically
organize precisely because they are effectively oppressed in the
factory.[4] And organized class antagonism is in his view one of the
powerful levers which will transform capitalism into the society of
the future.

The conceptual constructs of Marx and Weber, then, provide
us with the starting points for an analysis of the industrial labour
process. Theoretical models or ideal types more than detailed
historical analyses of early capitalism, they identify major
parameters of work organization in the context of the capitalist
system of production and exchange. We will now explore in greater
depth the conception of division of labour in industry as the result
of unequal power struggles. First we consider the conditions which
in general determine the relative power of the differernt parties.
Then we will review selected historical instances of transition in
the organization of the labour process in industry. Finally we will
ask how work organization in today's changed capitalist order
compares to the earlier conditions which are reflected in the
theoretical tools and arguments fashioned by Marx and Weber.

POWER RESOURCES OF THE PARTIES

The power of employers, in the early as well as in later forms of
capitalism, depends on their position in product and labour markets,
on the possession of capital without which labour power is worth-
less in modern industry, on a legal order guaranteeing property
rights and on a state apparatus capable of intervening more specifically in the relations betwen workers and employers. Their small
number – far from being a simple disadvantage – combines with
their position in society and their economic resources to ease
concerted action on the market and in politics. In addition, the
system of cultural understandings and the socialization of people
into society and culture tends to be biased in favour of dominant

interests, though as all the other factors this 'cultural hegemony' is subject to historical variation and it must not be misunderstood as a capacity of entrepreneurial interests to manipulate culture at will.

The power of workers begins with the ineradicable element of discretion inherent in virtually all work and with the spontaneous growth of small-scale solidarity among people who interact with each other and find they have common interests. Attempts to build strength from this basis, however, encounter the power disadvantage of any large number of people, the difficulty of achieving collective organization. This is not merely a matter of counterbalancing the employers' market power through the creation of a monopoly for labour: collective organizations are indispensable for identifying and articulating common interests which otherwise would remain inchoate, interpretable in different ways. They are needed for developing a realistic understanding of conditions, developments and future possibilities, for devising strategies and for mobilizing concerted action – within enterprises, on the market and in the political arena. Finally, organizations are critical for the growth of a common culture that is relatively insulated from the cultural hegemony of dominant interests and that nurtures the solidarities, commitments and understandings which make specific collective actions possible and effective.

The difficulty of organizing sufficiently large numbers of workers to make a difference would be formidable even without the intense competition of workers in the labour market and without active efforts of employers to discourage and disarray worker organization, often assisted by state action (see Olson, 1965). Competition on the job market not only pits one worker against the other; it also encourages those with special marketable skills to conceive of their interests as separate from the interests of other workers, and this tendency towards a fragmentation of the working class can be powerfully reinforced by employer stratagems of work organization, by state action and by cultural definitions of social solidarities and distinctions. Given these complex special obstacles, labour organization has been much more difficult than nineteenth-century observers – including Marx – anticipated.[5] In the admittedly extreme case of the United States, we find, after more than a hundred years of strenuous efforts to organize, that barely one out of five employees belongs to a union; and there is no viable party defined primarily by working-class interests.

The problems do not end once organization is achieved. The simple fact that a collective organization exists is no guarantee that collective interests will be pursued. On the one hand the organization has to take the initiative in the crystallization of common interests and in the pursuit of strategies; the organization has to assume a leadership role in order to serve common objectives. On the other hand, there is the chance – it is in fact a rather strong probability – that the organizational apparatus becomes independent of its constituency, a fact which Robert Michels formulated as the 'iron law of oligarchy' (Michels, 1908/49). Once this happens there always lurks the possibility that the apparatus pursues its own interests, merely mediates in conflicts between workers and employers or is in fact co-opted by the other side. Trade associations, guilds and unions have throughout history had this dual potential: to function as a tool of control over their members or to act as a means of protecting the members' interests.

Whatever their organizational strength, workers face other conditions on which their power in struggles with employers is contingent. We can think of them as a mirror replica of the factors relevant for employers: market constellations, especially the relation of demand and supply in the labour market overall and in its different segments; the possession of labour power and skills rather than capital (the critical difference being that the capital-owner is in a better position to 'wait'); and finally, basic legal guarantees and special state interventions which tend to be a given in most particular contests but in the long run are not unaffected by the outcome of labour struggles. The fundamental asymmetry of power between employers and workers, then, lies in two factors above all others – in the employers' possession of capital and in the workers' difficulties to organize collectively.

We have so far considered the resources of power which employers and workers have at their disposal. Yet when the issue at hand is the organization of factory work, would the narrower concept of organized domination not be more appropriate? Why not focus immediately on the more specific questions of formal organization and organized domination rather than deal with the 'sociologically amorphous' issues of power?[6] To review the power resources of both sides is critical precisely if the issues at stake are issues of organization: it is the broader conditions of power, however 'amorphous' and resistant to classification by limited principle, that shape the chance to find obedience for commands, the prerogatives of organizational authority and the arrangments of control and autonomy between managers and direct producers. At the same time, organized domination – command–obedience relations within an organization – has its own dynamics within the overall power setting. A few aspects of these dynamics of organized domination need attention here.

It is a common observation that neither workers nor unions are centrally concerned with the organization of enterprise and workplace. To the extent that this observation is accurate, and it seems to fit the facts for most times in the history of capitalism, it must be explained first and foremost by a simple power consideration: pay and employment security take precedence over issues of the organization and quality of work because they are issues of economic survival. Creating a 'linkage' between organizational issues and these more urgent economic interests is the most powerful leverage employers have to determine division of labour in the workplace. However, this advantage is greatly strengthened by the dynamics of organized domination. This is not just a question of 'outside' supports for the basic structure of property rights, command and compliance – supports that are legal, political as well as cultural in character; rather, once functioning, an enterprise generates consent to its system of rule by its very operations. We may view this as another aspect of the ultimately ineradicable fact of human subjects' discretion: every voluntary contribution to the organization's goals, however conditioned, implies acceptance of the organizational arrangement. Michael Burawoy has made this a central point in his analysis of the capitalist labour process, titled *Manufacturing Consent*:

> Within the labor process the basis of consent lies in the organization
> of activities as though they presented the worker with real choices,
> however narrowly confined those choices might be. It is participation
> in choosing that generates consent. As long as the application of
> force is restricted to transgressions of the narrow but specific and
> recognized limits of choice, it too can become the object of consent.[7]

Contingent on worker discretion, this generation of consent is the more effective the more choice is given to workers. The constraining structures, the division of labour and authority in the workplace, are in turn reinforced by the consent generated through such discretionary participation.

Together with the broader institutional structures established and guaranteed by the state and with the urgency of immediate economic needs, which removes social structural issues from most people's attention, this generation of consent to the very constraints of the game one participates in accounts for a peculiar 'nesting' of different levels of conflict and struggle. Struggles over remuneration on the job can be fought without touching on the structure of workplace division of labour. In fact they are likely to reinforce that organization of work via the 'manufacturing of consent' mechanism. The less frequent struggles over the organization of work (in Burawoy's formulation, over the relations *in* production) do not easily escalate into struggles over the relations *of* production – over the wider institutional framework of the relations between employers and direct producers. In fact, again, the former are likely to reinforce the latter via analogous mechanisms of the 'manufacturing of consent'. Yet while certain institutional patterns are thus removed from the immediate impact of dissatisfaction and struggle by several thresholds, they do reinforce and support organized domination at the lower levels.

One last point must be discussed here before we turn to selected historical instances of transition in the organization of work. It is easy, and yet utterly misleading, to think of struggles over the division of labour as conflicts between two parties, each having a blueprint of ideal work and production arrangements, and of the outcome of such conflicts as a point between the two conceptions that is determined by each side's thrust multiplied, as it were, with a factor representing the relative power of the two parties. Every single stipulation of this conception is problematic. We cannot assume that either side has clear-cut designs for the long-term future, or even a more or less complete understanding of relevant socioeconomic trends and of the attendant cause–effect relations. Differences in foresight may be considerable and constitute a power advantage, but to some extent each side improvises its strategies; and even the goals crystallize only as developments take place and new opportunities become visible. Furthermore, we must be prepared to think of more than two parties in these struggles. Not only can the state, autonomous in variable degree from the interests and demands of the parties, insert itself into the struggle, but professional groups within management may define themselves as separate from owners and executives as well as from workers in production, or skilled workers may constitute a distinct group at odds in its interests with both management and less skilled workers. The constitution of the relevant parties, the definition of their interests, their understanding of trends and possibilities, and the emergence, escalation and quiescence of conflicts over the organization of work are all interrelated in complex ways. The form such struggles take, as well as their outcomes, thus are likely to be more historically contingent than simple common sense would lead us to expect.

HISTORICAL TRANSITIONS

Assembly line production of Ford's Model T began in 1913 in Highland Park, Michigan. It completed the transformation of automobile production which had begun as the work of skilled mechanics and some helpers. Responding to very large and increasing demand, car production went through rapid division of labour, deskilling of work, and massive use of specialized machine tools. The conveyor belt solution of coordinating many subproductions was in some sense merely the ingenious conclusion of prior developments. Yet it was seen immediately as a change of great significance. It paced standardized work inexorably while at the same time reducing the need for direct command–obedience relations, for 'obstrusive foremanship' as two contemporary observers put it (H. L. Arnold and L. F. Faurote, 1915; quoted in Edwards, 1979: 119). The car assembly line came to symbolize both the unimagined productivity of industrial mass production *and* the extremes of fragmentation and degradation of work characteristic of such mass production. Charles Sabel (1982: 29) has described its historic impact:

> By the time Henry Ford achieved a practical synthesis of nineteenth-century advances in mass-production techniques, his solution seemed a triumph of the inevitable...Ford's ideas would fascinate the Bolsheviks and German Social Democrats, Louis Renault no less than Giovanni Agnelli. The first automobile factory in Czechoslovakia to use assembly-line techniques, built by Skoda in 1925, was called America.

Even though Ford's assembly line could be seen both as a mere further step in the evolution of industrial work and as the inevitable consequence of mass markets and mass production, it did meet with resistance. This resistance came in unorganized fashion, as turnover; but it was massive: 'By 1914 so many workers were fired or quit that five hundred new workers had to be hired every day to replenish the fifteen thousand-person workforce; the payroll office maintained records on nearly one hundred thousand persons previously employed at Ford' (Edwards, 1979: 121). This resistance declined soon – an outcome one could expect in view of the lack of worker organization; in addition, in 1914 Ford curbed the foremen's arbitrary power of dismissal and announced the famous Five-Dollar-a-Day wage, while unemployment was rising nationwide to 15 per cent; ten thousand people sought jobs at Ford the day after the new wage was announced.[8] Not surprisingly Arnold and Faurote could observe in 1915 that the workers at Ford were

> absolutely docile. New regulations, important and trivial, are made almost daily: workmen are studied individually and changed from place to place with no cause assigned, as the bosses see fit, and not one word of protest is ever spoken, because every man knows the door to the street stands open for any man who objects in any way, shape, or manner to instant and unquestioning obedience to any direction whatever (quoted by Edwards, 1979: 121).

Overwhelming market power thus ended this initial resistance to assembly line production. Yet the system was challenged time and time again, especially when management attempted speed-ups of production. The famous conflicts which erupted in 1972 at the General Motors Vega plant on Ohio are a recent example.[9].

Assembly-line production was part of a larger transformation of the labour process in the decades around the turn of the century, a transformation which wrested more radically than ever before *de facto* control of work from workers and transferred it to management. Harry Braverman has concentrated scholarly attention on this transformation in his seminal *Labor and Monopoly Capital: the degradation of work in the twentieth century* (1974). On this account a radical reorganization of work came about in these decades because of two interconnected and continuing developments: massive technological innovation leading to machine-dominated production and a managerial drive towards efficiency and control of which Taylor's *Scientific Management* was the outstanding manifesto. Together, the two developments separated the conception and design from the execution of work and arrogated to management and engineering departments the work knowledge and the relative autonomy hitherto held by industrial craftsmen. These changes are related to the broader transition from more competitive forms of capitalist production and exchange to 'monopoly capitalism', characterized by the emergence of the large corporation and, more importantly, by the establishment of monopoly, oligopoly or price leadership by one or a few companies in most of the important industrial sectors. In retrospect it is clear that this transition did not remain confined to new forms of market exchange. It reshaped the whole social order – the role of the state, the interrelations between social classes and, last but not least, the organization of production at the workplace.

Before we turn to a fuller discussion of this major transition around the turn of the century in order to explore the role of power and conflict played in it, we have first to gain an understanding of the changes that ushered in the industrial system of work. There is no obvious baseline discernible in the complex sequences and juxtapositions of early modern industry, and most attempts to delineate one end up with a simplified and often idealized picture of a previous 'old order'. What separates capitalism, in one of several possible definitions, from other and earlier forms of production is that owners of capital funds insert themselves between direct producers and consumers: attracted by the profit chances this market access provides, capitalists thus come to organize the production of workers who cannot afford to supply themselves with the means of production and who are in need of advances for the means of subsistence before their product is sold. By this definition, capitalist forms of production antedate by many generations the industrial revolution proper with its factories, machines and mechanical sources of power. Such early manifestations of capitalism, currently the subject of intense discussion under the name of 'protoindustrialization',[10] took many different and often quite modest forms, including cottage industries with 'putting out' capitalists and workshops with ignored or eluded old legal limitations of apprenticeship and equipment, but kept still to a moderate size, at least by later standards.

It is important to realize that the medieval and post-medieval guild and craft system was maintained by legal constraints. Far from being a simple organizational reflection of the available technology, it rested on coercive regulation; and when it broke down the political struggle between capitalists and workers over whose interests would be protected by the coercive machinery of the state was a decisive phase of the transition. To cite but one example, the English Weavers' Act of 1555 made it illegal for people outside of towns to have more than one weaving loom. Stephen Marglin (1974: 41) comments:

> To be the occasion of parliamentary repression, the loom shop must have been a real economic threat to the independent weavers even in the sixteenth century. By the same token, there must have been a class that stood to profit from the expansion of factory organization. The differences between the sixteenth and later centuries was in the relative power of this class and the classes that opposed the development of capitalist enterprise.

By the beginning of the nineteenth century the power balance had shifted radically against domestic workers and independent producers. Some excerpts from the account of E. P. Thompson (1963: 526-9) make this graphically clear:

> Every attempt to enforce statute law favorable to the workers' interests ended in failure or financial loss. The west of England woollen workers raised subscriptions to empower attorneys to commence actions against gig-mills and against unapprenticed men, but none were successful. The masters, however, were disturbed enough to petition for the repeal of all protective legislation covering the woollen industry. In successive years, an annual suspending Bill was pushed through the House with almost no discussion, waiving all protective legislation on the workers' behalf, while the quasi-legal Institution incurred endless expenses trying to resist the masters' progress.

By 1806, support for the workers' effort had broadened. The weavers' organization, the 'Institution', now cooperated with colliers, shoemakers, cabinet-makers and many other trades.

All artisans saw this as a test case, indicative of the restoration or the total abrogation of the old protective or arbitrative labor code which alone afforded any hope of legal defense against the full impact of wage-cutting and labor dilution...The witnesses all converged in a general detestation of the factory system...It would be a sad understatement to say that the men's witnesses before the 1806 Committee met with a frosty reception. They and their counsel were browbeaten and threatened by the advocates of *laissez-faire* and the anti-Jacobin tribunes of order. Petitions were seen as evidence of conspiracy...It was held to be an outrageous offense that they had collected money from outside their ranks and had been in contact with the woollen workers of the west. They were forced to reveal the names of their fellow officers. Their books were seized. Their accounts were scrutinized. The committee dropped all pretense of judicial impartiality, and constituted itself into an investigating tribunal. 'Your Committee need scarcely remark,' it reported to the House of Commons, 'that such Institutions are, in their ultimate tendencies, still more alarming in a political, than in a commercial view'...Finally, in 1809 all the protective legislation in the woollen industry – covering apprenticeship, the gig-mill, and the number of looms – was repealed. The road was now open for the factory, the gig-mill, the shearing frame, the employment of unskilled and juvinile labor.

There is, of course, a ready-made interpretation which dismisses these conflicts as ephemeral skirmishes, hopelessly quixotish attempts on the part of workers' to fight against the tide of technological innovation and, ultimately, against the phenomenal increase in the satisfaction of their own needs and wants. Their resistance, in this view, is only understandable when seen as growing out of their non-rational attachment to an established mode of work and life; indeed, does not E. P. Thompson himself speak of a 'general revulsion against the great employers who were *breaking down customs and disrupting a settled way of life*'? (1963: 528, my emphasis).

This argument overlooks the stark fact that very similar struggles, though with quite different outcomes, had been carried on for several centuries before the capitalists won. It does not appreciate that the material cornucopia in a future which we know by hindsight could not very well convince workers whose lives were upset and whose living standards remained low or even diminished; we might remember here that contemporary learned opinion – from Adam Smith to Malthus and Ricardo, not to mention Marx – did not foresee a sustained rise in real wages above the subsistence level. Finally, the argument fails to see that, while custom and tradition remove many aspects of the social patterns they stabilize from rational scrutiny, they typically correspond to important underlying interests of the people involved. If the traditional pattern becomes upset, not only do these interests assert themselves, but they can count on the 'non-rational' attachments created by custom and tradition to help overcome in part the organizational disabilities of 'the many'. It is this partial and temporary solution to the Olsonian problem of collective action that accounts for the fact that resistance is strongest in transition periods, when individual responses are still coordinated, in a fashion, by commitments to shared customary expectations and to the social bonds associated with them.

Stephen Marglin (1974) has offered an analysis of the early capitalist forms of division of labour, which pursues radically a perspective similar in important ways to the one proposed here. He argues that both the specialization of work in the putting out system and its centralization in the factory developed not because these were technically more productive forms of work organization but for reasons of entrepreneurial control and profit. Too little is known, perhaps, about the emergence of division of labour in the putting out systems to make a decisive argument about the causes and motivations that stood behind this development. Marglin provides only some anecdotal direct evidence for the divide-and-conquer view of specialization and points to the lack of specialization in coal mining as indirect support because here capitalist control rested on property rights in the land and did not need the prop of minutely specialized work without access to the market.

Evidence on the rise of the factory system is much more detailed, however, and it is strong. The early factory entrepreneurs were explicitly bent on controlling pilfering, wanted a closer supervision of work and its pace, and sought to leave workers only the choice between long hours of work and no work at all. These goals could be, and were, accomplished with factory organization. Furthermore, the concentration of work in factories often came about *before* technical changes, such as the use of new sources of energy, which in the alternate view are the primary cause and rationale for the factory system. (Most authorities agree that the desire for more discipline and supervision played *some* role.) Finally, factories were resisted by workers in a struggle that was lost because of an abundant supply of labour, because union organization broke down, and because the state guaranteed capitalists' interests while actively destroying past regulations protecting the interests of labour and the workers' right to organize (see Thompson, 1963: 296–305, 311–12, on the case of the weavers). But did not the factory organization in fact constitute a framework suitable for technical innovations and thus prove its efficiency? Marglin argues persuasively that invention followed rather than led the process: 'The steam mill didn't give us the capitalist; the capitalist gave us the steam mill' (1974: 41).

Why did workers resist the factory? E. P. Thompson observes about the woollen weavers: 'They resented, first, the discipline; the factory bell or hooter; the time-keeping which over-rode ill-health, domestic arrangements, or the choice of more varied occupations.' Even more important was their distaste for obedience to orders: 'To "stand at their command" – this was the most deeply resented indignity.' Other reasons derived from the history of factories and the image that history had created: 'There had been a time when factories had been thought of as kinds of workhouses for pauper children; and even when this prejudice passed, to enter the mill was to fall in status from a self-motivated man, however poor, to a servant or "hand".' And finally, the mills 'were held to be "immoral" – places of sexual license, foul language, cruelty, violent accidents, and alien manners' (Thompson; 1963: 305, 306, 307).

These reasons and resentments were closely intertwined with the ways in which the factory system was imposed. The poorest and the hardest-pressed workers submitted to factory discipline, and that very fact lowered the status of factory workers. 'All persons working on the power-loom', said a witness before the Select Committee on Hand-Loom Weavers' Petitions in 1835, 'are working there by force, because they cannot exist any other way; they are generally people that have been distressed in their families and their affairs broken up.' Contemporary opinion referred to the groups from which factory workers were recruited as 'the dishonorable trades': 'a pool of surplus labor, semi-employed, defenseless, and undercutting each other's wages' (Thompson, 1963: 307 and 280). The concern with the factories' impact on morality and on the upbringing of children cannot be separated from the imperious disregard of profit-oriented employment policies for the inherited structure of the family which resulted in massive factory employment of children and women, and in discrimination against adult men because of their higher customary wages. Thompson speaks of 'the weaver's shame' which was increased by 'his dependence upon his wife and children, the enforced and humiliating reversal of traditional roles'.[11] Employing children – more malleable and defenceless than adults – was critical to the establishment of the factory system; as Andrew Ure put it in 1835 (Marglin, 1974: 30):

> Even at the present day, when the system is perfectly organized, and its labor lightened to the utmost, it is found nearly impossible to convert persons past the age of puberty, whether drawn from rural or from handicraft occupations, into useful factory hands. After struggling for a while to conquer their listless or restive habits, they either renounce the employment spontaneously, or are dismissed by the overlookers on account of inattention.

During the one hundred years from 1750 to 1850 'the bargaining position of labor was generally poor'. This is the lapidary conclusion of Sidney Pollard's (1978: 103) review in the *Cambridge Economic History of Europe*, which assiduously pursues the complexities and contradictions of labour history during the industrial revolution. Supply and demand on the labour market shifted to labour's disadvantage because of immigration, because of indigenous population growth and because of the limited geographic mobility of many workers. The market disadvantages were reinforced by the advances of the factory system itself – by its long hours, by its more intense pace of work, and by the substitution of technology for labour.[12] In the middle of the nineteenth century Pollard estimates that one-third of the workers in London were unemployed and another third had only part-time employment. Averaging good and bad years and the varying conditions in different industrial centres, he concludes that 15–20 per cent of labour capacity was not used (1978: 125 and 127).

Such pressures on the job market undermined customary wages, and they made people ready to undercut collective organization and established work patterns. A weakened collective response was finally subjected to assaults by courts and parliament, of which only a few indications have been given above. Actually, Pollard (1978: 150) considers the fact that during the hundred years of the industrial revolution 'the political power...came increasingly to be in the hands of the owning and entrepreneurial classes' even more significant than the social and economic advantages of the employers. 'The state apparatus of coercion', he finds, 'was used, whenever necessary, and whenever economic and social forces alone could not have achieved it, to make sure that there was an overall abundance of labour, so that the market was rigged against labour.'

These are the major immediate reasons why labour's resistance to the factory system did not win. It is not necessary to subscribe to Marglin's absolute rejection of technical superiority of the new forms of division of labour and organization of work as an important factor in the situation; yet even an analyst as much inclined to give neoclassical economics its due as Max Weber insists on the coequal role of power:

> Historically, the expropriation of labor (from the means of production) has arisen since the sixteenth century, within the context of an economy developing through extensive and intensive expansion of markets, because of the absolute superiority and actual indispensability of a management individually oriented to market situations on the one hand and because of sheer power constellations on the other.[13]

The early factory, once it persisted past the resistance of the initial generations of workers and settled into an accepted pattern, had a simple structure of control. It relied on direct command and supervision, buttressed by legal coercion and the economic leverage derived from market conditions more or less favourable to employers. In smaller firms the relation between masters and workers was a personal one, in larger enterprises foremen mediated between employers and employees. Actually we find a great variety of arrangements, with several forms of subcontracting and different pay and incentive schemes. Furthermore, the levels of skill, as well as the attendant relative power of workers, varied between industries and changed over time, with massive deskilling processes in such fields as weaving running side by side with the emergence of new skilled occupations in other lines of work for which mechanics and engineers are good examples. Still, for broad comparative purposes one can, as Richard Edwards does in his brilliant study of changes in work control, *Contested Terrain* (1979), group the manifold variations of work control in the early factories into the broad category of direct, hierarchic control. This pattern constitutes the baseline for Braverman's analysis of the *Degradation of work in the twentieth century* in the United States.

While Braverman's work has ushered in a veritable renaissance of the social and historical study of work, subsequent research and discussions[14] have revealed flaws in his analysis that are critical for the issues which occupy us here. That he gives a somewhat idealized picture of the role of craftsmen in industrial work prior to the 'rationalization' of work around the turn of the century and in turn neglects the creation of new skilled jobs in this transition to modern mass production (see Montgomery, 1979: 177–19; Stark, 1980) is of less concern here; more important is that his conception of a transformation in North America according to inherent laws of capitalist development neither leaves room for class resistance and struggle over the organization of work nor permits him to recognize other historical contingencies which co-determined the outcomes of the transformation.

Edwards (1979) begins his account of this transformation in North America with an analysis of the increasing tensions within the system of direct control. The growth of companies and workshops destroyed the personal element which had become both buffer and cement in the relations between workers and employers in smaller factories and shops. The role of the foreman, mediating between management and the worker, became problematic from both sides. Not any more tied to the capitalist by personal bonds, the supervisor wielded formidable power, though mostly through negative sanctions.

> The internal structure of the firm thus came to mirror more accurately and more harshly the class division in society at large. The continued growth in the firm's workforce extended this process to crisis proportions. At both Pullman and U.S. Steel, the harsh and oppressive quality of shop-floor life and the total absence of positive incentives provoked almost perpetual conflict and, eventually, spectacular outbursts. Intimately connected to this conflict was the increasing difficulty that capitalists encountered in ensuring that foremen would use their power in the firm's interest rather than their own. Foremen were notoriously unpredictable in this respect, as the complaints of workers seem to bear out. Foremen's identification with management was never assured, for they had goals of their own quite different

from the firm, and favoritism, idiosyncrasies, prejudice, and grudges all seemed to flourish under this system. The result was arbitrary and personal punishment and undoubtedly widespread abuse of power (Edwards, 1979: 54).

The first aspect of the problem, the foremen's loyalty to the firm, particularly problematic in large and in multi-plant companies, is of course exactly analogous to the issues discussed in the previous chapter; but the solutions that were developed for the upper echelons of administration in the state apparatus and in private management were not easily extended to the lower reaches of the hierarchy. The second aspect, the arbitrary use of power on the shop floor, untempered by personal ties or effective managerial control and increasingly resisted by workers in the growing firms, was a new but less stable form of the old pattern of direct hierarchic control. What is significant for us is that the very impetus for changes in the organization of work came from increasing conflicts between workers and supervisors.

This crisis of control within the firm occurred in a larger context. Increasing conflict within firms coincided with middle-class opposition to trusts and the monopolization of the economy. Agrarian interests mounted the powerful challenge of populism. This convergence of several thrusts of opposition to the emerging new economic regime made each movement stronger and created anticipations of far-reaching reform.

Yet corporate business was still in a very powerful position *vis-à-vis* labour, for reasons that are by now familiar because they differ only in their relative weight from the conditions which favoured employers in the early development of capitalism in England. First, in a country with roughly double the population of Great Britain, union membership in the United States amounted to less than half the British figure in 1900.[15] Immigration was massive since the middle of the century and increasingly brought unskilled workers into the job market, who had no tradition of collective organization nor shared customary expectations about acceptable working conditions. Another important migration stream was that of Blacks, freed since the Civil War, who moved north to seek industrial employment. Racial and ethnic heterogeneity added further obstacles to collective organization. At the same time, these migrations continuously fed competitive pressures in the job market, and this effect was probably even more important than the difficulties ethnic diversity created for union organization.

One might expect that under these conditions business would settle the issues largely on its own terms. This is too simplistic a view, however. Solutions to the problems of social control were not obvious. Several were tried; none could be implemented without conflict; and all were modified in the process. At several junctures third parties entered the situation – above all the state, but also newly organized professional groups – and conflicts turned into multifaceted confrontations because both management and labour became internally differentiated. Among the different remedies tried were attempts to secure the loyalty of workers through paternalistic welfare schemes, the organization of unions under company control, the introduction of 'scientific management' as a means to break the craftsmen's control and to intensify labour, and the increased use of machine-paced work processes as mechanization advanced in great strides. Different recent analyses have given one or another of these developments the central role in transforming industrial work around the turn of the century. Braverman sees Taylorism and deskilling as the major change; by contrast, Edwards considers scientific management, welfare capitalism and company unions as failed attempts to deal with the new industrial control problems, while 'technical control' through mechanization achieved a temporary solution which only later ran into mounting problems. Rather than enter into this dispute about broad characterizations and the periodization of labour history in the United States, we will just briefly discuss some power aspects of the implementation of 'scientific management' and similar forms of rationalization.[16]

The movement towards scientific management was an ambitious attempt to gain full and detailed control over the labour process and to rationalize – study and rearrange – work literally move by move, time fraction by time fraction. In the process, engineering knowledge and planning would replace the knowledge held up to then by workers and skilled craftsmen. Rationalization of work was thus a major advance in the division of mental and manual labour. The thrust for the movement came from industrial engineers who emerged during the late nineteenth century as a sizeable occupational group and – with the growth of large enterprises, increased mechanization and the rationalization of the work process – carved out a place for themselves in the overall industrial division of labour.

Their number grew from 7000 in 1880 to 136,000 in 1920 (Layton, 1971: 3).

Scientific management was not only a scheme to be imposed on workers; it also challenged, at least by implication, the exclusive organizational prerogatives of the old management. In Taylor's programme engineers were inserted into the firm's hierarchy which now would be a hierarchy of expertise. This not only altered the existing structure of authority, but it had troubling substantive consequences: adopting Taylorist principles frequently led to strikes and other disruptions of production.

If management, then, had in these conflicts its internal divisions, so did labour. Opposition to Taylorism and to the broader thrust towards increased industrial efficiency came from the craftsmen, many of whom were being displaced out of positions of control. David Montgomery (1979: 9–31) has portrayed how the work culture of American craftsmen gave them both the motivation and a certain capacity to resist increased control and rationalization. Similar opposition arose among less skilled workers whose work became more intensive as a result of these innovations. However, the interests of these groups were not the same, their informal relations and formal organizations were quite different, craft culture had strongly exclusive tendencies, and workers with different levels of skill often differed in ethnic background (see Palmer, 1975; Montgomery, 1979; and Stark, 1980).

Major gains for the rationalization movement came during World War One, which also was a time of increased unionization. Massive standardized production demands arising from the war effort created opportunities for mechanization and rationalization of work. State war production boards sought and secured the cooperation of capitalists, industrial engineers and union leaders. Scientific management was expected to provide an objective basis for cooperation. The AFL unions, which had opposed scientific management vigorously before the war, came to accept and to endorse it during this period. They did so even as rank-and-file opposition persisted. Opposition continued until the recession of 1921–2 when unemployment rose to 20 per cent and unions, still largely under craft control and declining in membership, had to fight for survival. Leftist organizations, of some importance until the end of World War One, were now opposed, persecuted and effectively smashed by corporations, craft unions as well as the state apparatus.

What came to be implemented in the organization of work was not, except in a quite small number of firms, Taylor's original programme. Worker opposition had succeeded in preventing that. Yet even Edwards, who stresses the failings of Taylorism (which was in his words 'fought to a standstill' by workers), concedes that scientific management had accomplished changes of lasting importance:

> One important element that did endure was the aggressive attempt to gain management control over the special knowledge of production – what Harry Braverman has brilliantly described as the 'separation of conception from execution'. Another element that survived was the notion that each worker's job should be carefully defined, including standards of 'adequate' performance. The basic impulse to define jobs in terms of output rather than simply obedience to the foreman's orders would be picked up later by the structural control systems. Yet another lesson was the need to subject management itself to management control, specifically by breaking the power of foremen to act as absolute rulers of the shops (Edwards, 1979: 104).

In the perspective adopted here, several aspects of this development stand out as specially important. First, the very invention of solutions to new problems, rather than just flowing from the interests of capital-owners, is intertwined with the autonomy and power interests of different occupational and professional groups. Taylorism cannot be understood except in the context of the emergence of industrial engineering as a profession. Second, the relative strength of different groups of workers is of critical importance for the outcome. 'The structure of jobs – their stability or instability, who is employed and who unemployed – is shaped by economic, political, and ideological relations determined by the conflicts and alliances between struggling groups' (Stark, 1970: 116).[17] Third, even an ethnically and occupationally divided work force with a weak collective organization could offer sufficient resistance to force modifications in the new designs for the labour process. More investment in productive capital and a more complex organization of firms increase – other things equal – the need for cooperation from workers and thus reinforce the core of worker strength, which is grounded in human discretion. Fourth, the union leadership pursued policies that were at odds not only with the interests of a large proportion of their members as defined by some outside observer, but also with the views of the rank and file as expressed in unsponsored strikes, sabotage and other acts of resistance. The new alliances with industrial engineers and state managers not only led the union organizations away from broader political goals but also permitted them to continue with organizational forms best suited for skilled workers and at variance with the industry-wide interests of un- and semi-skilled workers. Fifth, state intervention played a critical role in the transition, first by creating a massive war demand for standardized products and by bringing together the previously opposed camps of industrial engineers and union leaders, later by combating leftist tendencies in the workers' movement. In contrast to the state interventions typical of the early decades of capitalism, this episode cannot be viewed simply as an action on behalf of capitalist interests. During the war the state apparatus pursued with a certain autonomy interests of its own reflecting neither the will of capital nor that of labour in any simple and straightforward way; and the pursuit of these state interests had a decisive impact on the course of the movement to rationalize work and management.

CURRENT PATTERNS OF WORK ORGANIZATION

The various forms of work organization and control we have discussed historically continue to exist side by side today. In different lines of work, in different types of firms and in different industries we find direct supervision and command–obedience relations, fairly self-directed craft-like production, highly mechanized work in which pace and discipline are technically determined, and various types of labour whose standards are set by engineering design and time--motion studies. At the same time, new patterns of work organization have developed since the 1920s. Especially in large firms with secure market positions new forms of production control have emerged which can best be described as bureaucratic (Weber, 1922/68; Edwards, 1979. Burawoy, 1979, 1981).

The outlines of this organization pattern are familiar: some degree of employment security, hierarchic gradation of positions, promotion from within the firm based partly on seniority and partly on performance, rules defining obligations and rights which cannot be changed by management at will and which in part replace commands and obedience, and corresponding provisions for internal adjudication or arbitration of complaints. This system grants workers a certain autonomy and maximizes in turn the generation of consent, reaping for the employer the benefits of worker loyalty and voluntary cooperation.

Organizational innovations which, as we saw in the last chapter, responded originally to the problems of division of authority, are here extended from the top down to the lower echelons of the firm. In many large companies such as IBM, Polaroid or General Electric this includes not only lower white-collar employees but direct production workers, too. Even though the advantages granted in this extension of bureaucratic control are greatly attenuated in the lower ranks compared to the privileges bestowed at the higher levels, the fundamental logic remains the same: issues of trust, which grow in importance with organizational complexity and the value of capital investment, find a solution of sorts through a system of mutually binding rules, material and symbolic incentives, and eventually the emergence of an ethos which is impersonally oriented to performance. Organizational encouragement of voluntary cooperation replaces the threat of negative sanctions, of loss of employment in particular, as the major motivation for compliance. While this bureaucratic control compares favourably with the autocracy of owners, who themselves are pressed by the market, and perhaps even more favourably with the human deprivations of fragmented machine-paced work, which in some sense could be seen historically as its closest cousin, it is well to remember that Max Weber – using the standards for a humane life current in the cultivated bourgeoisie of the turn of the century – saw bureaucratic organization as a system of domination that stifles individuality and freedom even as it grants circumscribed spaces of autonomy.

The conditions for this development were foreshadowed already in the issues of work organization that arose around the turn of the century. Increasing numbers of white-collar workers and of technical and professional employees were absorbed into the early bureaucratic patterns; and the implementation of modified forms of scientific management on the shop floor pointed towards an extension of rule-oriented forms of control to direct production wherever valuable machinery or the intractable problems of direct hierarchic control put a premium on any kind of labour organization which could elicit consent and cooperation.

Developments in the larger society since the Great Depression and World War Two contributed to the same outcomes in important, if often indirect, ways. The New Deal encouraged union organization;[18] and the extension of bureaucratic organization to production work became a way to stabilize negotiated gains and to integrate union strength into the day-to-day affairs of the firm. In other cases bureaucratization of work control was used as a means to fend off unionization of the work force. The conglomeration and monopolization of production, which began in the nineteenth century, continued into the twentieth century. This is of critical importance for the patterns of bureaucratic control because even limited employment security presupposes some insulation from the vagaries of the market.

Centralization and monopolization had of course much more far-reaching consequences for the political economy as a whole. We cannot adequately discuss here all the issues of the transition from competitive capitalism to monopoly capitalism. Suffice it to point out that as the role of the market automatism declined, two systems of domination gained in functional importance – that of the firm and that of the state. Expanding its activities beyond guaranteeing the bare institutional infrastructure of capitalist employment and exchange, the modern state not only engages in economic intervention and planning to an extent never known before yet indispensable to the maintenance of high production and employment levels; it also has become deeply involved in human services and the reproduction of labour power – in education and training; the maintenance of physical and mental health; and the provision of income during illness, unemployment and old age. Together with a much higher level of material want satisfaction, these state activities strengthen the bargaining position of labour, especially of skilled labour, and stimulate demands for an 'industrial citizenship' analogous to the citizen's role *vis-à-vis* the state.

The emergence of bureaucratic control of productive work has critical importance for the present and the future, but does not define the whole of current patterns and tendencies in industrial work organization. It would be preposterous to attempt to paint here such a comprehensive picture. One recent development which has received much attention deserves brief comment, however. Especially in the automobile industry there have been various attempts to reverse extremes of job fragmentation, to 'enrich' work by reducing minute specialization and to make workers participate in limited production planning and work redesign. These changes, though often described grandiosely as 'humanization' of work, seek to increase the efficiency and profitability of production. In a simple view, one might see them as reversals of earlier 'mistakes'; but that raises the question why these 'mistakes' were made in the first place and why they spread throughout whole industries and around the globe. A better interpretation seems that the current changes reflect an improved bargaining position, and, possibly, changed preferences on the part of workers and organized labour (see Stephens and Stephens, 1982). Even an analysis that uses efficiency and productivity as its master concepts cannot escape the fact that preferences may and do change, and that it is the leverage workers derive from their position in production and the power of organized labour (if the priorities of workers are articulated into union policy), which translate given preferences into costs. How productive a work arrangement is, and whether a reduction of job fragmentation leads to greater productivity, depends then on worker attitudes backed by power.

'Fordism' is, however, not likely to disappear once it has taken hold because of such minor reversals in the minute specialization of machine-paced work. A bigger challenge to this mechanical control of the labour process may come from competing production forms which respond to more varied and more specialized demand than is compatible with standardized mass production. This is the prospect which Charles Sabel (1982) opens in his study of the current division of labour in industry, significantly titled *Work and Politics*. In an analysis that covers market change and technical developments as well as political and labour market conflicts, Sabel shows for instance that in central Italy a high-technology 'cottage industry' is taking hold, which involves a complex cooperation of owners, engineers, technicians and skilled workers in small enterprises and represents an extremely flexible division of labour.

The very coexistence of radically different forms of work organization within the same economy points to underlying differences in power relations. Bureaucratic rule orientation and job security, however fragile in major recessions, constitute a costly pattern of employment which presupposes that the firm has monopolistic or stable oligopolistic market advantages *and* is dealing with a work force whose bargaining position is vastly superior to that of other segments of the labour market. Large firms in the less competitive core of the economy, which employ high proportions of workers with special skills, depend on worker cooperation for the maintenance and full utilization of very large investments and either face strongly organized workers or anticipate the possibility of effective unionization, are the most likely to move in the direction of the bureaucratic employment type. Access to employment in these firms tends to be limited because of the practice of internal promotion and because hiring at the entry points typically relies on standardized qualification certificates. At the opposite extreme we find small firms in competitive markets dealing with a labour force in a much weaker bargaining position due to lower levels of skill, intermittent labour force participation and – in part because of these first two circumstances – weaker union organization. In these firms the old patterns of direct hierarchic control by owners and supervisors are often still flourishing. [19]

Comparisons across countries similarly suggest that the relative power of employers and different groups of workers, as well as power considerations of the dominant groups responding to different problem situations, make for more or less clear-cut differences in national patterns of work organization. The impact of power factors often plays itself out over long periods of time and is in complex ways interrelated with other causal conditions; still it will not do therefore simply to invoke 'cultural differences' in order to account for national differences in work organization. A few indications of some contrasts and similarities between countries must suffice to illustrate the point.

As the first instance we can use some broad observations of Burawoy (1981: 103–4) which assess the different strength of labour in Britain and in the United States. They support the same theoretical argument even as, in some detail, they give a variant perspective on developments discussed earlier:

> In Britain the working class was shaped through its struggles with capital. It developed its characteristic strength by evolving along with capital as the latter passed through its various phases: handicraft, putting out, manufacturing, and modern industry...The ravages of the industrial revolution threw workers together into

powerful political movements. The English working class more than any other was forged through a prolonged period of political struggles aimed at transforming the state – struggles over combination acts, factory acts, poor-law reform, corn laws, and the extension of suffrage. Capital, although early on forced into employers' associations, was continuously weakened by its relatively small scale. The legacy of being the first nation to industrialize was a competitive structure of industrial production in which labor managed to resist the untrammeled power of capital.

In the United States constitutional, geopolitical, social structural and demographic conditions of the struggle between labour and capital were very different from the start and resulted in very different class relations:

> The widespread presence of political rights and the politics of an open frontier (which made labor relatively scarce) meant that working-class combination was not the matter of survival that it was in England. Violent though they were, the struggles of the late nineteenth and early twentieth centuries were an expression of the weakness of the American proletariat, not of its strength . . . Capital was able to launch into technological development, new forms of industrial organization, and changing market structures relatively unhindered by resistance from organized labor . . . The rapid mechanization not only presupposed weaker resistance from labor but further undermined the resistance that did exist. Thus, unions were frequently crushed by the advance of capital in the era of transition between 1890 and 1920 . . . Only after the completion of the first phase of the scientific-technical revolution and the breakdown of welfare capitalism did industrial unionism establish itself in the corporate sector. But this was a form of unionism shaped in accordance with the needs of capital, and took the expropriation of control over the labor process as a fait accompli.

The second instance concerns the case of Japanese factory organization, often seen as the paramount example of culturally determined exceptionalism (Abegglen, 1958; but see Dore, 1973, and Marsh and Mannari, 1976). Company welfare capitalism – most strongly developed in large Japanese firms in the first half of this century and retained in changed form until the present, but not without lesser parallels in Imperial Germany, the United States around the turn of the century, and even early British industrialization – could invoke in Japan pre-industrial value traditions and model itself after public employment. But there was little direct institutional continuity (Dore, 1973: 401). Scarcity of skilled labour, regulations and massive pressures by the state, and the emergence of strikes and unions in 1897 and in the years after 1918 were at least as important as cultural traditions in and of themselves; pre-empting the development of a strong working-class movement and open class conflict was an important rationale for lifetime employment and paternalist company welfare (Matsushima, 1966; also Dore, 1973: 375–403). These power factors interacted in complex ways with value traditions and ideologies as well as with certain consequences of late development, which cannot be taken up here (Dore, 1973).

Less well known are national differences between high-trust and low-trust work cultures, to use the categories of Alan Fox (1974). A study comparing work and work organization in French and German factories with similar technical equipment confirmed earlier impressionistic judgements of German work culture displaying high trust relations and French work culture low-trust ones (Maurice, Sellier and Silvestre, 1979; see also the discussion by Sabel, 1982: 22–5). It is very unlikely that such differences are simply an expression of contrasting national cultures; a more plausible explanation should probably first look at the strong state involvement in vocational and technical training in Germany since the nineteenth century. These efforts initially responded to drastic shortages of skilled labour in the 'first developing country', but later created a highly skilled labour force which is still characteristic of both West and East Germany. The aspirations of skilled workers and craftsmen for greater freedom from detailed regulation and close supervision today are likely to receive organizational support from unions and factory workers councils, in which skilled workers are over-represented.

Finally a glimpse at labour control in East European state socialism. In the German Democratic Republic, as well as in the other countries of Eastern Europe, workers are represented by unions which at the same time serve as instruments of controlling and mobilizing labour for centrally planned production goals. Freedom of association and other means of affecting state action from 'below' are severely curtailed. State, party and union seek to implement fully the scientific–technical revolution in industry and to gain workers' cooperation for the required reorganization of work.

At first sight it might seem that workers here are reduced to the rock-bottom capacity for resistance with derives from the leeway of discretion in everyday work and from the spontaneous solidarity among people who have similar interests and who are in close contact with each other. However, there is one factor which – as we know from the opposite case of capitalist economies in recession – should strengthen the bargaining position of workers considerably: the absence of unemployment. Due to the consistent full-employment policies of the socialist state, and perhaps reinforced by the contradictory functioning of centrally planned economies, there is a persistent labour shortage in the GDR as well as in most other East European countries.

What are the consequences? We have too litle reliable information to answer with certainty, but it seems clear that secure employment does improve the position of workers in the day-to-day mini-bargains of the shop floor (see Sabel and Stark, 1982). It also appears that the work collectives – union-organized work groups which seek to integrate work planning at the point of production, arbitration of grievances, the informal social life at work, mutual help, and leisure activities – protect some autonomy of workers on the shop floor and even become to a certain extent channels for grass roots influence on company policy (M. Rueschemeyer, 1982; M. Rueschemeyer and B. Scharf, forthcoming). Yet the absence of working-class organizations more strongly responsive to worker interests than are the East European trade unions seems to have far-reaching disruptive consequences: the considerable power potential which arises from guaranteed employment is reduced to expressions that are individualized and passive – high turnover, apathy, slow work and forms of official participation which merely mimic the appearance of real cooperation. Next to the problems of coordination in centrally planned economies, this may well be the most important cause for their notoriously low levels of productivity.

CONCLUSION

The industrial organization of work has come a long way since the beginnings of capitalism. Does it still make sense to analyze it with the concepts that were fashioned by Adam Smith and Karl Marx, or even Durkheim and Weber? There is no doubt that the most ambitious attempt to forecast history in the long run, that of Marx, has failed. It was an attempt which centred around the relations between capital and labour and had at its core problems of labour control and organization. That it failed became evident since before World War One; and the resurgence of a changed capitalism since the Great Depression and the destructive cataclysms of World War Two has convinced everybody but a few post-Stalinist believers protected by ignorance and political discipline.

As it turned out, competitive capitalism was pregnant not with socialism but with a new form of capitalism – monopoly capitalism – in which the patterns of struggle and competition have been transformed. What Marx missed was the possibility of tempering the worst effects of competition without undermining competition completely and the possibility that class struggle not only could be contained within the parameters of capitalism but could be harnessed to the reproduction of capitalism if workers extracted concessions that would make it more tolerable. Class struggle was not the gravedigger of capitalism but its savior (Burawoy, 1979: 195).

Marx failed more fundamentally than by missing the containment of both market competition and class struggle. His was a prophecy about the course of history; it *had* to fail despite his astute analyses which shaped much of subsequent social science. That anticipations of the historical future turn out wrong would not be astonishing even of social analysis were more scientific than it is. It is easy to point to mistaken forecasts in the work of Smith and Spencer, Durkheim and Weber, and even Tocqueville. What sets Marx apart is a Hegelian view of history, a conception of history as an organic whole with an end inherent in its law of development. It is this view that has been shattered – by arguments and events. Few open minds can entertain the idea that Soviet state socialism represents the penultimate stage in the destiny of mankind. Nor is it plausible to take the new corporation-dominated and state-managed capitalism as the fulfilment of human history, an illusion which sometimes seems implicit in the unspoken premises of a shortsighted and ahistorical social science.

However, the concepts fashioned in the century-long response to the transformation of Europe by capitalism can be separated from the philosophy of progress – straight-line or dialectical. That separation was one of the major achievements of Max Weber, aided both by his broad comparative historical vision and by his stoic pessimism. Yet as we have seen, his conceptual framework for analysing the industrial labour process, while by no means identical, showed important similarities to that of Marx.

The central ideas of Marx and Weber remain useful for understanding division of labour in industry even after several generations of massive socioeconomic change. The concern with power, including the power derived from one's position on the market, the focus on organized domination expressed early in Marx's distinction between division of labour in manufacture and division of labour in society, the questions raised about collective organization and about the relation between what happens on the shop floor and in the job market and what happens in the political determination of state action – these problem formulations and strategies have not lost their intellectual power in the new political economy of advanced capitalism and state socialism. In fact, power and domination, resistance and conflict are perhaps even more important categories today, when two systems of organized domination – the corporation and the state – have taken over a good part of the functions previously met by competitive market exchange.

A whole group of fresh studies on the development of industrial division of labour has in recent years documented what role was played by managerial design and imposition but also by organized opposition as well as uncoordinated resistance of workers. Power and domination remain real even when resistance and open challenge are not strong. The analysis of consent and accommodation, of their origins and their consequences, is an integral part of the study of power. Power and domination would become irrelevant to the study of division of labour in industry only if we could assume complete harmony among the interests of all parties. That assumption, we can safely assert, has been rendered implausible by the history of conflict over division of labour in industry.

Power struggles involve collective organization as a critical variable. Collective organization is of special significance for 'the many', and it is specially difficult for them to achieve it; but the matter does not end there. Collective organization is not only necessary for the effective pursuit of given interests of a large number of people. It also plays a significant role in defining and shaping these very interests and in delineating the set of people whose interests are to be served. The very constitution of the parties to conflict, then, their social identity and their interests, is partly the result of the process of collective organization. From this it follows that the unity of the working class can never be taken for granted and that its fragmentation, where it occurs, is not just a reflection of 'objective' differences in skill, industry, place, racial and ethnic affiliation, or nationality (themselves subject to continuous social construction and reconstruction), but depends on the political processes of collective organization. This has further consequences for the balance of power and the impact of different interests on the division of labour. Given the fragility of collective organization on the working-class side of struggles over division of labour, the greatest influence should lie with the other side, whose organization is more stable and whose interest in the division of labour is most direct – with corporate management.

Yet we cannot end with the conclusion that now more than ever management will impose those forms of division of labour most desirable from the point of view of the corporation (or the state). We have seen that market changes may limit the potential for standardized mass production and open opportunities for less routinized and fragmented work. We have seen that even subtle expressions of worker dissatisfaction can become sufficiently costly to induce a search for alternative arrangements. We have seen that state intervention and state regulation, in varying degree autonomous from direction by the dominant class, have an increasing impact on markets as well as class relations and even on the organization of work directly, while the political processes shaping state action vary greatly from country to country. In sum, while we recognize an overwhelming imbalance of power in the relations between employers and workers in advanced capitalist countries (as well as in state socialist ones), the constellations of conflict are too historically contingent to allow simple predictions of the future. The future of work in industrial society is not determined by technology in conjunction with an overall efficiency calculus, nor is it dictated by bureaucratic elites in corporations and government. As in the past, it will be the outcome of conflict, even if the parties to these struggles are very uneven in strength.

6

The Political Economy of Professionalization

'Knowledge is power' – the by now trite slogan of nineteenth-century popular thought identifies very well one fundamental aspect of professional work. Experts who possess knowledge which helps in solving urgent problems of others can exert a price, and that price may well be much more than a good fee; it nearly always includes honour and esteem and often influence and power, especially if the experts use their common expertise and social honour as a foundation for collective organization. Furthermore, since knowledge is never a simple, 'objective' reflection of reality but always represents selection and interpretation, and since it shapes (as well as reflects) our ideas of what ought to be, groups in control of a certain body of knowledge have far-reaching influence also in another way: they define the situation for the untutored, they suggest priorities, they shape people's outlook on their life and world, and establish standards for judgement in the different areas of expertise – in matters of health and illness, order and justice, administration of the commonwealth, the organized use of force, the design and deployment of technology, the organization of production.

It is no accident that insights into the relation between knowledge and power became popular in the nineteenth century. The rapidly increasing use of knowledge is characteristic of the modern world; and 'professionalization' – once we push the concept beyond the parochial confines of the historical experience of England and English-speaking countries, where it took one particular form (see Freidson, 1983, and Rueschemeyer, 1983) – professionalization can best be considered as the development of institutional forms for this vastly expanded use of knowledge. The specialization of learned pursuits is of course much older than professionalization in the context of the rise of the modern state, expanding market exchange and increasingly complex industrial production; but the changes in learned work induced by these developments were dramatic and gave a particular salience to the educated classes and their new role in society. This is reflected not only in popular thought; what became visible in the transformations of the European social order is theoretized in the work of the classic social theorists.

Karl Marx is not normally counted among the major students of the professions and of professionalization; yet once we push our questions beyond the narrow framework of a latter-day specialty in sociology we find in his work, as in that of all the classics, illuminating insights about the specialization of learned pursuits, its power implications, and its relation to larger patterns of division of labour. In *The German Ideology*, where he and Engels seek to set out their conception of the fundamentals of historical change, the division of intellectual from other work is given a central role in the overall process of the division of labour: 'Division of labor only becomes truly such from the moment when a division of material from mental labor appears' (1945–6/1978: 159). Marx adds in a marginal note to the manuscript: 'The first form of ideologists, *priests*, is concurrent.'

That religious and intellectual pursuits acquire a socially specialized place is for Marx significant in several ways. Such specialization, first, impoverishes the life of the common people and adds to the advantage of the rulers. 'The class which has the means of material production at its disposal, has control at the same time over the means of mental production, so that thereby, generally speaking, the ideas of those who lack the means of mental production are subject to it' (op. cit.: 172). Second, the division of mental and material labour differentiates within the ruling class the producers of ideas from those who more directly exercise power. 'This cleavage can even develop into a certain opposition and hostility between the two parts, which, however, in the case of a practical collision, in which the class itself is endangered, automatically comes to nothing, in which case there also vanishes the semblance that the ruling ideas were not the ideas of the ruling class and had a power distinct from the power of this class' (op. cit.: 173). While this passage seems to take back in the end what it has given initially, the assertion that specialized intellectual pursuits attain a certain autmomy, we may note that the concluding negation speaks of the rather rare historical situations in which the dominant class as a whole is endangered. Though in the context of their argument the third effect of the specialization of intellectual work – that it creates illusions about the autonomy and the transformative power of ideas – is for the authors the most important, we have here an interest in rescuing the differentiation-within-the-dominant-class hypothesis from being overwhelmed by the anti-idealist polemic agenda of Marx and Engels in 1846.[1]

The emergence of a specialization of intellectual and religious pursuits unquestionably added to the resources of the few in ruling the many. Yet at the same time it represents a power base different from coercion and wealth, one based on mystery, charisma (however routinized), and cultural inheritance. As such it carries the potential for tensions and conflicts within the elite and for a dispersal of power at the top. The conflicts between religious and secular authority in the Middle Ages are perhaps the most dramatic example – one that had extremely powerful and long-lasting consequences as most recently Harold Berman has reminded us with his study of *The formation of the Western legal tradition* (1983).

Marx focused in his comments on the influence knowledge experts have as 'ideologists', on their influence on the ideas prevalent in their society. He neglected their bargaining power as purveyors of useful, and often in fact urgently needed, knowledge. This is quite understandable if we consider the major pre-modern professions – priesthood, law and medicine. Their knowledge rested largely on belief and traditional construction rather than on pragmatically relevant scientific research, and was embedded in diffuse social authority relations, maintained jointly by dominant ideas and organized coercion in addition to habit and custom. The services of the modern professions are much more (though never completely) detached from diffuse relations of authority, social honour and established economic inequality. They are typically delivered in the impersonal market or in meritocratic organizational settings where the practical usefulness of their knowledge more starkly stands out as salient. The modern professions' power rests primarily on this knowledge even though, as we shall see, establishing the validity and the practical value of expert knowledge is itself a political process and not just an intellectual matter. Collective organization is of course a critical power resource for the professions, too, as it is for any other set of people with parallel interests. Bargaining strength based on expertise and collective organization shapes the major foundations of professional power – alliances with powerful groups and class fragments and privileged relations with the major institutional structures of society, expecially the large business corporations and the modern state. As is typical of the arrangements of the powerful, professional institutions and professional privilege are relatively well protected against erosion and tend to persist over time. From this it follows that older expert groups will have significant power advantages – and they do so in fact (see Portwood and Fielding, 1981).[2]

The modern professions, as well as their learned, less knowledgeable but more charismatic ancestors, constitute a critical element in the power constellations of their societies. They represent a challenge to the power of the elites who use their services: Gerhard Lenski (1966: 316) sees in the broad-based expertise of professions and similar occupations a probable cause for the lesser power concentration and lower level of inequality in industrial as compared to agrarian societies. If they do not impose their conceptions and designs, they codetermine major developments in industry as well as in the modern state, a condition which is indicated but not much affected by recurrent condemnations of 'technocracy'. Finally, the various institutional forms for the delivery of expert services are, and have always been shaped by power and conflicts; and this applies also to the process of specialization within the professions (see Bucher and Strauss, 1961).

The professions do not see themselves in this light. They tend to view their role as determined by the logic inherent in problems, circumstances and technology. Power concerns do not at all figure prominently in their self-understanding; and since the dominant ideas of our age are strongly shaped by the ideas of the most educated classes, both the public and much of scholarship take this understanding of professional work for granted. In fact, the appeal of the efficiency conception of division of labour owes much to the self-understanding of the professions, which is in effect just a particular version of that conception. We will see that power plays a large role in this area, too, a much larger one than these ideas allow.

KNOWLEDGE AND POWER

Is knowedge inherently a basis of power? Are there circumstances which enhance that power or diminish it? What is the relation of knowledge as a power resource to other bases of power, especially those of an economic and a political nature? How does it compare with them? What are the possible and likely interrelations among the different bases of power? Ultimately, these questions have to be answered before current disputes about the social role of knowledge experts can be resolved.[3] The following will consider these problems, but attend to only the first questions in any detail and give merely suggestive and sketchy indications about the latter ones.

At the beginning of our discussion of division of labour on the shop floor we encountered the ineradicable element of discretion in even the simplest and the most oppressed forms of human labour. Where complex knowledge is used in the performance of work, it magnifies significantly this element of discretion. It makes control and supervision very costly if not impossible since detailed control of experts requires equally well-qualified controllers. 'Lay' customers – however rich, prestigious or powerful – cannot themselves exercise this control because they often do not know enough even to define what their problem is, not to mention monitoring its solution. If they wish to supervise the expert's work they have to rely on a duplication of services, on trusted expert advisors, second opinions, and other such means.

Of course, not all customers of expert services are lay customers. They may themselves be engineers or lawyers using for a specific problem another engineer or lawyer as a consultant whose work they can in large measure evaluate even if they cannot do it themselves. Similarly, at a lower level of expertise, 'lay' customers may be sufficiently well educated to have a reasonably discriminating judgement of the services they receive. This ability of customers to evaluate expert services is greatly enhanced if there is a close relationship between the quality of work done and the success achieved. In turn, if 'the tree' cannot reasonably 'be judged by its fruit' – as is the case in much of the work of doctors, lawyers or priests – the client is that much more dependent and vulnerable. Dependency and vulnerability are further increased to the extent that the intervention of an expert requires faith and trust in order to succeed. In much of teaching and general medicine, for example and even more in psychotherapeutic work, the interpersonal relation is itself a tool of the intervention, while legal counsel often requires that the client entrust the lawyer with confidences which, if the trust is not justified, expose the client to further harm.

In variable degree, then, the expert is not only a specially helpful but also a potentially dangerous figure since it is often difficult to control his work. This does not matter much if the issues are of moderate importance; but it becomes salient in more significant expert interventions, and the costs of expert services tend to focus them on the more weighty concerns. The contrast between a car mechanic's botching his job and a surgeon's doing so points to a difference in what is at stake as much as, or perhaps more than, to one in the amount of expert knowledge deployed on the occasion. This comparison suggests a critical question for the analysis of continued division of labour in areas of professional work, namely whether a given speciality still deals with some potential high risk (as the primary care physician does even in a world of medical specialization) or is reduced to more limited stakes (as most nursing work is).

So far our discussion suggests two interrelated conclusions: that knowledge experts are likely to enjoy a large degree of autonomy in their work and that many of them – because it is difficult to control their performance, while the stakes are very high – represent a potential threat to their customers' interests. Both of these conclusions are subject to variation and do not simply follow from the fact that knowledge expertise is employed for some practical purpose. Both are the stronger the greater the competence gap is between practitioner and customer, the less certain the outcome is even with excellent work, and the more a successful intervention requires faith and trust on the part of the customer.

These conclusions represent as yet only a modest result about the power implications of using knowledgeable expertise. The expert's greater autonomy in his work constitutes a certain freedom from the power of others; and intervening in the affairs of the client often entails influence – through a determination of what the problem is and through advice that may border on command ('doctor's order'). The two conclusions do, however, set the stage for a fuller understanding of the role power plays in the division and institutionalization of intellectual work. A first step is the proposition that a relation thus characterized – by autonomy on one side, need and not quite calculable risk on the other – is unlikely to be stable, unless further institutional features are built into it. It can be stable if one side or the other has an overwhelming power advantage on other grounds. In that case, which is typical of traditional agrarian societies, the expert service may be rendered by a dominant patron to a dependent client, together with other benevolent and often largely symbolic actions, or by an expert who is at the disposal of a lord on whom, perhaps in addition to a few others, his livelihood depends. In both cases the issues of the expert –client relationship are absorbed into the comprehensive inequality of a broader relationship which gives few options to the dependent client and creates powerful incentives for the dependent expert to do his best (and to hope for the best where the outcome is only loosely related to his efforts). These old patterns of expert service, imbedded in relations of diffuse inequality, gave way to new ones under the impact of expanding market exchange, urbanization, growing prosperity, and the emergence of the modern state.

In expert–client relations with a less one-sided power balance the constellation of expert autonomy, urgent need and potential harm will encourage customers to search for safeguards against the threatening aspects of expert work, and experts in turn will seek to protect their autonomy against unwanted control.[4] In addition, both sides will of course try to protect old and acquire new economic advantages. The search for safeguards and the experts' reaction may take many forms; and so will the outcomes, which depend in large measure on the political power resources of the two sides as well as on the demand for and the supply of expert services, both of which are not independent of state polices.

In these contests over changing institutional forms for the delivery and control of expert services the experts tend to have a significant power advantage in dealing with a clientele composed of many individual customers: they have less difficulty in achieving corporate identity and collective organization. Fewer in number, they share a similar education, often come from comparable origins, occupy a similar place in the division of labour and thus in the structure of society, and encounter similar difficulties and problems – among them the ambiguities of the relations with their clientele and various attempts at regulating the experts' work. The early modern professions thus tended to form a more or less homogeneous status group, joined together with other professional groups and set off from the rest of the population by their advanced education. At the local level, professionals typically cultivated close social relations. On this basis organizational entrepreneurs can construct effective assocations and cultivate support for collective action with relative ease, even though in a given field and locality most practitioners compete with each other in the same market.[5]

Among the most important tasks to which this organized strength of a group of experts can be put is the maintenance and development of the primary base of their power – of the knowledge they claim. The issues that here need attention are not just questions of setting and enforcing educational standards. There is also the problem of convincing the potential clientele, as well as the public at large and strategically located elites, that the expertise offered is built on valid knowledge and that it is relevant to critical problems. This is by no means simply a matter of making a true treasure known to those for whom it may be of value. Rather, the very criteria for validity and relevance are a social construct which is developed not merely by argument but also by the use of authority claims, by exploiting respect for status and reputation as well as by manoeuvring for the best position in the market of competing promises. Andersen's tale of the emperor's new clothes has a moral not only for judging astrology but also for understanding the appeal of psychotherapy, economic policy advice and surgical intervention. We saw in the previous chapter how 'scientific management' was urged and promoted by the emerging profession of industrial engineering; it was by no means the obvious solution to management's problems once it was tried out and tested. Even in the case of established scientific knowledge it is a political achievement to have its validity and relevance widely accepted and acted on by customers and (potential) regulators alike.

Of course the knowledge offered by the professions, today as well as in the past, consists of many different components – of common sense, knowledge of precedents and established practices, skill in dealing with people, command of inherited wisdom (as well as inherited prejudices); and only parts of it are subject to a discipline akin to that of scientific research. Furthermore, advice of experts inevitably contains elements of evaluation which can never fully be justified in purely cognitive or scientific terms. Being learned in major cultural traditions, which are consensually accepted as valid and pragmatically relevant, confers a quasi-charismatic prestige (Shils, 1965) and constitutes a powerful source of expert authority and legitimation of privilege. Expertise in specifically scientific knowledge represents one variant of this more general phenomenon, one that carries a special authority today but also one which allows critical outsiders to separate more easily cognitive from evaluative components in the 'knowledge' of experts and through such decomposition to increase the chances of control. The composition of a given body of expertise thus has complicated consequences for the position of experts, and therefore is of critical importance in the politics of continued division of labour and of changing the organization of expert services.[6]

CREATING KNOWLEDGE: THE CASE OF SCIENCE

If the applied knowledge of the professions is subject to the pulls and pushes of interest, are these not absent or at least much reduced in the institutions devoted to the creation of knowledge? Are the major institutions of science and learning, universities and academies, not places in which the pursuit of knowledge has become an objective with its own weight and is largely detached from the different social interests with their varied ways of exerting power and influence? A few reflections on these matters will not only be helpful in deepening our analysis of the role of knowledge experts in society, but will also throw some light on broader issues raised by technological determinism, another strand of contemporary thought which, together with functionalism in sociology, neoclassical utilitarianism in economics and the benevolent rationalism of the self-image of the professions, forms the backdrop from which our ideas about the role of power in division of labour must be set off.

Limiting the following observations, which have to be fragmentary in any case, to the extension of scientific knowledge is not only appropriate for reasons of space. Science is the intellectual pursuit of which many believe that is has emancipated itself from divergent interests and from the influence of the powerful and privileged; and assumptions about the independent and inexorable advance of science underlie the widespread ideas of technological determinism.

The modern university, academy of science and other institutions which give institutional suport to scientific research are a relatively recent phenomenon. Continuous scientific growth over long periods of time did not exist anywhere before the seventeenth century. Ben-David (1971) has shown how modern science, after discontinued beginnings in fifteenth-century Italy, was first established as an accepted activity in seventeenth-century England and France. Leadership in science shifted first from England to France, then in the nineteenth century to Germany and from there to the United States. If in England and France science became 'institutionalized' in the sense that it was accepted as an important activity, well articulated with the rest of society and regulated by its own norms, it was only in the reconstituted universities of the nineteenth-century German territories that it became rationally organized – with systematic training for young scientists, professional careers for those trained and selected, and effective bureaucratic arrangements.

Both of these main stages of the institutionalization of science in the modern world were pushed forward by conspicuous concentrations of power, though these took a very different form in each case. The political strength needed for the first institutionalization of science in seventeenth-century England and France came from broad-based intellectual movements. Science became for powerful groups both a means for, and the 'symbol of, an open and advancing society' (Ben-David, 1971: 78).

In Central and Eastern Europe no movements of this kind emerged, an indication of the much lower level of socioeconomic development in these areas. However the rulers of several absolutist states and their managers soon saw advantages in scientific research even though they had no use for the 'scientistic' ideology that promoted science in the West and extended in hopeful anticipation the procedures of scientific inquiry to economic, social and political issues. Paradoxically, then, modern science found its first full-fledged organizational establishment not in the societies that were the most developed countries of Europe but in imitating late-comers where a powerful state apparatus adopted Western advances selectively. Providing a large and steady flow of resources, the sponsoring states could insist on a depoliticized version of scientific research, on science without enlightenment scientism – as stark an example as any for a process of social differentiation that was instigated by power interests. At the same time, state sponsorship offered science protection from interference by the forces of a far more backward society that surrounded it.[7]

'Development of empirical knowledge is always upsetting to some vested interest. Hence, unless it is positively institutionalized in itself it is likely to develop only slowly and sporadically, in spite of the fact that on the other side there is an obvious interest in its development.' This is how Talcott Parsons (1951: 333–4) states the peculiar need of science for institutional protection against interference even in societies that have come to rely on its uses. The 'vested interests' referred to include commitments to religious belief as well as political power interests, a profession's stake in established practices, workers' interests in job security as well as capital-owners' and business managers' fear of product obsolescence. These interests clearly have an impact on the application of newly won knowledge in technology, an impact that depends for its effectiveness on the power balance of contending parties. If the creating of knowledge is to a large extent protected against such interference, this clearly represents a form of institutionalized power: the process of inquiry advances even against objection. Such protection of scientific research can be secured in different ways, and typically we find a combination of different modes – by investing roles and organizations of research with a large degree of autonomy, by combining research with elite education thus securing a measure of loyal support from dominant groups, by cultivating alliances and privileged exchange relations between institutions of learning and the state, large corporations and possibly other dominant institutions and groups, and by articulating the scientific enterprise with the cultural heritage and popular values in such a way as to maximize legitimation and moral support.

The autonomy of research, however, is never complete because even the most autonomous institutions of science do not sever all relations with the rest of society. Even the most established scientific institutions are open to some outside influence. In fact, while the early amateur science of the seventeenth and eighteenth centuries was a fragile phenomenon, the very move towards full institutionalization of science in complex organizations and full-time careers, which assured continuity and made more complex undertakings possible, at the same time opened the scientific process to greater outside influence from certain quarters because it became so much more costly. Shryock (1948–9) argues in his famous essay on the American indifference to basic science in the nineteenth century that short-run utilitarian attitudes of business tycoons and political leaders turned American science into a more applied cast as the amateur scientific culture of the eighteenth century came to an end and science became too complex an enterprise for self-supporting gentlemen and intellectuals to pursue. The need for outside funding opened the door to outside influence, especially since the funding came from sources that more than others expected a return on their money.

The short-sighted view of the uses of fundamental research has changed, but this mode of outside influence has not. In fact the cost of scientific research has grown so as to dwarf the outlays for science in the nineteenth century.[8] Of course, the political will expressed in funding decisions does not simply determine the direction taken by research. It is filtered through complex lines of advice and consent, partly formalized in review committees, partly informally constituted in the interstices between various institutions and communities of science and the groups and institutions in control of funds. Even a system of funding science that approximates a 'command mode', such as that of the Soviet Union, must rely on the advice of trusted experts and generally encounters all the problems of the control of experts.

Yet the constraints of scarcity – of funding and of access to public notice and recognition – have consequences within the realm of science also. Individual scientists as well as institutions and groups of scientists with similar ideas and orientations vie for eminence; and their success is not simply determined by 'objective truth'. Success in this competition means increased control over access to publication, influence on the criteria of what is worthwhile and promising work where these criteria are not yet settled by an established consensus, and a greater voice in funding decisions (see for instance Bourdieu, 1976).

Scientific knowledge itself is not unaffected by these conditions. Without entering into the full complexities of these questions, we know that scientific knowledge ineluctably derives from the questions asked. And these are in large part shaped by economic and political interests as well as by broader cultural premises and, finally, by the *social* processes within the realm of science which in turn are interrelated with cultural, political and economic factors. Even the rigour of standards of empirical testing, and thus the reliability and validity of specific explanations and predictions, are to a significant extent shaped by such 'extraneous' factors. Scientific knowledge is inevitably contingent on what Kuhn (1970) has called the 'paradigms' of fundamental concepts, assumptions, problem formulations, accepted modes of investigation and standards of empirical adequacy. Even though the interrelations are not at all well understood, it is more than likely that both the consolidation of a paradigm and its eventual abandonment are developments which are not simply determined by the cognitive promise and the eventual exhaustion of a paradigm, but are also influenced by the social process of science, its internal power structure and patterns of conflict, and by the way science is embedded in a broader political and economic context.

Stressing the role of non-cognitive factors in problem formulation and in the mode and direction of research is not to deny the part played by the structure of existing research results. The questions that it is possible to investigate are indeed determined in part by previous knowledge. Research cannot pursue any and every question imposed on it from the outside. To be effective it must proceed from what is known already and from the tools developed in past investigations. The more research is integrated theoretically, and the stronger the body of recognized knowledge, the more will the direction of future research be shaped by internal criteria. The nature of the body of knowledge, then, is one major determinant of the autonomy of science. Yet such self-determination of the research agenda varies greatly from one field of inquiry to another; and it is never complete, not even in the most advanced areas of natural science. Aside from the shaping of the research agenda, funding always is a major factor that determines the pace with which knowledge expands in different areas. That chemistry, for instance, developed in close interrelation with its uses in an expanding textile industry is well known.

A likely response to the arguments outlined is that the potential uses of science are such that they override the influence of the factors discussed and reduce them to mere wrinkles in the overall picture. Large corporations and state apparatuses sponsoring research are under intense competitive pressure to elicit the best research results. In this situation they will copy not only research methods, findings and applications, but also the most effective modes of organizing research.

The reasoning contains more than a kernel of truth, but it complements rather than invalidates the arguments advanced so far. A first observation is that the competitive constraints have by no means led to the same patterns of organization and funding of research in all countries, not even in all the major industrial countries. Research and development function very differently in the United States, the Soviet Union, England, France and Japan. Scientific research in England, for example is steered in a much more centralized way than in the United States and it is, once differences in resources are taken into account, equally successful (or more so) albeit in a less applied direction.[9]

A second observation has even greater theoretical significance. It will by now have a familiar ring. That corporations and states act in their science policies under severe competitive constraints does limit their freedom and discretion. This does not mean, however, that the role of power in the directions taken by research is eliminated. It is the interests and visions of powerful business and state elites which primarily set the goals for research and development, not the interests of weaker though much more numerous groups, unless these are taken into account by the policy-makers. The assumptions of the self-balancing pluralist model of politics apply even less to the politics of science than to the politics of farm prices or occupational safety. The tremendous amount of research that is geared toward war is only one indication of this pattern.

Even from this crude sketch of our thesis emerges a picture of scientific advance that is very different from the dominant ways of thinking about science. In the dominant imagery science is not only ultimately autonomous but it is also fundamentally a force for the 'common good'. It is an objective enterprise both intellectually and morally. Of course, it can be abused, but that then is the fault of forces outside of science. That the substance of knowledge and research is itself shaped by powerful interests does not come into sharp focus in this view.

What our argument means for technological and scientific determinism should be clear by now. It is not an autonomous advance of knowledge, perhaps hindered or pushed forward by extraneous forces but moving along a path predetermined by the structure of reality, that shapes our lives. If there is an exorable force that expresses itself in technological change, it is the inexorability of interest and power constellations which shape even fundamental research and which determine translations of knowledge into new products and new ways of production.

Finally a question that will return us to issues of the professions and the social control of expertise. If our argument began with expert power that is based on knowledge, does it not become circular if we can show that knowledge itself is not independent of social power? This would be true only if the expert groups themselves had sufficient power to shape their knowledge base to their own advantage. Even the most established professions, however, do not belong to the most powerful groups in any modern society and they are internally divided; knowledge is in modern society much less the preserve of the closed monolithic groups that it once was.[10] Professional interests do affect the creation of knowledge as well as its public acceptance as valid and relevant. Exaggerated claims of validity and effectiveness, selective development of knowledge (say in curative rather than in preventive medicine) as well as pro- tective maintenance of mystique and complexity and the derogation of alternative approaches are indeed among the tools of professional self-advancement. And it is furthermore true that the professions have a special voice in determining what constitutes a problem fit for, and in need of, expert intervention: doctors shape our con- ceptions of what constitutes illness, and lawyers foster a more procedural or less substantive view of justice and order than most common citizens would otherwise entertain. However, to conclude from this that pragmatically relevant knowledge and the definition of occasions requiring its use are simply a function of the interests and the power of expert groups would be a fundamental mistake. Expert groups can affect these matters at the margin but they cannot shape them at will to their advantage. Such a view not only underestimates the degree to which their own expertise is inter- twined with stable components of culture, secured in part by the institutionalization of science and other scholarship in differentiated institutions. It underestimates also the impact of the dominant interests on the same issues.

CONTRASTING INSTITUTIONAL PATTERNS OF PROFESSIONALIZATION

We return to the starting point of this chapter: the modern world is characterized by a vast increase in the use of knowledge – however characterized by a vast increase in the use of knowledge – however complex the intellectual, social and political underpinnings of the different kinds of knowledge considered pragmatically useful. This development gives knowledge-bearing practitioners a peculiar power, which they are likely to consolidate and enlarge through collective organization. Conversely, the recipients of knowledge-based services find themselves potentially in a situation of dependence and vulnerability, since they are often unable to evaluate the experts' services. This dilemma of control is aggravated if the stakes are high – for the immediate customers and even for the community at large.

What are the major institutional forms that emerge in response to this dilemma, and which forces determine the development of alternative patterns? Both sides will mobilize whatever resources they have to shape the outcome to their advantage; and inevitably public institutions, in particular the modern state with its claim to make binding collective decisions guaranteed ultimately by coercion, will be involved in setting institutional arrangements between expert groups and their customers. Differences in outcome will partly derive from the relative strength of the contending groups and the way in which they and state agencies see their interest and mission. They will also depend on prior institutional forms and constellations of interest as these affect the power as well as the perceptions and goals of the various groups and institutions involved. The institutional patterns for the dispensation of expert services will therefore quite likely vary a great deal for different knowledge-bearing occupations and different groups of clients, and they will take different forms in countries with contrasting historical legacies.

These simple considerations, then, make it unlikely that we will find one modal pattern of organizing professional work in all modern societies, as much earlier work on the professions suggested though not explicitly maintained (Parsons, 1939, 1968; Merton, 1960; Goode, 1957; Goode, Merton and Huntington, 1956; Greenwood, 1957). These analysts took their lead from the self-understanding of the dominant professions in England and North America and argued that expert practitioners, organized in professional associations, strike a 'bargain with society' in which they exchange competent service and integrity for the trust of client and community, freedom from lay supervision and interference, protection against unqualified competition as well as substantial remuneration and high social status, which are secured by a strong influence of the organized profession on expert education and by their monopoly over broad areas of work. Careful recruitment and training, professional organization and informal relations among colleagues, as well as codes of professional ethics and formal bodies enforcing such codes are offered as the means through which the profession ensures that its side of the bargain, the promise of competent and devoted service, is fulfilled.

This functionalist model of professional autonomy has been criticized on many grounds, not all of which have to be rehearsed here. It took the knowledge base of professional work for granted and left it unanalysed. Its benign view of the relation between the experts' profession of ideals and the reality of the professions' behaviour left little – too little – room for exploitative actions on the part of professional monopolists.[11] And it assumes too easily that professional privileges are contingent on the delivery of competent service and the maintenance of a professional ethos. These privileges rest on the considerable cultural and political resources of the professions; they are quite immune to a good deal of public suspicion and even plausible accusations of incompetence and unethical behaviour. Above all, however, this model does not recognize that its assumptions – however idealized and theoretically incomplete – were abstracted from the particular historical forms professionalization took in the Anglo-American world. This last feature it shares with many of the more critical counterpositions it provoked. A few sketches of how professional work has come to be organized in different historical situations and of the interconnections of different forms of professionalization with the rise of the modern state, the expansion of capitalist market exchange and production, and the emergence of large corporations will give us a broader perspective. Different patterns of power gave rise to contrasting institutional forms for the dispensation of expert services.

Professional organization with a high degree of autonomy was most characteristic of late nineteenth- and early twentieth-century Britain and North America. Building on a heritage of corporate status privileges, especially notable in the case of lawyers,[12] modern professional groups skilfully exploited the opportunities that presented themselves in the course of urbanization, expanding market exchange, and capitalist industrialization. Both the needs of industrial production and the higher levels of living stimulated the demand for competent expert services in many fields. The professions, increasingly organized in voluntary associations, responded to these new opportunities by upgrading and standardizing their services through more systematic education and with attempts to secure a collective monopoly through state-enforced licensing and exclusion of unauthorized practitioners. The state was used to provide a framework for private exchange relations. It had no role in shaping the substance of the work of the professions nor in regulating the content of the professions' exchange relations with their clientele. While these strategies are completely in line with the dominant features of the early capitalist order, the modern Anglo-American professions espoused an ethos that was partly grounded in precapitalist and anticapitalist ideas and principles – the ideal of service, a conception of work as intrinsically meaningful, and a view of one's social bonds with colleagues and clients as transcending mere instrumental consideration.[13] This ethos served to legitimate the interests and the public demands of the professions, but we should beware of therefore dismissing it too easily. It also shaped the outlook of the practitioners themselves even if it did not determine their behaviour in a comparable way; and it had pervasive and lasting effects on the moral premises of the modern social order as a whole – testimony to the share of the professions in the cultural hegemony of modern societies. Among these effects are the ideas of modern individualism, which did not simply grow out of entrepeneurial ideologies; the central role of higher education in modern society and the conceptions of what it means to be an educated person; meritocratic legitimations of equality of opportunity *and* inequality of results based on educational qualifications and occupational performance; and the impact a generally increased standing of expert knowledge has on the interrelations between democratic opinion formation and political decision-making.[14]

On the European continent professionalization took place in a quite different way. Here it was the early modern state that provided the context for the growing utilization of expert services. The beginnings of professionalization in Prussia–Germany, France and other continental countries were shaped by public bureaucracies which directly controlled education and professional training, provided employment for most persons with a higher education, and closely regulated the rest. The extent of the state's involvement is illustrated by the fact that in Prussia–Germany most schools and all universities were (and are) run by the state, ministers were (and are) employed by the state, and even lawyers serving private clients were quasi-civil servants until 1879. Such close relations between knowledge-bearing occupations and the state shaped the institutional forms of professional work and the cultural orientations of professional groups. These had lasting effects even after capitalist modes of exchange and production came into their own on the continent and professional groups acquired more autonomy from the state. Against this background we can understand why in Prussia–Germany, to stay with this example, the ethos of the civil servant has informed the outlook and orientation of professionals (*Akademiker*) and other white-collar occupations throughout the nineteenth and well into the twentieth century (see Rueschemeyer, 1973; Kocka, 1980; Kaelble, 1978).

More than in England and the United States, professions on the European continent kept a greater distance from the morality of the market place. Precapitalist and anticapitalist principles were generally strengthened by their orientation towards the state. Organizational loyalty played a central role in the state-centred professional ethos. This loyalty, more than the moral mission of an autonomous professional group, gave legitimation to the experts' claim to act in the public interest. Loyalty to the organization to which one belongs could well prevail if in conflict with the values germane to one's field of expertise. If the moral failure of market-oriented professional self-control is represented by the exploitation of monopolistic advantage and the reinforcement of the interests of the strongest clients, the perversion of the state-centred professional ethos expresses itself in moral indifference when the goals of the loyalty-demanding state are at odds with the mandate of morality.[15] Despite such differences, however, many elements in the outlook of the state-oriented expert occupations resembled the orientations of the more autonomous professions. This similarity, engendered by the general character of professionalization, pertains not only to ideas about the centrality of expertise and to educational qualification as the basis for rank and career but also to notions about learned cultivation and individuality and even, though here with important qualifications, to individualist conceptions about a person's relation to society.

The different paths of early professionalization can be explained to a large extent by the relative timing of, on the one hand, bureaucratic rationalization of rule and, on the other, the extension of market exchange, followed or accompanied by the transformation of production under the control of capital owners (Rueschemeyer, 1973). The relative timing of the emergence of the modern state and the expansion of capitalist market exchange had profound consequences for the power constellations that shaped the organization of professional work. Where a centralized bureaucratic state emerged in advance of full-blown capitalism, it set the cast for the expanding role of expert occupations; where the entrepreneurial transformation of exchange and production took place in the presence of a weaker administrative state apparatus, much more autonomous professional groups reorganized themselves so as to seize the new opportunities In both patterns the actual use of knowledge in social, economic, technical and personal affairs increased greatly, but the forms of control of expert services were quite different. In both, the control of professional work involved a mix of actors and agencies: state licensing and regulation were an important underpinning of the market-oriented pattern of professional autonomy; professional independence and self-control had a place even in the state-centred forms of professionalization; and the choice of consumers among different practitioners was a significant force in both patterns. Yet the different character of the modern state and its relations to knowledge-bearing occupations in different countries had a profound impact on the course of professionalization; and in turn, the institutional forms created for the growing use of expertise shaped the development of the state apparatus.

In a broad-based comparative historical study, which builds on earlier work on the origins of the modern Japanese state, Bernard Silberman (1982) has reconceptualized the same difference in state structure. What we just saw as a consequence of the different relative timing of bureaucratization of rule and commercialization of exchange and production, he treats as alternative modes of state bureaucratization, one built primarily on lifelong organizational loyalty, the other on partially autonomous professional expertise. Silberman seeks to explain the alternative paths of state-building with differences in the political risks the ruling elites encountered during the formative decades of the modern state. Radical upheavals in state–society relations, such as social revolutions or even threats of revolution, made the ruling elites opt for a maximum of loyalty, while lesser risks left room for a less tightly controlled use of expertise. Such differences in risk set England, the United States and Canada apart from France, Prussia–Germany and Japan. This argument is well grounded in recent organizational theory; it moves towards a theoretical analysis and explanation of what in earlier studies remained the historical givens of relative timing; and it makes power considerations of the ruling elites the critical factor in shaping different modes of state-building and – by extension – different patterns of professional work. Some reservations about the argument derive from the fact that it gives so much weight to the *intentions* of dominant groups and classes. There are also as yet unresolved tensions between the particularities of certain cases and the general theoretical argument; and the relative timing of the spread of capitalism and the emergence of a modern state apparatus does seem of critical importance, however the different patterns of timing can themselves be explained.

EXPERT OCCUPATIONS IN ADVANCED CAPITALISM

The transformation of competitive capitalism into new forms dominated by large corporations in favourable market positions and managed by a vastly extended state has changed the course of professionalization. It raised the demand for knowledge and knowledge-based services to a new level and it transformed the ways in which professional services are delivered and controlled.

It is a constitutive characteristic of advanced capitalism – and actually of industrial state socialism as well – that systematic knowledge is used more than ever before. Post-elementary education is available to, and expected of, the majority of people and quite large minorities move on to higher education and professional training. Furthermore, more and more occupational groups claim to be, and are considered as, 'professions'. True, both the expansion of education and the acquisition of professional status by ever-growing numbers of people represent partly an inflation that is fuelled by individual and collective mobility projects but at the same time reduces the value of what is being obtained: In the United States a college degree of the 1980s entitles the graduate to little more than a high school degree did in the 1930s; and many of the new professions do not even come close to the old ones in income, power and prestige. However, important as the inflationary outcomes of such mobility efforts are, they must not be allowed to obscure the major fact – that the practical use of knowledge has reached a level unheard of before in human history.

At the same time, the institutional forms in which expert services are made available and subjected to one or another form of special control, have changed profoundly with the transformation of capitalism. They have become more similar in different advanced capitalist countries, though within each society there are large differences among the various groups of knowledge-bearing occupations. The greater similarity across countries does not go so far as to eliminate important differences that are rooted in each country's institutional heritage and shaped by different current power constellations, but it is real nevertheless. In all advanced capitalist countries the large business corporation has become a major consumer of expert services and has attained such a concentration of resources that it, too, has been able to establish bureaucratic controls over most of these services similar to those created earlier by absolutist rulers and then transformed by the modern state. The proportion of self-employed practitioners has declined drastically. This is in part due to the fact that occupations which never had many members in private practice expanded more than others, as did engineering, nursing, social work and teaching; but the proportion of self-employed professionals diminished also in such fields as law and medicine, where self-employment had once been the rule. The role of the state in the provision of knowledge-based services has greatly increased. Though there is considerable variation across countries and across different expert occupations, it is nevertheless true that everywhere the state provides a very large share of the funds necessary for the practical use of expert knowledge – for the creation of new knowledge, for the education of practitioners, for the equipment and institutional infrastructure needed for professional work, and for the direct employment of professionals.

These developments have given rise to a number of sharply divergent interpretations. Some analyses emphasize primarily the unprecedented use of knowledge and project knowledge-based occupations as the dominant elites of 'post-industrial' society (for instance Bell, 1973). Others focus exclusively on the change in institutional patterns. They often see bureaucratic controls as incompatible with professional work and view the decline of self-employment and the rise of corporate and public control as a twentieth-century crisis of the professions. It is not without irony that for certain neo-Marxist interpretations the model of professional autonomy, which was abstracted from market-oriented forms of professionalization, has provided the baseline against which the spread of bureaucratic control can be diagnosed as deprofessionalization and at least incipient proletarianization of knowledge-bearing occupations (Oppenheimer, 1973; Haug, 1975; McKinlay, 1982). Actual changes towards managerial control of professional work, new uses of computers affecting the role of experts, and the adverse effects of an oversupply of highly trained people in the recent experience of many Western countries are taken as components of a consistent development that subjugates knowledge-based occupations to corporate interests paralleling the domination of manual work by managers and capital-owners. More circumspect analyses, which use a similar analytic framework (Larson, 1980; Derber, 1982), acknowledge that most expert occupations have not been deprived of their knowledge-based discretion and autonomy at the workplace in either public or corporate employment; and they distinguish clearly between proletarianization and the sense of loss due to a diminished labour market position or the frustration of mobility hopes that is engendered by an expansion of the educational system not synchronized with changes in the occupational structure.

Max Weber recognized long ago the structural similarity between the positions of workers in capitalist forms and of officials and employees in bureaucratic organizations: both are separated from the means of their work and subject to discipline defined by those who control the means of production and administration (1922/68: 224; 1919/58). However, this structural similarity did not lead him to see both bureaucratically employed professionals and industrial workers as members of the same class. Nor did he consider bureaucratic organization and professional expertise as incompatible opposites. To the contrary, he was emphatic about their consonance: 'The primary source of the superiority of bureaucratic administration lies in the role of technical knowledge which, through the development of modern technology and business methods in the production of goods, has become completely indispensable'; and: 'Bureaucratic administration means fundamentally domination through knowledge' (Weber, 1922/68: 223 and 225). Neither do advances in the utilization of knowledge establish the bearer of knowledge without fail as the dominant groups in society, nor does bureaucratic control constitute the end of professional privilege. Each of these trends is relevant indeed for the changing position of different groups, but they are far from being the only determining factors and they do not typically outweigh other important considerations.

We saw in the last chapter that industrial workers find themselves in advanced capitalist countries in a great variety of workplace regimens – with bureaucratic work and career patterns, incidentally, one of the more favourable among the currently prevalent forms. Expert practitioners of various kinds generally have greater leverage in the market and at work than industrial workers do; but on a more privileged level they probably match manual workers in the diversity of work arrangements. Different professional groups vary greatly in the degree of autonomy they can maintain for individual practitioners and for the profession as a whole, and there are considerable differences in the power they derive from their respective places in the social division of labour. This diversity is often neglected in current discussions of the changing position of the professions. A few sketches will have to suffice here to give at least some indication of such differences in power, autonomy and socioeconomic privilege and of several of the factors that determine the contrasting outcome.

Of all professions, medicine is today in the most advantageous position. An ancient art, it acquired during the past hundred years a scientific base for a good deal of its procedures and dramatically improved its effectiveness. The purposes it serves are subject to little conflict and rank very high among most people's priorities: everybody, high or low, can fall ill, and most conclude a review of their luck with the observation that good health is the most important of gifts. In view of these simple facts it is not surprising that in all modern societies medicine has attained a position of professional eminence and power rarely equalled by other occupations.

In all modern societies scientific medicine has become the established form of treating the ill; non-scientific practitioners, if tolerated at all, work only at the fringes of the field and under severe restrictions. All industrial countries have a variety of schemes for funding doctors' services in such a way that medical care becomes less dependent on the sick persons's ability to pay at the time of illness. In most advanced countries – the United States being a notorious exception – tax-supported plans are available to all or nearly all inhabitants. This corresponds to the depth of the concern for health, the perception of medicine's impressive and expanding capabilities, and powerful egalitarian demands for general availability of health care. At the same time, such funding schemes buoy the income chances of physicians considerably.

Medicine has become a capital-intensive industry. Perhaps the greatest tribute to the professional power of physicians is the fact that by and large hospitals and their equipment are put at the disposal of doctors by public and charitable funds. In hospitals doctors control, but with few exceptions do not own, the means of their work. The degree of their control varies across and within countries and over time, but it is the strongest control exercised by any occupational group that does not own the means of its production – the most powerful university faculties constituting perhaps an exception.

Specialization and complexly organized division of labour in the practice of medicine are closely associated with the advent of the large and technically well-equipped hospital. There is no doubt that the power of certain groups within the profession and their professional and economic interests were decisive factors in the development of medical specialties. As David Mechanic (1983: 433) put it in his recent review of the literature: 'The establishment of boards and subspecialties is as much as political process through which physicians come to dominate a specific domain and restrict competition as it is a reaction to the mandates of an increasingly sophisticated technology (Stevens 1971).' If knowledge and technology were the foremost determinants of medical specialization, one would expect a much more orderly division of labour than we actually find, as well as greater similarities between countries at similar levels of wealth and development.

Equally and perhaps even more important, the medical profession maintains control over nurses, medical technicians and other new health practitioners and dominates the process of increasing division of labour in these 'auxiliary' health occupations (Freidson, 1970b). This professional dominance rests on the physicians' 'superior' knowledge but also on their organizational control of the hospital and on the historical sequence of increasing division of labour, in which doctors came first. If, as is typical, physicians are mostly male and the auxiliary practitioners mostly female, the doctors' dominance is strongly reinforced by discrimination against women and by deep-seated differences in the way men and women relate to others. Eli Ginzberg (1983: 487) is one of many observers who note that the 'predominance of women in the field [of auxiliary health work] has a depressing influence on the salary structure'. While the exact division of tasks is determined by many factors, including the countervailing power of the subordinate professions as well as technical and organizational exigencies, one common feature is the shedding of routine tasks and the retention of the more complex and more lucrative work by the dominant profession.[16]

The power even of doctors is not unlimited, however. It is historically constructed, and it is contested by others. It is circumscribed by the effectively pursued interests of other – even if subordinate – health occupations, by patient interests expressed in the market, in health organizations and in politics, by insurance and drug companies, and above all by the state – once health expenditures become a significant and growing part of the budget.

The power of doctors as well as the institutional forms of health care are historically constructed. They depend on the changing constellations of interest and power as well as on institutional arrangements of the past even though the concern for health- and science-based medical technology are fairly universalistic elements in the equation. That the latter are important is expressed in the fact that doctors have a very privileged position in all technologically advanced countries. However, health policy is not determined by such simple givens, but is shaped by past institutional structures and by the balance of power of different interests. As Rosemary Stevens observes in a comparison of Britain and the United States (1983: 301) 'The. . . sense of egalitarianism that pervades the British NHS [National Health Service] – the sense that limited resources for health care should be shared out, as far as possible across the whole population, may never be part of the larger system of health services in the United States.'[17]

The different public policies in the health care area, which are partially grounded in such institutions as the British National Health Service and thus more insulated from volatile political changes, do not only affect who benefits. They also shape profoundly the process of division of labour in the health field. To give only one example, which is an indication of other far-reaching contrasts, the ratio of specialist physicians to general practitioners is far larger in the United States than in Britain, and there is no question that institutional history and public policy are the main causes of this difference. In spite of a slight increase in the proportion of specialists between 1963 and 1978, Britain had in both years about one specialist for every two physicians in general practice, while in the United States the ratio was reversed and is increasing: 2 : 1 in 1963 and 4 : 1 in 1977 (Stevens, 1966: 357; 1983: 285). Similar differences in institutional structure, the flow of benefits, and the medical division of labour obtain between the health systems of the United States and Germany, although the contrasts are not as radical as those between 'socialized medicine' in Britain and the 'capitalist' system of the United States. In West Germany the considerable power of doctors, organized privately as well as in the state-established chambers, is unevenly balanced by the countervailing power of publicly constituted sickness funds. Deborah Stone concludes her case study of the West German system with an observation that exactly coincides with the thesis advanced here: '. . . the political power of the medical profession is an artifact of political arrangements as well as [derived from] technical expertise' (1980: 181).

Law presents a very different picture, even though it is a profession of equally long standing as medicine and was also favoured by fundamental, if different, changes characteristic of modern society.[18] Law deals with contested issues. Not only does it directly pertain to social conflicts, but the ideals of justice and order are subject to disagreement in a way that health and even health policy are not. Furthermore, while lawyers do have expert knowledge, their expertise does not derive its authority from science but from socially established norms and procedures, which are experienced by some as coercive impositions and by others as expressions of the common good. Aside from their knowledge of 'the language of the state', as John Austin (1832/1954) called the law, lawyers use in their work a good deal of common sense and experience with the ways in which various institutions function – an expertise that does not involve systematic knowledge and that is not much different from the skills of many of their clients.

The professional autonomy of lawyers, one should conclude from these observations about the knowledge base of their work and about its relations to conflicting social interests and values, is likely to be weaker than that of doctors; and their power will be largely derivative – derived from the power of powerful clients or from that of the state. Autonomy and independent power of lawyers in private practice are likely to be greatest where the administrative state apparatus is small and not prone to invervene in society, where there are many clients of roughly equal clout, and where legal advice and judicial decisions are needed to adjust many exchange relations not any more regulated by traditional social conrols. Such autonomy and power of lawyers reached a zenith in the American legal elite of the first half of the nineteenth century. Themselves a leading element within the commercial bourgeoisie, these lawyers fashioned through litigation and legislation the civil law of competitive capitalism out of the more traditional legal material of eighteenth-century English common law.[19]

The professional independence of attorneys rests, aside from their expertise in the law, in a particular way on the requirements of dispute settlement. These stipulate a certain independence for intermediaries who need the trust of the parties they counsel and represent, and who at the same time have to maintain a minimum of loyalty to the framework of law and judicial institutions and to the public policy these serve. Here we find the reason why even in the Soviet Union attorneys work in cooperatively organized private practice (Barry and Berman, 1968) and why in the late eighteenth century an experiment of the absolutist Prussian state seeking to replace partisan advocates with appointed junior judges had to be abandoned after only a few years (Rueschemeyer, 1973: 149–50). Yet this delicate balance may be tilted and upset from either side. Strong client influence may undercut the public service commitments of lawyers and subvert the interests of justice and public policy; and public conrols over the legal profession may become so powerful that they endanger the lawyers' service to individual rights and conflict settlement. A cohesive culture and organization of the bar can help to counterbalance these forces while it also supports the socioeconomic interests of the profession.

Professional cohesion is difficult to achieve for lawyers in private practice. Though they work primarily for the well-to-do, they serve clients with sharply divergent interests and outlooks, and devoted service will divide them in their own views and commitments. In most capitalist countries a significant part of the bar – typically its elite – serves the legal needs of the dominant interests of large corporations and major capital-owners. Others deal with the legal affairs of middle-sized and smaller business firms and affluent individuals, and yet others with matrimonial law, accidents and criminal cases. The most important form of specialization in the law is the specialization by type of client rather than a specialization in terms of particular fields of expertise. The latter flourishes where large corporations demand such specialized expertise, which then is often bundled together in law firms serving those clients more or less exclusively. Differentiation in terms of clientele correlates closely with differences in legal ability, and it determines gradations in prestige and income within the bar. This internal stratification reinforces other divisions in the profession and may result in deep rifts. [20]

Given these centrifugal tendencies, social cohesion of the bar and thus its autonomy and power actually may be strengthened by state regulation and control, largely because such regulation often limits the areas of work and attendant involvements of lawyers, counter-balances identification with divergent client interests, and moderates the internal stratification of the bar. The bar's autonomy *vis-à-vis* client interests will also be enhanced if the law enforcement by the state is strong and rather immune from the influence of the interests affected.

Even though self-employed, the bar in private practice then is strongly shaped by outside forces. The balance of strength among client interests, law enforcement, administrative state action, and state regulation of the profession influences how far the work of lawyers extends beyond court work and related advice; it sets the parameters for different degrees of autonomy and power lawyers have *vis-à-vis* clients and state agencies; it shapes the development of specialization and the size and organization of law firms; it strongly influences the distribution of income and prestige among lawyers; and, through all of these effects, it determines to a large extent the chances for professional cohesion. Located at the inter-section of market and state, lawyers in private practice see their work setting and the surrounding institutional structures often shaped by others, primarily by powerful clients and by the state. Unless these forces are relatively weak or neutralize each other, the autonomy and power lawyers do have are largely derived from the strength of the interests they serve.

Today most professionals are not self-employed. Especially in the new and newly expanded fields employment by private corporations and by the state predominates. The situation of these employed experts differs considerably depending on whether they work in the private or in the public sector and, if in the private, how strong the market pressures are to which their organization is exposed; where they find themselves located in the bureaucratic structure; and finally what the character of their expertise and of their professional community is.

Very roughly, we may distinguish three types of location in the bureaucratic structure: first, professionals in managerial and executive decision-making roles; second, professionals in staff positions who advise officials in the line of authoritative decision-making, that is to say, whose clients are their superiors and in a broader sense the organization as a whole (research scientists or lawyers in a corporation's legal department are classic cases); third, professionals who serve clients outside the organization or rank-and-file workers inside, but are subject to controls from the bureaucratic top (social workers, teachers, and school or factory nurses illustrate this type of employment).

Professionals as managers and executives rarely figure in the sociology of the professions because in a perspective premised on the antagonism of professional and bureaucratic principles of work and organization they have 'moved to the other side'; yet they were the knowledge experts of greatest interest to Max Weber, and understanding their role is critical for any analysis of the place of expertise in the division of labour and in the structure of power of modern societies. Weber never made a sharp distinction between expertise and bureaucratic office – in contrast to both Lenin and Talcott Parsons. Parsons (1947) took Weber to task for not separating conceptually authority based on bureaucratic position from authority based on superior knowledge, a critique that shaped the later course of the sociology of the professions. Lenin, viewing the old state as part and parcel of the capitalist system, argued in *State and Revolution* that the state bureaucracy must be crushed. He believed that it was possible to separate in organizational reality sheer technical expertise from bureaucratic oversight and control. Expertise would continue to be available, but bureaucratic oversight and control would be replaced by the direct democracy of worker committees, and policy-making was to be reserved to the vanguard party.[21] Weber's tendency to see expertise as part of the concept of bureaucratic office certainly reflects the fact that in continental Europe professionalization took place in the framework of the early bureaucratic state. However, there are also very good theoretical reasons for it when it comes to the analysis of bureaucratic domination. The power of bureaucrats rests, in Weber's view, precisely on the *fusion* of three elements: the bureaucratic office with its specific authority; technical expertise based on systematic knowledge; and the knowledge of procedure, precedent and particular facts – the 'secrets of office' (Weber, 1922/68: 225).

We have to ask whose power it is that is thus founded. It is clearly not just that of the individual bureaucrat with technical knowledge, though his or her autonomy at the workplace benefits from the same factors. The collective subject is either the bureaucratic organization as a whole or a group of officials with an *esprit de corps*, a shared outlook, and more or less clear-cut policy inclinations. Something approaching such a corporate spirit is, as we saw in chapter 4, necessary in any complex organization in order to overcome the problems associated with division of authority and to achieve corporate cohesion for the organization. It may originate in the outlook and the standards of a professional group or – more likely in today's complex division of labour – in the orientations shared by several such groups.[22] Yet this professional ethos is likely to be transformed by the bureaucratic system. Career concerns in the particular environment of a firm or government department reinforce organizational loyalty. To the extent that organizational incentives and controls and the bureaucratic ethos of loyalty prevail, the wider professional community from which individual orientations derived some sustenance will be splintered. This outcome is very likely in the case of experts in managerial and executive roles; if, however, executives rose to their position from a strong professional base within the same organization, as is often the case with university, school, or social work administrators, this 'deprofessionalizing' effect of holding executive office in an organization may be moderated.

The relative weight of either of these sources of orientation is difficult to assess. Even where apparently one or the other side prevails, what typically takes place is a mutual penetration.

Capitalist interests are in a corporation probably as much modified by the outlook and standards of its managers and executives as royal interests were by the corps of higher civil servants once a complex bureaucratic apparatus was established (Rosenberg, 1958). At the same time, dominant interests will use whatever means seem practical in order to domesticate the body of managers and executives and turn it into a pliable instrument of their goals. Cooptation through payment in capital shares is one common response. Among other important factors that shape the balance and at critical junctures of organizational expansion or restructuring often set a pattern for the future, are the relations of supply and demand on the market for executive and managerial work as well as the specific mode of their education and the distinctive affiliations and orientations it may or may not engender.

The power and autonomy of professionals as managers and executives is not only determined by their position within the bureaucratic structure. To the extent that they play in fact a dominant role in their organization, they partake of its autonomy *vis-à-vis* the wider environment. A corporation with monopolistic control over the markets for products and inputs has much more leeway for policy options than one that finds itself under tight competitive pressures. State organizations, too, vary a good deal in their autonomy *vis-à-vis* dominant socioeconomic interests and the formal political process.[23] And the specific place of a government organization in the patterns of influence and constraint is of great consequence for the power and autonomy of its leading administrators. If a central role in the organizational and political matrix of the state comes together with cohesive policy orientations of the top officials, the concentration of effective power can be impressive. The role of the military forces in recent Latin American history, or that of the British Treasury in the 1920s and 1930s, are among the many illustrations that come to mind.[24]

Experts employed in organizational locations other than those at the top are subject to a control that is bureaucratic in form but at the same time informed by technical expertise. Informed oversight loyal to organizational goals neutralizes much of the specific power professionals derive from their expertise. Yet such oversight is costly, and since it also interferes with the morale of professional workers it typically confines itself to the broad outlines of performance control, leaving individuals and groups a good deal of autonomy. This does not preclude, of course, that corporate and public management will often try out bureaucratic forms of oversight and discipline that clash with workers' conceptions of professional autonomy. Repeated examinations of teachers, or moves to evaluate teachers by detailed before-and-after tests of their students are examples much discussed recently in the United States. Where professional autonomy is respected, professional status may be circumscribed as narrowly as possible. The pressure of costs leads to ever new attempts to separate routine tasks from complex professional work, using the process of continued division of labour as a cost-reducing mechanism.

Research scientists and other professionals with the organization as clients are typically organized in staff departments where professional patterns of interaction enjoy a certain autonomy from bureaucratic supervision. Staff departments are relatively insulated from the bureaucratic styles of work and control that predominate in the 'line' between different levels of bureaucratic authority. Expert groups enjoying this privileged enclave space usually have particular leverage. Their work is important for the organization's goals. They have employment alternatives, for instance in university research or in private law practice. They are part of a larger professional community which supports their claim to professional autonomy. And their work is not easily evaluated by the results.[25]

Bureaucratically employed professionals, whose clients are outside the organization or among the rank-and-file inside, tend to face a different control situation. The most typical case are public or non-profit private organizations for human services. If the interests of the clientele – of students, people on welfare, clients of psychological case workers – are at all represented in the organizational management, it is typically through the professional commitment of administrators rather than in more direct ways. At the same time, the management of schools and welfare agencies tends to be exposed to outside pressures to contain costs. Where these pressures are intense, where the prestige and influence of the clients are low, and where the professional expertise actually used is rather shallow, professional autonomy and influence are at their lowest, penetrated easily by crude and effective bureaucratic controls.

Many social service occupations excel more in devotion to the welfare of their clients than in potentially threatening expertise.

On any analysis of the professions' power this is a disadvantageous combination. It is often reinforced by the fact that women predominate in many of the social service professions. The high devotion/low power syndrome articulates well with traditional conceptions of women's roles, and the subtle patterns of selective recruitment and of discrimination against women can therefore easily coalesce with the disadvantages of this constellation.

A weak position cannot, however, be generally attributed to professionals in the service sectors of the modern state. There are important variations across expert occupations as far as the nature of their expertise and the standing of their clients are concerned. Thus, the autonomy of research and teaching in the top universities is far more resistant to economizing bureaucratic controls than that of welfare workers and elementary-school teachers. In addition, well-organized occupational groups can exert pressure within the state apparatus as well as in the political arena. This is a critical factor in shaping public policy as well as in determining the situation of different professions in public employment. In fact, professional groups throwing their organized weight behind the causes to which their work is dedicated constitute one of the major forces pushing the expansion of the service state forward and resisting attempts at containment and reduction. The fact that top administrators in these fields often come from the professional ranks strengthens such professional influence within the state apparatus; and the idealistic service orientation, while a liability in many concrete power battles, can be a significant asset in struggles over cultural hegemony. Since the institutional patterns within which human service professionals work are shaped by such broader political struggles, it is clear that we should expect important variations across countries primarily determined by the historical development of state structure and policy, and by the balance of class forces.

CONCLUSION: DIVISION OF LABOUR AND THE PROFESSIONS

A closer look at professional work enhances our understanding of division of labour significantly. It is not only that here are highly specialized occupations quite differently embedded in the institutional structure than managerial executives or rank and file workers; or that we cannot understand modern bureaucratic organizations without an appreciation of the peculiar part played by professional expertise; or that the work of knowledge experts has risen to unprecedented importance in modern societies. Rather the professions represent patterns of division of labour that inform the dominant understandings of the phenomenon. Given the strategic location of the professions, the experience of expert practitioners with the realities of the division of labour and their reactions to them inevitably exert a major influence on the prevailing conceptions of division of labour. What emerges from their experience is fundamentally a happy view, not – as Robert Dingwall (1983: 4) put it when characterizing the work of Everett Hughes – 'the pessimistic vision of Marx and Weber but [a conception of division of labour] in the optimistic spirit of Durkheim and Simmel who saw its possibilities for the extension of human freedom and cooperative interdependence.' It is also a view that knows little of power, coercion and conflict, that emphasizes instead objective issues and opportunities as conditions of division of labour and that implies a value consensus about problems and their solutions. The professional experience, then, may be seen as a particular challenge to the understanding of division of labour advanced in this book.

If we look at the broad contrasts between professionals and most blue- and white-collar workers, the differences among professionals, on which we have focused in much of our discussion, recede into the background. Professionals enjoy a higher degree of autonomy and of trust in the workplace. Their work is interesting and demanding. Specific contentions aside, they largely see merit play the role in rank-and-file remuneration that in their view it should play. They experience specialization of their work not as an imposed limitation, but rather an enabling structure that makes it possible to be good in what one does and to accomplish solid results. At the same time, specialization is seen as determined by the objective requirements for the solution of problems shared by all, not as a cost-saving device that serves some interests more than others and not at all as an instrument of power. As a consequence of these beliefs and experiences, and as further corroboration, most professionals are convinced – in fact they take for granted – that their specialized work is part of a whole that makes sense. Their self-respect is sustained by an identification with the larger social order, whether it is state socialism in the Soviet Union or advanced capitalism in the United States. Most expert practitioners in most industrialized countries, then, embrace the actual course of the division of labour as objectively necessary, as resulting neither in job fragmentation nor in oppressive regimentation and control but rather as the welcome condition for individual accomplishment and success and as a development that is healthy and progressive for society as a whole.

This was, of course, precisely the version of modern division of labour that Durkheim advanced in 1893. Given sufficient time, advanced societies would eliminate coercion and drastic inequality of opportunity and develop a moral order fitting with their basic structure. Durkheim saw modern society move towards a state in which both imposed, or forced, and unregulated, or anomic, division of labour have been abolished. This industrial society, when it had found its equilibrium, would encourage at once free individual self-realization and a very high degree of social solidarity.

Yet the realities of power and conflict shape the division of labour still, nearly a century after Durkheim stated his vision of the future. The self-understanding of the professions conceals these realities. Very different power constellations rule the division of labour of manual workers, office employees with routine jobs, and professionals; but our review leaves no doubt that it is power constellations that shape the position of different knowledge experts in society, their immediate work situation, the development of specialization in their work, their relations to other occupations, and the institutional protection of varied prerogatives. Their knowledge expertise gives the professions a particular power potential based on cultural tradition and intellectual innovation. But the acceptance of professional knowledge as valid and pragmatically relevant does not simply follow from the results of scholarly investigation; it is the outcome of complex social and political processes. Even the very creation of knowledge is a social process shaped by conflict and the exercise of power.

The varied, though usually advantageous, positions of the professions in the division of labour at large are largely due to the ways in which different expert occupations succeeded in utilizing and exploiting their advantages of knowledge and collective organization. Taken together, the power sharing of the different knowledge-- bearing occupations has probably diluted the concentrations of power based on property, coercion and popular appeal; but that is a far cry from saying that the power of partial interests and the conflicts between them have become irrelevant or even muted.

7

On Dedifferentiation
Diverse Explorations

After discussing the role of powerful interests and conflict among contending groups in the division of labour at the apex of organizational structures, on the shop floors of industrial production, and in professional work, our argument takes a sharp turn and focuses now on dedifferentiation – on reversals of specialization and the fusions of functions. If power constellations are indeed of critical importance for advances of the division of labour and the forms it takes, they should play a similar role in reversals of division of labour, and in stagnation and structural stability as well. In fact, examining instances of blockage and reversal should help in understanding the causation of differentiation *and* dedifferentiation and reveal more about the role of power and contest in both.

At the same time the scope of our questions will broaden. While until now I have used the narrower concept of division of labour (though on occasion pushing its limits), in this chapter I employ the broader concepts of differentiation and dedifferentiation in order to explore similarities, contrasts and interrelations among a number of quite diverse developments. Structural differentiation encompasses division of labour, but it goes in two respects beyond the older concept. While division of labour pertains to work roles, and in complex societies primarily to full-time jobs and occupations, the concept of differentiation is not confined to the economic sphere and includes political, cultural, and other social roles as well. Furthermore, differentiation refers to the specialization of organizations and institutions as well as of roles. If we want to discuss the structural location of religious and political concerns in the same or in different social structures, the concept of differentiation gives us more purchase than division of labour. Similarly it is more helpful in examining such important developments as the emergence of citizenship as a universal role in modern societies.

Reversals of specialization and declines in institutional complexity have found much less interest in social theory than advances in division of labour. Modern social science arose as the intellectual reflection of the rise of capitalism, and even where it was critical of the developments analysed, trends towards more division of labour and greater complexity of institutions occupied the centre of its attention.[1] True, one can argue that in a sufficiently broad and long perspective the history of human social life shows patterns of 'general evolution' – from small social units to large ones, from few tools to many, from little to high energy use, from simple social structures to ever more complex ones, and from low to high levels of division of labour (see, e.g. Lenski and Lenski, 1974). Yet while these patterns of change hold true *grosso modo*, one does not have to delve into esoteric and minute historical detail to make a case for the importance of processes of the opposite kind, for reductions in complexity and specialization, for 'devolution', for 'dedifferentiation'. (The awkward terms betray the neglect of the issues they name.) After all, cyclical theories of history have been dominant in most recorded social thought outside the Judaeo-Christian world, and as a counterposition they persisted even within that eschatological tradition and into the most recent phases of Western intellectual history. W. H. Dray (1967: 250) observes:

> it is less from Greek philosophy than from Judaic and Christian religion that most Western discussion of the meaning or significance of history derives. Where reason and observation could find, at most, the orderliness of historical cycles, the eye of faith discerned in a unique historical process the redemptive activity of God.

Before we proceed further it is necessary to resolve a common conceptual confusion. Bringing together a number of tasks and functions in one role or organization is often viewed, especially at the level of control and coordination, as an instance of integration; rather than a process of dedifferentiation, it represents a necessary complement of differentiation. This view does not recognize that differentiation and integration are logically heterogeneous concepts. To put it in the language of structural functionalism itself, differentiation is a concept of *structure*, while integration refers to functional issues and responses. Integrative problems may be solved by newly specialized roles and organizations, that is by differentiation, as well as by a structural fusion of functions and tasks in one role or organization, by dedifferentiation. This simple conceptual distinction opens new perspectives on seemingly well-explored territory.

Dedifferentiation is a topic of vast dimensions. To explore it I will not attempt a systematic overview of problems but rather make a number of different cuts into the subject-matter. It will begin with certain broad and encompassing patterns of dedifferentiation focusing on the decline of historic empires. From there the discussion moves to a consideration of partial countertrends within global developments of devolution and evolution. Expanding on the idea which emerges from these considerations, that developments and counterdevelopments of differentiation and dedifferentiation do not just happen to coexist but are causally interrelated with each other, the third section examines the simultaneous emergence of moral–political individualism and the most complex system of division of labour known in history. The last section looks at some responses of the modern state to social mobilization as revealing instances of dedifferentiation. In each case our interest centres on the importance of dedifferentiation and, again, on the role of power and power interests in blocking or reversing trends towards greater division of labour and structural differentiation.

LARGE-SCALE STAGNATION AND DEVOLUTION

History is full of instances of stagnation as well as of decline after advances in division of labour. Accounts of social change that end with the refrain 'there is nothing new under the sun' match especially well the historical experience of agrarian societies, which covers the largest part of the whole of recorded history. True, social life based on settled agriculture and centred in cities did eventually become the basis for cumulative technical and social change, and in latter-day retrospectives covering many civilizations and millennia at once it is possible to discover patterns of slowly increasing technical and social complexity. If, however, the focus in time and space is narrowed only a little, long stretches of repetition and stagnation emerge as particularly characteristic of agrarian forms of social life. And the fascination of myth and historical tale is the rise *and the decline* of great systems of civilization. Both phenomena, the experience of long-term stagnation as well as the rise and decline of civilizations, are of interest to us though both are far beyond the reach of a detailed discussion in this volume.

It may be futile to search for an explanation of so broad, and vague, a phenomenon as the technological stagnation and social status that are found frequently in large-scale agrarian societies. Yet one extant account should be noted at least in passing, if for no other reason than that is focuses on power structure as the major explanation. Building on arguments of V. Gordon Childe (1953) and drawing also on ideas Thorstein Veblen developed in his *Theory of the Leisure Class* (1899/1934), Gerhard and Jean Lenski reason:

> the cause [of technological stagnation] apparently lies in the emergence in agrarian societies of a highly exploitative social order in which few of the rewards for work or innovation went to the worker or innovator. Rather, they were monopolized by the members of a small, powerful, and wealthy elite that knew little about technology and cared less. Under these conditions, people's natural inclinations to maximize their rewards were diverted into other channels. Potential peasant innovators knew that they could seldom hope to benefit from inventions or discoveries they might make. And the elite were so unfamiliar with the mundane world of technology that they were incapable of making any significant contribution. (Lenski and Lenski, 1974: 87–8; see also Lenski, 1966).

There is no need to quarrel here with the Lenskis' simple rational choice model and to amend it with a number of social structural and cultural factors such as the impact of traditionalization and its bases in agricultural production. What is worthwhile to keep in mind is that the interests of the powerful may not only steer advances in technology and division of labour in certain directions but can also block them, and can do so for very long periods of time. Furthermore, such blockage is in this argument not the direct result of conscious strategies to guard the collective self-interest of the powerful; rather it is an unintended – but for that perhaps especially long-lasting – consequence of certain alignments of privilege, motivation, opportunity, and rewards for technical and social innovations, alignments that tend to arise and solidify with special frequency in agrarian civilizations.[2]

The role of power constellations and of the interests and actions of privileged groups are also the central elements in the most sophisticated accounts of the general declines in division of labour and institutional complexity in a society or civilization. Such wholesale devolutionary processes are not rare; nor are they just brief interludes in secular advances of division of labour. For instance, little is known beyond ruins, weathered sculptures and some inscriptions about the civilization that flourished in the Indus valley two thousand years before the Common Era; but we can date its destruction and relate it to invasions; and we know that division of labour and technology declined precipitously; writing, for instance, was not used again in the era for more than a thousand years. The fall of the Roman Empire is another instance of vast devolution. It has occupied centre place in European historical reflection for good reason: the subsequent decline of trade and productive division of labour in Western Europe lasted for centuries, and comparably differentiated systems of rule were not developed again until the rise of the modern European states. The other half of the original system of Roman rule, the Byzantine Empire, lasted a millennium longer, but eventually it too, disintegrated, with similar consequences for the division of labour in society. Further examples of long-lasting devolutionary periods are found in the histories of Egypt and Persia.

In all these instances of large-scale dedifferentiation, the decline and finally the breakdown of the system of rule were the critical developments. The rationale for that is indicated by a comment of Norman Baynes on the Roman Empire: 'The civil service and the army together formed the steel framework which maintained the entire structure of civilization' (1943: 34). The early bureaucratic states not only gave military protection to trade and thereby secured the flow of resources and demand that made increased division of labour possible; they also actively transformed social organization and culture so as to free human and material resources from the fixations of established privilege, inheritance, and tradition – a precondition both for increased rationalization of rule and for advanced division of labour. At the same time, such a 'mobilization' of people and of resources entailed risks for the stability of rule. These risks were the greater the more the ruler's power rested on the very traditional fixations that bureaucratization and market expansion undermined. As discussed earlier (see chapter 4), this may be seen as the central dilemma of early bureaucratic rule (Eisenstadt, 1963). It introduced contradictions into the system of legitimation of the central rulers as well as into their policies; and it often set the interests of older aristocratic groups (and of administrative elites with opportunities to gain a tradition-alized aristocratic status) against the rationalizing policies of the centre.

The common factors which Eisenstadt (1963: 342–60) sees as causing, in variable combination, the decline of early bureaucratic systems are now easily understood. The balance of the tensions and contradictions characteristic of historical bureaucratic empires tilts toward the 'conservative' side. Here is a brief restatement of his hypotheses: first, the state's needs for revenue and manpower, often occasioned by wars, exceeded the free resources available. Second, strong traditional components in the legitimation of rule made it difficult to tolerate newly mobilized groups and their non-traditional orientations and actions. Third, elite strata with some social and political clout (older aristocratic groups, administrators, religious elites) developed more traditional orientations as well as more traditional bases of power and either competed with the centre or withdrew into apolitical ways of life.

The first factor – the drain of resources, usually due to wars – was of paramount importance in some cases. It could destroy the central state without significant change in much of the rest of the social structure. In Persia and in the ancient Egyptian empire the demise of the central bureaucracy led, according to Eisenstadt's (1963: 352) review of historical studies, to a resurgence of more decentralized forms of patrimonial domination, which had been little affected by the superimposition of the now exhausted central state. In other cases, like Rome and Byzantium where culture, society and economy had been much more deeply transformed by the bureaucratization of rule, complex developments in the interrelations among elites were of critical importance, though the precipitant causes of the final breakdown were, here too, external wars. In his summary comments on Byzantium, Eisenstadt focuses on an 'aristocratization' of elite groups and on the incompatibility of those developments with the bureaucratic rationalization of the central state:

> The internal aristocratization resulted in concentrating economic productivity in semi-feudal units, shrinking internal trade activities, and incessantly withdrawing free resources from the central political institutions. These [developments] weakened the state until it was no longer able to withstand foreign invasion, and facilitated alliances between [local] powers, war lords, and the invaders (1963: 352).

What Eisenstadt describes here is a pattern of wide significance – a concentration of resources in the hands of elites whose outlook and interests are unfavourable to further structural differentiation and division of labour in society.

The account of the decline and fall of the Roman empire by A. H. M. Jones (1955; see also 1964) comes to similar conclusions. He begins his analysis with quite different concerns and first discusses 'psychological' factors such as the decay of the civic spirit in the cities due to increasing centralization and the growth of highly individualized and otherworldly religious orientations in both Christianity and pagan religion and then adds to these factors economic weaknesses – an impoverished peasantry supporting a larger and larger landlord class and a growing state apparatus. Ultimately he points to a simple reason, however, why these often-invoked factors cannot be considered decisive. They were as prevalent in the Eastern Roman Empire as in the West. 'Yet at the very time when the western empire was staggering to its fall, the eastern was making a recovery' (Jones, 1955: 220). What, then, were the critical differences? First in Jones's view is the difference in external threat. The burden of barbarian attacks was greater in the West (see also Baynes, 1943). Secondly, the East was richer in manpower and resources; it was more fully developed and had suffered less from devastation by war. Finally, Jones argues at least as a working hypothesis that a set of interrelated differences in social structure weakened the Western empire. And here we encounter again the consequences of change in the internal structure of power.

Since the second century BCE the Roman senatorial aristocracy had accumulated vast estates which were concentrated in the West. Corresponding to such greater concentration of landed property, there were fewer peasant freeholders in the West. These differences in the distribution of landed property had three critical consequences. Landlords took in rent what otherwise could have been increased tax revenue. Landlords also competed with the state for manpower and succeeded in having their tenants legally and effectively tied to the land as well as excluded from military service. And members of the senatorial families pursued aristocratic self-interests when they served in public office. The combination of greater external threats than the East experienced, of lesser economic resources and of stronger tendencies towards 'artistocratization', then, was the set of decisive factors in this view of the fall of Rome, even though cultural and psychological developments were also part of the overall constellation.

That the fall of historic empires was closely related to internal and external power relations may not be very surprising; yet it is critically significant for our understanding of the role of power in large-scale declines in the division of labour, since imperial orders for long constituted the necessary framework in which market expansion and advances in social differentiation could take place. The picture becomes more complex if we now turn to less comprehensive developments, to counter-currents that run against the mainstream of change. We will ask how these contrasting developments are related to each other and we will again inquire into the role played by power and contest.

PARTIAL COUNTERTRENDS WITHIN GLOBAL DEVELOPMENTS

The coexistence of trend and countertrend, of differentiation and dedifferentiation, is common indeed. Within the patterns of dedifferentiation and decline just examined we find partial developments of increasing division of labour and growing institutional complexity and vigour. Thus, the Christian church consolidated itself as an institution during the same generations as the Roman Empire declined. Its growth into a vigorous institution with a complex internal division of labour is but one of many examples. Another instance, even more intimately connected with the overall decline of imperial organization, are the households and courts of aristocrats and quasi-aristocratic officials who benefited from the demise of central power. As they attracted more revenue they became in minor, and occasionally not so minor, ways centres of splendid consumption, and the expansion of demand locally increased the division of labour.

As in global devolution, so in global advances of division of labour: while central institutions of far-reaching impact become more differentiated, others are reduced in complexity. As some occupations and offices proliferate and subdivide, others wither and disappear. These currents and countercurrents are not merely simultaneous processes. They involve competition for resources and often entail conflict and coercion so that the rise of one contributes to the decline of the other. We will examine a few types of such developments.

If government is becoming more centralized as division of labour and market exchange advance (this is often the case but does not occur with necessity), smaller units of community and governance frequently lose importance and may actually decline. Village, city and region often lose as nation and empire gain. Kin-based organization, local courts, indigenous law, cooperative civic ventures, and traditional forms of regional rule are often displaced by the expansion of central government (Jones, 1955: 210–12; Tilly, 1970: 453–4, 463; Diamond, 1971). The histories of empires and nations are replete with the struggles such changes entail.

Why struggle and conflict? Decline and displacement will be resisted by established communities and organs of smaller-scale governance. These are after all well prepared to engage in collective action and fight back. They often enjoy deeply rooted loyalties of members and officials, and they are organized for action.

The outcomes of such struggles are not forgone conclusions. The smaller units of community and governance may lose, decline in importance, and dwindle in their internal division of labour or even vanish. But they may also win or hold out and thus check the growth of large-scale centralized government and impede the expansion of division of labour associated with that political centralization. And many outcomes may fall between these extremes. The new political centre may avoid bitter struggles and use the existent forms of local collective organization and governance for its own purposes while leaving them much of their earlier autonomy. In colonial administration such patterns are known as 'indirect rule'. They may appear inconsistent and clumsy to the twentieth-century eye, but they are less costly than more thorough centralization and they often met the intentions of central rulers adequately. On occasion, such cooperation between new centre and older periphery may actually strengthen local community and governance far beyond the previous condition, thus creating the apparent paradox of a growth of traditional solidarities and traditional political roles as a consequence of political centralization and rationalization.

As division of labour advances in economic production, it has an impact of similar complexity. It gives rise to new jobs and occupations as well as new types of productive organization while exposing older forms of work to decay and even creating in some areas incentives to return to much simpler and poorer ways of making a living. The handloom weavers' troubles in competition with the new British textile factories are the most celebrated example. The pattern they represent is much broader, however. Domestic industry had spread through the countryside in many areas of Europe since the seventeenth century and even earlier. This 'protoindustrialization' had shaped rural social and economic life profoundly. Factory-based production undermined that industry and ultimately wiped it out, drawing some workers into the factories while leaving others to return to agriculture. Tilly describes one region:

> In the west and south of France, at least, hundreds of communities which entered the Revolution of 1789 humming with industry and deeply involved in international markets left the Revolution of 1848 isolated, depressed, and chiefly engaged in what appeared to be 'traditional' agriculture. In and among these communities, the economic changes of the early nineteenth century produced dedifferentiation, disintegration, and perhaps even particularization. The evolutionary growth of industry produced a devolutionary countercurrent through important parts of Europe (1970: 461).

These changes, too, were subject to struggle and conflict, though once they were defined as the product of the impersonal, 'natural' working of the market, legal and political remedies could be dismissed as ineffective, and if they were sought nevertheless they were, in a new constellation of power, quickly exhausted. Occasional outbursts of protest appeared less than rational because they lacked a clear target and – going against the 'natural advance of progress' – seemed futile and quixotish. We have seen in chapter 5 that the emergence of the factory system met with worker resistance and why that resistance failed. We have paid less attention to those whose domestic industrial work faded away and who had little choice but

to hold on to a declining trade, return to peasant work or migrate.
Tilly reminds us of their political reactions:

> They did not always return to the land peacefully. Thompson's great
> portait of English working-class radicalism and rebellion in the early
> nineteenth century gives pride of place to the dying class of handloom
> weavers. Their German counterparts lashed out in the Revolution
> of 1848. In France, the massive resistance to Louis Napoleon's coup
> of 1851 fed especially on the anger of rural artisans. Throughout
> Europe, the rural worker's anguished sense of being squeezed out,
> of losing his identity, lent a curiously reactionary tone to the
> otherwise radical protests of early industrialization (1970: 460; notes
> omitted).

This displacement of domestic industry through factory work
exemplifies an aspect of advancing division of labour that is critically
important. As noted earlier, in chapter 4, division of labour often
does not go foward through a simple subdivision of existing roles
and organizational forms, but it gains ground through bypassing
old organizational forms and making a fresh start. Whether the
new forms will later coexist with the older ones or displace them
depends on a number of technical and economic, but also on
political, conditions. Such developments offer fascinating opportunities for studying how organized power and uneven economic
exchange relations are woven together and, at critical junctures,
clash with each other.

One reason for such 'fresh starts' is that the established patterns
of production are often well protected against change and interference. Yet such social, political and religious 'fortifications' as
for instance the medieval guilds developed, rarely cover all the
ground from which innovations may be launched. This proposition
actually applies to the very origin of the rural protoindustrialization
whose decline we just considered. It seems that one major stimulus
for domestic industry outside the cities was the resistance of
organized urban producers against changes in the established
division of labour and organization of work. The guilds fostered
and maintained a fairly detailed division of labour, but it was a
division of labour among autonomous producers, with limitations
on the numbers of apprentices and employees and with restrictions
on the permitted range of work within each shop. Competition from

the countryside was later one of the factors that caused the demise of this craft system of production.[3]

We have so far developed several ideas that are simple yet have considerable reach. Long-term stagnation and long-term declines in division of labour are common historical phenomena, both for whole societies and for certain segments of the social fabric. Early bureaucratic empires, based on complex internal and external power constellations, provided the historic context for broader social differentiation, and the dissolution of their rule was followed by large-scale devolutionary processes. Power constellations are equally crucial in more delimited contests over differentiation and division of labour, both in the political realm and in the organization of production. Partial devolutionary processes often stand in a close relationship to advances in division of labour. Many instances of dedifferentiation represent favourable conditions or inescapable consequences of concurrent advances of division of labour. In the next section we will see that certain forms of dedifferentiation, intimately related to advances in division of labour, are crucial features of the emergence of modern society.

INDIVIDUALISM AND GENERAL RESPONSIBILITIES

Is modern social life characterized by major trends towards structural dedifferentiation? The question seems to beg for a strong and definitive negative answer. However, there are fundamental developments in modern society that go decisively against specialization. I do not think here of economic production. Nor do I refer to the growing proportion of time when people are off work duty – the larger proportion of time spent in general education and in retirement, the longer vacation periods, and the increasing number of hours of free time devoted each week to rest and recreation but also to family concerns and do-it-yourself tasks, all activities in which people differ less from each other than they do in their various trades and occupations and in which they enjoy more freedom from external control and domination. These are important changes, but the following will focus on other, if not completely unrelated development. The argument to be made moves even further away from 'labour' in the conventional sense, though it does fall within the broader meaning that 'division of labour' has long had in social thought and that Durkheim, for instance, indicated through his formulation of 'division du *travail social*'. We will speak of the growing bundle of tasks and rights that fall to every person by virtue of being a member of society, at least ideally. This is a prime instance of dedifferentiation and yet it is a major characteristic of modern society.

Consider citizenship. The modern state has leveled the distinctions of birth amd merit, of family descent, ethnic affiliation and occupational status and treats all citizens in fundamental respects as equals. This equality of basic rights and obligations, inherent in the general role of the citizen (see T. H. Marshall, 1950), represents a form of dedifferentiation. It negates Plato's ruling class of specialized 'guardians' and his philosopher kings as well as Hegel's conception of the bureaucracy as 'the universal class', recruited by knowledge and proof of ability and charged with 'the universal interests of the community'. The body of equal citizens, and not any specialized agency, is the source of legitimate authority in modern societies; even – with some modifications – in the USSR. The authority of an equal citizenry stands against any claims of professional or administrative experts to the right to rule.

Of course, a picture of politics and domination in which citizen rights and obligations and the associated theory of legitimate authority stand out as the paramount features does not describe realistically the actual system of rule in any country. However, the rights to vote, to go to court or to receive welfare payments, the obligations to pay taxes, to obey traffic and contract law or to serve in a country's armed forces, and all the other entitlements and duties which together constitute the role of citizen in modern countries, are real nevertheless – even if they are very unevenly realized, even if they are counterbalanced by other social patterns more differentiated and unequal, even if in critical respects they are more important in theory than in reality. Ideals and principles held by some people and acknowledged by others have a significant reality even if they are not universally followed and implemented.

The citizen role has its counterpart in typical developments in modern morality and religion. The individual conscience is the ultimate guide to moral action in virtually all modern views of morality. At a minimum, the individual must take responsibility for drawing conclusions from general principles about problems and situations only she or he can fully appreciate. What Parsons

(1966) called 'value generalization' – the development of conceptions of what is desirable and obligatory which cover a widened range of concrete problems and situations – is indeed a correlate of increasing social differentiation; yet it contributes at the same time to dedifferentiation since it entails a greater moral autonomy of the individual. The autonomous moral person is a close cousin of the citizen. This concept similarly negates external authorities. The dictate of conscience replaces the authority of specialized guardians of morality; at most they retain the status of consultants.

Religion has undergone similar transformations. Robert Bellah (1964: 373) sees in the last of five stages of 'religious evolution' he constructs an 'increasing acceptance of the notion that each individual must work out his own ultimate solutions and that the most the church can do is provide him a favorable environment for doing so, without imposing on him a prefabricated set of answers.' In fact the moral autonomy of the individual person has important religious roots – in the options given to individual choice by religious conflict and pluralism but also in powerful religious ideas. These go far back within the Christian tradition and into its Jewish and Greek origins, but they gained special strength in the Reformation. A. D. Lindsay's sketch highlights the negation of specialized office in these ideas as well as their connection to democratic thought:

> The central doctrine of the Reformation was the universal priesthood of believers, a doctrine in implication individualistic and democratic ... The church is a fellowship of believers, each the direct concern of God, each directly responsible to God, each guided by the illumination of God in his own heart and conscience ... Compulsory religion and compulsory morality both become contradictions in terms (1932: 676–7).

We can here leave open whether these developments should be understood as a critical phase of 'religious evolution' or are better analysed as contingent historical changes that are now of far-reaching consequence but could have taken a quite different course.

The generalization of moral, political and religious concerns in the complex of obligations and rights of the individual is an important aspect of modern individualism.[4] Its correlate is a similarly dedifferentiated collectivity – a congregation or political community which consists, in the individualist view, of members who are similar and equal and in which specialized authority is problematic unless it is derivative of the will of the members. It should be clear by now that individualism in the sense used here does not necessarily mean a ruthless pursuit of self-interest and a lack of collective identification. To the contrary, devotion to the community can be specially intense because it is experienced as a homogeneous 'we' composed of equals.

It is only an apparent paradox that both these interrelated patterns of dedifferentiation – moral–political individualism and identification with collectivities conceived as homogeneous and egalitarian – emerged together with the growth of the modern division of labour. In fact, not only do they still coexist with very high levels of structural differentiation, but each side seems to reinforce and strengthen its opposite counterpart. We can only touch on some of the causes and consequences of egalitarian individualism and its interrelations with overall advances of division of labour and institutional complexity.

Modern individualism has cultural foundations in the Greek philosophy of the fifth century BCE when an old social order disintegrated, in Judaism after political autonomy was lost, in the continued relevance and repeated revivals Christianity lent to these ideas, and in their radicalization during the Reformation. Specifically cultural preconditions of the religious, moral, and political autonomy of the individual, then, can be traced with little ambiguity. At the same time, social structural factors have also contributed to these developments. Among them are changes that undermine a settled moral order, such as prolonged and multiple contacts with other cultures. But especially important are developments which change the system of domination and shift the balance of power away from established authorities.

With several such developments we are familiar from earlier discussions. The division of authority which becomes necessary as organizations grow and which requires voluntary, intelligent, and devoted cooperation of deputies often results in the emergence of an ethos of loyal autonomy of officials. The ideology of professionalism with its emphasis on independence, competence and personal commitment gives an answer to similar problems that emphasizes the individualistic elements even more. Such changes in the ethos of elites are relevant in themselves but also because broader changes in moral orientations are often prefigured in elite subcultures. Individualistic conceptions tend to be generalized in part because their intellectual structure is universalistic in character. Yet they also spread because in other situations of life, too, people who think for themselves, who have good judgement, and can take initiative in line with common purposes become more and more valuable. These developments, which still correspond rather directly to the pursuit of dominant interests as division of labour advances, are complemented by others which independently strengthen the autonomy and the relative power position of broader groups.

People engaged in trade encounter special risks but also gain more freedom from political control when market exchange expands beyond the scope of single political units. Improved means of transportation and communication, the concentration of people in factories and cities, and rising educational requirements in social and economic life make voluntary collective organization easier; and collective organization is the means *par excellence* for the many to gain leverage against the few. As social differentiation advances, people encounter within the normal course of their lives a greater variety of others with different outlooks and moral orientations; this contributes strongly to an individualization of their own positions and views (Simmel, 1890 and 1908/1950; Bott, 1957). In many complex and complementary ways, then, advances in division of labour diffuse power, strengthen individual autonomy, encourage ideas that posit the intrinsic worth of the individual human being as a supreme value, and support the universalization of the new morality. This intimate connection between individualism and division of labour was stressed by Durkheim long ago, even though he did not recognize the shifting balance of power as a major factor in these interrelations.

The dedifferentiated roles of the citizen and the morally responsible person coexist with other roles of the individual that are highly specialized and form a part of complex hierarchical systems. While this coexistence is not without problems, there are ways in which it contributes to the functioning of differentiated institutional forms. It is quite reasonable to consider this pattern of dedifferentiation as an integrative mechanism. It integrates high levels of specialization at the base. If we look at a complex social structure as a whole, the individual is the linkage point for variable combinations of disparate roles – of, for instance, mother, professional worker, neighbour, friend, church member, officer of a political organization, etc. All of these can come into conflict with each other and need articulation; all require initiative and energy of which there is never enough; and the appropriate responses are hard to standardize in custom and convention. The more complex the pattern, the more fitting – and the more likely – are the individualistic conceptions of autonomy and responsibility.

Yet the coexistence of the two types of roles is also riddled with problems and tensions. The subjective experience of alienation (see chapter 2) is aggravated by the expectations associated with moral and political individualism. Increasing division of labour, one might say, nurtures a moral and psychic sensibility that makes it harder to bear the experience of work in highly specialized, routinized and subordinate jobs. True, the fact that the one effect is stronger among the more privileged and the other among the less privileged members of society limits these contradictions, but there are large areas of overlap where they do matter.

More important contradictions emerge between hierarchic forms of social organization and the egalitarian character of political and moral individualism. As the latter spreads and becomes established in strategic social locations, it creates profound problems for the legitimation of authority. It was for these reasons that the French Revolution of 1789 shook the foundations of rule throughout Europe. Authority in industry, too, became repeatedly problematic quite aside from the conflict between the material interests of workers and owners (Bendix, 1956). However, crisis situations aside, the egalitarian implications of moral and political individualism tend to be submerged in the routines of everyday social life. As most value orientations most of the time, the tenets of moral and political individualism are, in Parsons's appropriate formulation, 'latent'. They may be celebrated on ceremonial occasions, taught to the young, and can be mobilized in situations of stress and conflict; but in everyday life they often are of little direct consequence even though they may stand in tension with the experience of people and with people's actual behaviour. Nevertheless, the egalitarian character of the individualistic complex of standards, values and ideas is a reality, a reality that can be activated even if normally it is 'latent'.

The bundle of rights and duties that in modern societies fall to every individual, then, represents a pattern of dedifferentiation that has critical if complex implications for the funtioning of modern social structures even though it pertains primarily to the level of ideal normative orientations. Growing out of distinctive cultural origins yet at the same time resting firmly on social structural conditions associated with advancing division of labour, it profoundly affects the legitimation as well as the realities of rule. It makes a critical contribution to the integration of highly complex institutional patterns and yet it stands in ineradicable tension to fragmentation and routinization of roles as well as to the hierarchical relations in ever-larger organizations.

MOBILIZATION AND DEMOBILIZATION

If we look at the same developments that are involved in the emergence of modern individualism in a slightly different perspective, we encounter the phenomenon of 'social mobilization', which has been a major concern of political modernization theory in past decades. Karl Deutsch has used the mobilization of a citizens' army for a major war as a metaphor to designate the destruction of old forms of social organization and the concurrent emancipation of people from the constraints of past customs and traditional authorities, both of which are correlates of economic development in agrarian societies. He defines social mobilization as 'the process in which major clusters of old social, economic and psychological commitments are eroded and people become available for new patterns of socialization and behavior' (1961: 494). Mobilization increases the proportion of people who count in politics. New groups of people now become able to organize themselves and collectively pursue their interests.

Social mobilization threatens the interests of political elites and their managers and it undermines the stability of the political order unless the newly released social forces can be securely tied to, and controlled by, mutually compatible political institutions and organizations. Existing institutions may have to be reformed and strengthened in order to be up to these tasks of cooptation and incorporation. Whether and how established parties and parliamentary institutions were, for instance, able to incorporate an increasingly mobilized working class was a critical factor shaping the course of political change in England and in Prussia–Germany during the nineteenth century no less than in Brazil and Chile during the twentieth.

We are already familar with the dilemmas of social mobilization – necessary for economic development, it tends to undercut established political patterns and to create conflict and turbulence – from Eisenstadt's discussion of the contradictions in the policy problems faced by early bureaucratic rulers. Eisenstadt's 'unfreezing' of human and other resources out of the fixations of tradition represents exactly the same phenomenon as social mobilization under a different name and in different historical circumstances; and the central dilemma he identified for bureaucratic rulers was precisely the problem of gaining sufficient resources freely available for rational allocation and reallocation without losing control over newly emancipated groups and without radically undercutting traditional support for existing patterns of authority.

Recalling the parallels between these two arguments is useful because Eisenstadt's analysis is sensitive to the power implications of these issues in a way that most political modernization theory is not. Scholars in this tradition tend to remove questions of power from centre stage by focusing on 'system problems'. In its most elementary form this argument states that high levels of uncontrolled social mobilization are incompatible with the dutiful loyalty and the subordination of private interests to public purposes without which no political system can function. On one level this is without question a sound argument. No group, no organization and no political system will function well unless individual goals and behaviours are to some extent socially integrated. But the argument misleads us if we do not consider different forms of such integration and if we do not ask at the same time who is to be loyal and dutiful, whose interests are to be subordinated to common goals, and who can effectively participate in defining what are to be the public purposes. There are more ways than one to go about defining and reaching 'the public interest'; and major redefinitions come about by crises – crises of 'the system', but also crises of dominant interests defended by tooth and claw. Less well-equipped interests may suffer critically and chronically, without a system crisis and without change.

Samuel Huntington does not pursue these latter questions with particular verve, but he stands out among political modernization theorists by being emphatic about the fact that system integration entails rule. 'I do know', he quotes Walter Lippman, 'that there is no greater necessity for men who live in communities than that they be governed, self-governed if possible, well-governed if they are fortunate, but in any event, governed' (Huntington, 1968: 2). Huntington's own discussion of how political order can be achieved in the face of massive social mobilization is instructive even though he neglects the question of who gains and who loses in the process; it is instructive about issues of organizational structure and in particular about the interrelations between the maintenance of power and structural dedifferentiation.

The antidote to the political turmoil and decay that may derive from social mobilization Huntington calls 'political institutionalization', 'the process by which organizations and procedures acquire value and stability' (1968: 12). Institutionalization maintains political order in the face of increasing mobilization and increasingly diverse demands by incorporating the new political actors into a stable system of organizations and procedures. Huntington identifies four dimensions of institutionalization – the coherence, adaptability, complexity and autonomy of an institution. On closer inspection we find that these specifications of institutional strength and stability, on which scholars of widely divergent positions can agree, contain important elements of dedifferentiation in the normative order and in organizational structure.

The coherence and unity of an institution or organization may be supported, as Spencer (1876–97/1975) and Durkheim (1893/1964) have taught us, by the interlocking articulation and the interdependence of specialized parts. It does not derive exclusively from the cultural canopy of a *conscience collective* shared equally by an undifferentiated membership. Yet Durkheim later came to give greater and greater weight to consensual bases of integration even in highly differentiated societies; and most sociologists today would subscribe to the view that some degree of consensus is required for any form of cooperation, even if they disagree on the extent to which whole societies actually exhibit such consensus and on the sources of consensus where it exists; at one extreme consensus is seen to derive from human nature, the exigencies of social life, and the harmonizing effects of interaction, at the other from imposition and cultural hegemony. Consensus, however, whether it is spontaneous or imposed, whether it is focused on concrete and substantive expectations or on rather abstract values and formal procedures, represents a relative absence of differentiation in terms of normative expectations. Consenting views are the more important the closer a person is located to the institutional core of a system of domination. This form of dedifferentiation, then, is of particular significance at the controlling centre.

Adaptability as understood by Huntington reveals the elements of dedifferentiation it contains more easily. The less an institution is fixated to one specific purpose the more stable and powerful it is:

> An organization that has adapted itself to changes in its environment and has survived one or more changes in its principal functions, is more highly institutionalized than one that has not. Functional adaptability, not functional specificity, is the true measure of a highly developed organization. Institutionalization makes the organization more than simply an instrument to achieve certain purposes. Instead its leaders and members come to value it for its own sake, and it develops a life of its own quite apart from the specific functions it may perform at any one time. The organization triumphs over its function (Huntington, 1968: 15).

If functional adaptability involves the change and the accumulation of functions over time, the requirement of complexity for institutional strength and stability stipulates the bundling of functions in one organization at a given point in time:

> The greater the number and variety of subunits the greater the ability of the organization to secure and maintain the loyalties of its members. In addition, an organization which has many purposes is better able to adjust itself to the loss of any one purpose. The diversified corporation is obviously less vulnerable than that which produces one product for one market (Huntington, 1968: 18).

That organizations with multiple purposes have greater strength and stability applies to subunits as well – with interesting consequences for the internal organizational structure:

> The differentiation of subunits within an organization may or may not be along functional lines. If it is functional in character, the subunits themselves are less highly institutionalized than the whole of which they are a part. Changes in the functions of the whole, however, are fairly easily reflected by changes in the power and

roles of subunits. If the units are multifunctional, they have greater institutional strength, but they may also, for that very reason, contribute less flexibility to the organization as a whole (Huntington, 1968: 18).

The final issue Huntington sees involved in institutional stability and strength is autonomy. How well is an institution insulated from outside forces, protected against being overwhelmed by their demands and transformed by an influx of *homines novi*? Can it resist becoming an instrument of outside interests? A highly autonomous institution channels outside demands on its own terms and either is able to keep newcomers out or to transform their goals and orientations before they reach positions at the institutional core.

> In a sense, the top positions of leadership are the inner core of the political system; the less powerful positions, the peripheral organizations, and the semipolitical organizations are the filters through which individuals desiring accesss to the core must pass. Thus the political system assimilates new social forces and new personnel without sacrificing its institutional integrity. In a political system that lacks such defenses, new men, new viewpoints, new social groups may replace each other at the core of the system with bewildering rapidity (Huntington, 1968: 22).

Autonomy, then, rests primarily on secure differentiation of political institutions from other social spheres. But it is supported by institutional complexity – by an aggregation of functions in one organization; and what is protected with special care in a stable and strong institution is access to that core at the top, where – as we will see – specialization is inherently limited.

Dedifferentiation – in different forms and under various names – runs like a (not fully recognized) red thread through Huntington's discussion of institutional strength and stability. This is not an artefact of the choice of conceptualization and argument in this particular analysis as rendered and interpreted here. The logic of power dictates that the institutions of rule and the roles at the top of these institutions be less specialized than subordinate units if the relation of domination is to be secure. Specialization makes for good tools. Specialists and specialized institutions are not only more effective instruments for given purposes (set by decision-makers at the top), they also have (and know) 'their place'. 'Cobbler, stick to your last' is the demobilizing injunction *par excellence*. Furthermore, if indeed multifunctional institutions are stronger and more stable than single-purpose ones, specialized subordinate units of an organization are more pliable than those with broad purposes; they can be more easily redesigned and changed according to the purposes of the core managers because they themselves have less stability and power of resistance.

In turn, the dominant institutions and the dominant roles within them gain a power advantage from being less specialized than the subordinate organizational units and rules. This has long been recognized. Max Weber was emphatic about his thesis that the top of a bureaucractic apparatus is not itself bureaucratic in character. It cannot be as specialized and oriented towards the execution of directives as the body of the bureaucracy because what is at stake is precisely the setting of direction, the control of specialists, and the marshalling of political support for policies chosen – all of these at once.[5] The doctrine of the separation of powers acknowledges, as we have seen, the inverse relation between specialization and secure effective power in a different way. Insisting on the institutional differentiation of executive, legislature and adjudication was, and is, a means of constraining the power of rulers and state managers; it did not aim to enhance the efficiency of their apparatus of rule.

The arena of political debate – the 'public sphere' in which the collective good is determined and public policy is formed – is inherently generalist in character. Yet its boundaries, whether narrow or wide, are well guarded and often sharply contested. The political essence of mobilization or, as Karl Mannheim called this critical feature of the emerging modern political orders, of 'fundamental democratization' is precisely that new, broad-based groups seek and gain entrance into this public arena. Even in the most open societies such entry has been the result of struggle, and in no society is the eventual outcome equal access and equal participation. Even the mere right of suffrage for workers, peasants, women, and minorities has been the outcome of organized struggle.

In countries with a highly differentiated institutional structure, contests over the entrance into the arena of political debate often take a form that is of special interest for our discussion of dedifferentiation and power. Whether or not – and how – specialized organizations can participate in shaping the public will has been a matter of serious concern in recent political debates. It is typically treated as a matter of the integrity of the institutional structure in the face of impetuous mobilization, but it is also very clearly an issue that affects the balance of power. Examples abound: political and moral pronouncements of scholarly societies that go beyond the immediate sphere of their technical competence, attempts of students and professors to commit their university to a moral and political position on war and peace or on apartheid, the pursuit of political goals by unions that previously had a narrow 'business' orientation, the use of strikes to put pressure on parties, parliament and executive.

The underlying pattern is fairly general. Various specialized institutions and groups are strongholds for concerns and interests of a less narrowly defined nature. In critical situations they may try to throw the resources of their specialized organization into the balance in order to affect or shape public decision-making. Often such moves towards dedifferentiation are merely temporary or minimally successful in the first place. It usually takes a considerable exertion of power, sustained over a period of time, to bring about such dedifferentiating entries into the political arena and make them stick. Powerful interests are served by the specific delineations of the 'proper' functions of most institutions in stable societies, and moving beyond those limits may well provoke retaliation and do serious damage to the organization in question. These delimitations of institutional purpose are further typically buttressed by persuasive arguments about how political decision-making works, what the enlightened self-interest of the different parties is, and how the institutional structure ought to function. (Arguments against the entry of specialist organizations into the political arena might, for instance, invoke the principles of political/moral individualism and the attendant conceptions of the political arena as a homogeneous community of equals.) Whether we consider such arguments reasonable and legitimate or not, the activities of important institutions and especially changes in their relation to the arena of general political decision-making are also, and significantly, matters of power.

Political institutions as well as other institutions involved in generalized concerns, such as ideological and religious organizations, may engage in a different form of organizational dedifferentiation. Here a political, ideological, or religious organization seeks to secure the allegiance of its adherents and to broaden its following by offering intrinsically non-political, non-ideological and non-religious services and opportunities for association. Missionary schools and hospitals, religious or political fraternal and sororal associations as well as hiking, gardening and singing clubs under denominational or party sponsorship represent an assortment of examples.[6] We can see a similar logic in the growth of the modern welfare state to the extent that it is the creation of relatively autonomous state apparatuses or established political elites; this is not to deny, of course, the other major source of welfare state development, the organized struggle of previously weak classes and strata. Both of these causal configurations, we might note, are in turn the result of substantial extensions of social mobilization.

That such a broadening of institutional purpose often meets with little resistance, provided that the potential clientele is willing and interested, highlights by comparison what was argued before about the obstacles that stand in the way of previously non-political organizations when seeking to enter the political arena of power. Political, ideological and even religious organizations are typically already established in that arena, and their expansion of activities is then not easily interdicted nor frequently of much concern. On the other hand, great resources of power and coercion may be needed if the potential clientele is unwilling or, perhaps more important, if their interests are already served under the sponsorship of competing institutions. One might look from this perspective at the introduction of compulsory education under the sponsorship of the modern continental European state, which displaced church sponsorship of education, or at the imposition of ideological party auspices on most organized activities in the totalitarian states of the twentieth century.

Finally we return to the power advantages that a dedifferentiation of the functions of political institutions brings to those in control and apply this proposition to totalitarian regimes and similar attempts at rapid induced social change. It appears that certain forms of dedifferentiation at the level of control and direction are of strategic importance for large-scale and thorough transformations of a social order. Totalitarian control and penetration of all spheres of life is only one of these forms, one that is of particular importance in relatively developed societies where many people are potential political actors and where advanced structural differentiation makes elite control difficult without pervasive indoctrination and control of both behaviour and commitment. In less developed societies the fusion of different functional elites and the concentration of their efforts on certain goals of social change may be sufficient to create a similar potential for rapid and thorough institutional change.

In either case, one particular fusion of functions – or at least a very close coordination, perhaps through overlapping jurisdiction and multiple channels of command and communication – seems of special importance: the linkage of operative, 'managerial' policy concerns with new value orientations and ideological guidance. The insistence in Mao's China on not letting the role of 'red' and 'expert' drift apart is a powerful example. Social change that involves such a reduction in differentiation and complex mediation between concerns with ultimate orientations and the more realistic preoccupations with running the machinery of society might be called charismatic change, borrowing from Weber's conception of charismatic authority (Weber, 1922/68; see also Shils, 1965, and Eisenstadt, 1968). In analogy to Weber's theorems about the routinization of charisma, one should then expect that such processes of fusion of functions are followed later by new developments of specialization and differentiation, though their results are likely to be of a nature quite different from the social structure preceding the change.

CONCLUSION

We have in this chapter reviewed a perhaps bewildering variety of phenomena, held together by a single abstract tie – the concept of dedifferentiation. Yet these explorations yield a number of quite consistent results. Dedifferentiation is, to begin with, a common phenomenon – whether in the long or in the short run of historical change, whether in the global pattern of a society or in certain parts and segments, whether in social roles or in the structure of organizations and institutions. This has a simple consequence worth noting. It precludes attaching to dedifferentiation a negative evaluation, as has been done so often.[7] Dedifferentiation takes so many different forms that is is impossible to attach a single evaluation to it, whatever one's political and value position. Depending on the form they take and their context, reversals of division of labour and structural dedifferentiation may be as 'progessive', but also as inhumane as various forms of specialization and differentiation can be under different circumstances.

Perhaps a more important result is that recognition of the very high incidence of dedifferentiation processes and of the variety of their forms opens up opportunities for deeper inquiry into the causal condition of both specialization and fusion of functions in a given role, organization or institutional complex. Critical for a full use of these opportunities is the conceptual separation of dedifferentiation and integration. Even though specialization typically creates integration problems, integration is not the logical opposite of differentiation; integration represents functional problems that can be answered by different structural developments – by new forms of specialization, by a partial fusion of functions or by both in combination. Even a cursory exploration of the conditions of structural dedifferentiation helps us to go beyond analytic description of broad trends and contributes to a causal process analysis of changes in the division of labour and institutional complexity that go in either direction.

Our exploration of a few types of dedifferentiation amply demonstrates the importance of power constellations and power interests. Thus the fate of historical empires, which provided the framework for far-flung trade and for growing specialization, rested on specific internal and external power configurations. While market exchange and internal division of labour were important in building the early bureaucratic apparatuses, a high level of internal differentiation was not sufficient to secure imperial rule. The decline of both the Eastern and the Western Roman Empire illustrates the importance of changes in the internal constellations of power as well as the role played by the devastating invasions of much less differentiated forces, of 'barbarian tribes'.

Similarly, we have seen that partial processes of differentiation and dedifferentiation within a given society involve the exertion of power on the part of contending parties and often entail prolonged conflict between them. This applies not only to changes in relations between the political centre and local or regional authorities; it is also critically important when we study the persistence and change in the organization of economic production. Here the political structuring of economic relations, private power, and market competition, which often involves very uneven starting conditions, mesh in complex ways to determine structural outcomes.

Processes of differentiation and dedifferentiation may occur simultaneously and yet be closely interlinked. This becomes especially clear if we look at changes in the specialization of roles and of organizations and institutions at the same time. One frequent pattern is that while roles become more specialized the organization that contains them broadens in purpose; a recent example is the emergence of the modern department store. The opposite dynamic can be observed in the craft organization that was the goal of the medieval guilds; here increasing division of labour among shops went hand in hand with little specialization within them. The difference between these patterns has far-reaching implications for the relation between power and division of labour. Distinguishing between different levels and forms of differentiation and dedifferentiation – between the levels of roles and of organizations and institutions, between changes in patterns of actual behaviour and of normative expectations – has proved both necessary and useful in our discussions.

Modern societies are characterized by peculiar forms of dedifferentiation that arise with advances in division of labour. Citizenship as well as moral and religious individualism are paramount examples of such dedifferentiation. The closely related phenomenon of 'fundamental democratization' or social mobilization often was answered by important dedifferentiations in the structures of political authority. Their analysis yields further insights into the relation between dedifferentiation and power, which need not be recapitulated here.

Instead it may be useful to highlight in conclusion another point. Egalitarian individualism and social mobilization are both developments that were advanced by overall increases in division of labour and structural differentiation (even though it appears that relatively autonomous cultural and religious developments were significant factors in the growth of individualism). This has critically important implications. However weighty power constellations and power interests are at any given point as causal factors shaping the advance or decline in the division of labour and determining the forms it takes, they are in the longer run themselves changed by the developments they engender and steer. Broad advances of division of labour and structural differentiation have had consequences for the distribution of power which were neither intended by nor favourable to the most powerful groups of earlier periods. Such long-term dependence of power structures on changes in the division of labour raises issues that go to the heart of our argument. These we will consider with other major theoretical questions when we now turn to a concluding review and discussion.

8

Coda: Power and Division
of Labour

This book stands in a rather ironic relation to its subject-matter. It is hardly possible to choose a less specialized topic in sociology than the division of labour. Yet, going against the current of the prevailing intellectual division of labour in the field may not be as irrational as it appears at first sight. Specialization has become the iron rule in sociology as in the rest of the social sciences. It has developed to a point where we must confront the question whether the discipline itself persists as more than a formal label for congeries of specialized inquiries that are not only separate from, but irrelevant to, each other. Sociology has long been the locus of intellectual discourse among diverse inquiries within its own formal borders and, more broadly, it has been a conflictual arena of integration for the social sciences as a whole. Preserving that role seems a worthwhile goal, and this book makes perhaps a modest contribution to such an effort.

Yet this project is very different from what may be the most obvious, and certainly the most ambitious, way of responding to these problems – the systematic treatise on the analytic and methodological foundations of social theory.[1] We began with questions about division of labour that had a central place in the very beginnings of modern social science and that have remained central ever since. There are indeed few problems that held a place of similar strategic significance for more than two hundred years. However, the issues of division of labour are not coextensive with the set of problems that define sociology as a discipline; and in regard to division of labour, the strategy adopted was not that of the systematic treatise. Instead, we developed a particular thesis about power and division of labour and from that centre point made different cuts into the evidence in order to explore problems that follow from the core thesis and to demonstrate its theoretical reach.

The principal argument grew out of the critique of the efficiency explanation of division of labour. The association of efficiency and specialization must not be taken for granted. It is problematic not only because specialization may create problems whose solution can be more costly than the productivity advantages it also brings about. It is problematic most significantly because *efficiency is a meaningless concept unless one specifies the value of what is gained and what is sacrificed.* It is the preference structures of people – their needs and wants ordered according to priority – that determine the value of gains and losses; and these preference structures vary, not only across cultures but also across groups and classes antagonistically involved in the same projects of production and social life. What is efficient by one set of criteria is wasteful by another. Neither the shaping of needs and wants by a shared culture nor the aggregation of expressed preferences through the market eliminates this divergence of evaluations. The question, 'efficient for which interests.' leads to the introduction of power. *It is the most powerful interests that most determine which efficiency criteria will seclect among different forms of division of labour and thus shape the particular forms of social production and reproduction.* A concern that is likely to be given high priority is the protection of power itself. Less powerful individuals and groups whose needs and wants are affected adversely may succeed in blocking or modifying changes, but the outcome is still determined by constellations of power and cannot adequately be understood as the result of self-validating advances in efficiency.

This central idea was developed in chapters on the division of authority, on the changing organization of industrial labour and on the specialized work of knowledge experts. The next to last chapter examined reversals of division of labour and processes of dedifferentiation. Using the concepts of differentiation and dedifferentiation, it broadened the framework of analysis to include roles and organizations other than those involved in economic production. It demonstrated – contrary to still surviving notions of linear 'progress' – that devolution and dedifferentiation are of great historical importance and, furthermore, that differentiation and dedifferentiation stand in complex interrelation with each other, both in past history and most emphatically also in advanced modern social structures. Here, too, contests over power and interests in the preservation and expansion of power emerged as causal factors of supreme importance.

If these chapters succeed in detailing and developing the central argument, they do not fully cover the subject-matter. There are many aspects of division of labour that were not treated in any detail, including such major topics as division of labour by sex, the emergence of the modern state and its impact on unprecedented advances in division of labour, and changing patterns in an ever-widening international division of labour. These issues occupy centre stage in current discussion; yet they were treated here with benign neglect. Covering the subject-matter was not our intent. This book sought to pursue an argument about power and division of labour that has far-reaching implications for basic theoretical issues in sociology and the social sciences at large. However, a few brief comments situating the neglected issues in relation to the core argument are in order. These will be followed by two sections that review and comment on the results of our investigation. The final section will then return to questions raised earlier but left aside until now – questions of the humane value and the moral evaluation of alternative patterns of division of labour.

THREE LACUNAE EXAMINED

The division of labour by sex is – together with that by age – the oldest form of division of labour; the vast modern expansion of division of labour is unimaginable without the underpinning of power by the modern state; and an ever more extensive and intricate international division of labour points to a major outcome of the modern advances in social differentiation: the emergence of a single worldwide matrix of specialization and interdependence. Clearly, it was not for lack of significance that these subjects received a less-than-prominent place in our discussion. My rationale for that was twofold: standing very much in the limelight of current intellectual interests, all three topics have received frequent and varied treatment. More important, in each of these three areas the critical role of power is undisputed across a wide range of theoretical positions.

Division of Labour by Sex

Margaret Stacey attacks past analyses of division of labour for not coming to terms with division of labour by sex:

> There appear to be two separate accounts of the division of labour: one that it all began with Adam Smith and the other that it all began with Adam and Eve. The first has to do with production and the social control of workers and the second with reproduction and the social control of women. The problem is that the two accounts, both men's accounts, have never been reconciled (1981: 172).

> The problem exists, I shall argue, because the classical theories derived ideas from and focused on industry, the market place and the state. All other institutions and processes were secondary and of relatively trivial importance (1981: 173).

If this charge were accurate, treating division of labour by sex largely in passing would indeed be a major problem of omission. If there are indeed two different kinds of division of labour with radically different dynamics, it will not do to explore the role of power in only one of them. However, the thesis of two separate accounts pertaining to fundamentally different structures and processes of division of labour does not hold up under close scrutiny. The differentiation of male and female activities has always been viewed as critically important for the division of labour in economic production, especially in its early forms; and the differentiation of production activities from the more inclusive matrix of social relations in the household, sustained by kinship solidarity, has held a strategic place in most accounts of industrial division of labour.[2] There can be little doubt that the consequences of different historical changes in the division of labour for inequality between men and women have received less than full and systematic attention in the classic tradition. But the fundamental causal arguments discussed in the very productive current efforts at dealing with division of labour by sex stand in a relation of close continuity with the classic tradition, rather than breaking completely new ground.

Quite clearly, occupational division of labour by sex cannot be grasped simply as a problem of differential access of men and women to positions, whose structure is determined by an altogether different dynamic – one unrelated to the social identities of men and women, their relations to each other, and inequality of resources between them. If Canadian Eskimos are excluded from most urban jobs other than menial work such as car washing, one may well treat this just as a matter of differential access to jobs and regard the occupational structure as unaffected by the relations between Eskimos and other Canadians. The same separation between division of labour and access to differentiated positions becomes much more problematic where minority groups facing access problems are larger and provide the better part of the labour force for major job categories and even industries. The same approach is definitely impossible in the case of division of labour by sex. Not only numbers are relevant here. Given the interdependence of social life, role differentiation between men and women in one sphere of life inevitably shapes the options for division of labour in another. This is not to deny, of course, that the occupational structure is also influenced by factors unrelated (or only very indirectly related) to role differentiation by sex, and that therefore partial analyses may very well inquire into the differential access of men and women to positions whose structure was taken for granted in those studies. It is also reasonable to argue, as Engels did (1884/1972: foreword to the first edition), that sex-based differences and solidarities have a less determining influence on the social structure of more advanced societies, and in particular of class societies. But it remains impossible to give a full account of division of labour in any society, whether the analysis is confined to economic roles or is conceived more broadly, without paying attention to division of labour by sex.

Role differentiation by sex is universal; we do not know of any society without it. At the same time, the part played by men and women in social life is extremely variable. It is not fixed by biological differences. Child-bearing, breast-feeding and the uncertainties of paternity do make a difference, and they may represent more than 'hints' (as Ruth Benedict, 1934, has put it) for the development of cultural designs and the construction of social institions. But such biological differences do not dictate any particular role configuration for men and women. Even among societies in which the organization of family and kinship is the dominant foundation of social structure as a whole we find a variability of division of labour by sex that flatly contradicts all notions of 'natural' roles for men and women – notions which are prevalent in many cultures, including our own. It is true that we do not know of any society in which women were dominant over men, and there is lack of agreement about the existence of real sexual equality; but there is no theoretically sound reason to view this limitation of past variations as biologically determined.[3]

We are far from understanding the major factors that account for these different forms of division of labour by sex. There is even, as one might expect, disagreement on the basic ways of approaching such an explanation – from a Freudian starting point, for example, or focusing particularly on cultural patterns, or seeking to derive the different forms of sexual division of labour from environmental conditions and economic constraints. Across most theoretical positions, however, we find agreement that power constellations and interests in the preservation of power are of critical importance for understanding the dynamics of division of labour by sex. A few ideas may serve as illustrations. To the extent that women's activities are confined to the domestic sphere by an emphasis on the maternal role, women lose control over broader decisions and structures – the 'public sphere' – to men (Rosaldo, 1974). Women's power corresponds to their contribution to material subsistence and their related control over economic resources (Sanday, 1974; Sacks, 1974). Sexual domination is also closely related to unequal participation in warfare (Sanday, 1974, 1981). Of critical importance are social conditions that favour, or inhibit, the formation of separate associations for men and women (Engels, 1884/1972; Leis, 1974). Throughout the current discussion, and of course in established popular wisdom as well, it is recognized that resistance to power and struggle between the contending parties are critical elements in the conditions of sexual equality and inequality.

Role differentiation by sex has a peculiarly 'fundamental' character. It enters the experience of each individual early and thus forms a foundation on which later experience builds and by which it is shaped. It is of pervasive importance in all societies, the simplest as well as the most complex: our identities as men and women are irrelevant only in the rarest of situations. Highly salient in many contexts and relevant in most, what it means to be a woman or a man tends to be extremely change-resistant (though, of course, such resistance to change varies across historical constellations and perhaps across cultural traditions as well as class and ethnic subcultures). This is consonant with the fact that the division of labour by sex, and especially the norms pertaining to it, seem to correspond often to material conditions long past (for instance old patterns of mortality and family size). Taking off from such considerations, one may speculate that division of labour by sex is in a peculiar way grounded in the cultural tradition.[4] This idea would not negate the importance of power in explaining division of labour by sex; but it would point to a peculiar prominence of cultural power resources that is rarely encountered in the investigation of other aspects of division of labour (with the possible exception of symbolic political authority). If such a difference in resources of power did actually obtain, the study of sexual division of labour would acquire critical importance for a power-oriented analysis of division of labour because it would allow us to analyse better the specific role of culturally based power.

The State and Division of Labour

Comments relating the state to the concerns of this book can be even briefer than those on division of labour by sex. We encountered the state at every stage as the argument developed, even though no single chapter had the state as its exclusive theme. Quite obviously, this was no accident. The state represents the incarnation of a peculiar kind of power. At the core of this power is organized coercion, though all states also wield power derived from other sources – from economic assets, effective organization or moral conviction. The modern state seeks, more or less successfully, to monopolize the use of coercion; and it claims to put its power at the service of society. This latter claim constitutes the fulcrum of four hundred years of political theory concerning the state – from Hobbes's Leviathan averting the 'warre of everyone against everyone' and Rousseau's vision of a participation of free citizens in forming and realizing the 'general will' to the varied conceptions of the state in the renewed contemporary discussion among liberal and Marxist scholars, who respond to earlier critiques of their respective positions as well as the political realities of the twentieth century.[5]

It was Marx who insisted most sharply that the interests of civil society are inevitably divided, and that the power concentration which the state constitutes must always be analysed in relation to these contradictory interests. The state's claim to transcend the contradictions of civil society and to represent the universal interest is false, even though it reflects a longing the young Marx thought grounded in the 'species nature' of human beings. The limited state of the founders of liberalism, of Locke, of James and John Stuart Mill or of Bentham, could be seen as serving universal goals only on the premise that all individuals are in fact equal. In reality, even this minimal state of classic liberalism does not simply provide a neutral framework – the chessboard and the rules of the game – for interactions among individuals unaffected by social structure. It mobilizes force so that the players can 'play for keeps'; it protects property relations that are by no means already supported by common and spontaneous consent; and it enforces contracts no matter how unequal the economic power of the bargaining parties. It is a deterrent force not just to the random lawbreaker, but – given the existence of structured social and economic inequality – it deters in the first instance lawless action by the propertyless and those whose service to the privileged is secured by need and circumstance. I have already referred before to Horwitz's (1977) important study of the creation of the legal infrastructure of competitive capitalism in America, which documents in detail how a legal order that from liberal positions appears just to 'lower transaction costs' (North, 1979) or, more broadly, 'facilitate interaction' (Fuller, 1969 and 1971) had an impact on society that was anything but neutral; it drastically favoured entrepreneurs at the expense of farmers, workers and consumers.

The conceptions of liberal political theorists focused subsequent analyses on the role of the state in guaranteeing social and economic relations in such a way as to make vast expansions of division of labour possible. The social structures primarily favouring instrumental rationality – contractual market exchange and bureaucratic organization – are unthinkable without the coercive and, at the same time, regularized guarantees of state law. And without these new institutional frameworks, modern levels of differentiation are in turn unimaginable; without them, interests in advancing division of labour could never have overcome the obstacles to further differentiation inherent in kin-based and other ascriptive and multifunctional forms of social organization.

In a by now exceedingly complex debate, Marxist theorists have explored from a variety of positions the interrelations between state power and class power. There is no need to attempt even a sketch of this debate here, which on occasion (especially in France and Germany) has taken rather scholastic turns. It is clear, however, that once these problems are posed in a persistently empirical mode and with full appreciation for the historical variability of critical factors, the answers to these questions are ultimately very important for understanding division of labour and the forms it takes under different circumstances.

The state does not only provide the power-infused infrastructure for changing patterns of division of labour in civil society, nor is its impact on division of labour comprehensively understood when we take its relation to the class structure into account. The state is also itself a prime location for vast processes of division of labour. This was a major theme in Max Weber's political sociology, which has also found its way into both neoliberal and neo-Marxist political thought. The internal structure of the apparatus of rule and its changes are now generally recognized for their importance. Changes in this internal division of labour take place within hierarchical organizations. They thus belong to the same generic type of differentiation that Marx analysed as 'division of labour in manufacture'. What sets them apart from division of labour in business firms is that the organizations themselves are not under any direct market pressure. This does not mean that they operate under no constraints at all, but it does mean that here is a major instance of division of labour and organization whose dynamics cannot be understood in terms of preference structures unified by the operation of the market, however imperfect.

The main arguments that emerge from considering the state in relation to changes in division of labour, then, support the central thesis of this book. It is patent that this particular concentration of power – the state – has tremendous significance for the development of division of labour, both within the state apparatus itself and in civil society. The state, furthermore, is a phenomenon that cannot be understood in terms of an aggregation of individual preferences either through the market or through sociocultural consensus. Reflection on the 'functions' of the state is, in fact, the locus classicus for the realization that the idea of the common good may be inherently flawed, invariably hiding – and not overcoming – contradictory interests and value positions.

International Division of Labour

International division of labour stands at first sight in a very different relationship to our argument. Transcending the reach of state action, it may seem shaped (in virtually pure fashion) by the invisible hand of the market. If power had indeed only a negligible role in the dynamics of international division of labour, the thesis of this book would have to be severly qualified if it could be maintained at all. International division of labour – clearly of great importance in the capitalist world – cannot, after all, even be confined to modern history. Division of labour among clearly delimited and closely organized communities and tribes has always been considered one of the mainsprings of division of labour in human history.

Yet there is no question that the conception of international trade as market exchange in pure form – as exchange uncontaminated by power – is thoroughly mistaken. *International division of labour is shaped by power as much as any other form of division of labour.* Rather than entering into a discussion of dependency and world system theories, which have transformed the analysis of socioeconomic development,[6] I shall just make a few fairly simple points.

First, like other market exchange, international trade requires an infrastructure of guarantees that rests ultimately on coercive power. One might well argue that such guarantees are particularly important in international relations precisely because non-coercive social controls are less prevalent. The chances that this power-induced infrastructure is neutral *vis-à-vis* contradictory interests are slim indeed. It may be supplied primarily by one dominant state – as, for instance, it was by Britain in the nineteenth century – or by a set of states with unequal clout. Second, if at all possible, states will seek to affect international trade and the international division of labour so as to proctect their geopolitical interests as well as to pursue internal policies that are shaped by power constellations at home. Third, even if we neglect the role of state action in international trade and division of labour, power is not eliminated. The working of the market conveys power, too. I am not thinking here as much of shifts in the terms of trade due to changing supply and demand as of the dominance of firms and countries in given markets. Monopolistic, oligopolistic, and price leadership positions constitute economic power, which if stable has a tremendous impact on the changing division of labour.[7] These economic power relations may in turn provoke state action searching for the most advantageous insertion of a country's economy into the changing international division of labour – advantageous for geopolitical state goals as well as for a constellation of powerful (if in the normal case partly contradictory) social and economic interests.

International division of labour has a dynamic that is historically variable and that does differ from division of labour within a political community. It is of consequence whether or not a process of significant change is contained within the jurisdiction of single state. But beyond that the logic of international division of labour is not fundamentally different from that within a country. Much less does it put profoundly into question the ideas about power and division of labour advanced here. International division of labour does constitute a phenomenon of great substantive importance. Neither under modern conditions nor before the development of capitalism can changes in the division of labour be studied adequately without exploring the full scope of actual power and exchange interdependencies that shaped them in a given instance. Yet the purpose of this book was not to provide a comprehensive explanation of specific instances of division of labour, but to advance an argument about division of labour, power, and efficiency and to explore and substantiate the role of power in different aspects of the phenomenon.

CONCLUSIONS REPUGNANT TO COMMON SENSE?

It is time to return to the central argument and confront for the last time a number of critical issues, some of which have been only touched up on so far. The thesis of this book asserts more than that power has something to do with the advance of division of labour and the forms it takes. It is more than a plea to focus attention on the role power plays in social change. It departs from fundamental assumptions of major positions in social theory – functionalist as well as Marxist – and it contradicts common views about the impact of technology and knowledge on social change and its structural outcomes.

I began by questioning the view that division of labour is driven forward by the same efficiency gains it allegedly generates. This view, perhaps rarely encountered with all components explicitly stated in one place, was found wanting not primarily because it naively derives causal explanation from the results of the phenomenon to be explained. Not all functional analyses make that jump in argumentation. Nor is its main fault that it treats the relation between specialization and productivity as self-evident. Though a tendency to take this relationship for granted is quite widespread, the review of the multiple and contradictory consequences of increased division of labour in chapter 2 could draw on a rich literature, classic and modern.

A more radical departure from common assumptions is involved in the proposition that *efficiency is a formal concept, in its meaning inherently dependent on specific preference structures, and that the diverse preference structure of people are not objectively aggregated either through the market or through sociocultural consensus.* This was the point where power entered the argument. This also is the point where its implications seem at odds with good common sense, because it denies the notion of socioeconomic gains, costs, and productivity changes as objective givens, independent of people's contradictory priorities in needs and wants. Is it not obvious that the modern system of production yields so much more than was produced ever before in history? Furthermore, is it not obvious that the subordinate classes, too, are better off in industrial societies than in feudal and other agrarian social order? Why, then, should we not view the modern division of labour and organization of production as better adapted to the release of productive forces, as vastly more efficient in an objective sense, than the patterns they superseded?

This indeed is the position of Marx and Marxism, as well as of most liberal economic and social theorists. Marx never doubted that division of labour in capitalism led to greater efficiency in production. In his view, class power and class struggle shape the forms division of labour takes. Power and class conflict also can hold social transformation at bay or advance it. But this does not negate that the socioeconomic regime of capitalism allows the free development of productive forces to an extent undreamt of ever before. The idea of objective increases in productivity and efficiency presents no conceptual problems to Marx.

That the 'industrial society' of Spencer as well as of Parsons is seen as well adapted to the requirements of instrumental rationality is less of a surprise than that we can find in the work of both of these authors significant traces of an alternative view. Even Spencer, the prophet of *laissez faire* in the late nineteenth century, at least allowed for important costs of capitalism's productivity advances – costs that fall more on some than on others and that for industrial workers may well outweigh the gains:

> Though in his capacity of consumer the factory-hand, in common with the community, profits by the cheapening of goods of all kinds, including his own kind, yet in his capacity of producer he loses heavily – perhaps more heavily than he gains (Spencer, 1876–97/1975: III, 514).

Parsons, at least in his early writings, was much impressed with the continued resistance to high levels of differentiation and specialization in modern society. Faced with the threats of fascism, he considered the future of Western society for this reason as precarious. In his introduction to a selection of Weber's writings he states, with emphasis and implied agreement, that for Weber 'the high functional differentiation and specialization of roles in our society was by no means to be taken for granted as the simple result of ultilitarian "division of labour"' (Parsons, 1947: 80). However, neither Spencer nor Parsons allowed such considerations to escalate into a questioning – be it factually, conceptually or both – of the ideas of productive advance or greater 'adaptive capacity'.

Is it indeed possible to say that more clothes, more convenient and spacious housing, greater reach and ease of movement and communication, better control of pain, a lengthened life span, and fewer baby deaths do not necessarily constitute objective improvements? And if they are advances do they not have to be attributed, broadly speaking, to changes in the division of labour and technological innovation made possible by a thorough rationalization of the organization of production?

The position taken here does not deny that productivity and efficiency are meaningful concepts, nor that industrialization has brought tremendous efficiency increases. What is at issue is a comprehensive assessment of gains and costs, including those not expressed in market prices. The theoretical argument developed does insist that the preferences by which gains and losses are assessed vary;

they are not homogeneous across periods, cultures and social groups. With these premises a three-pronged argument suggests itself. First, differential power is critically important for what is produced as well as for the process of production. Second, the power diffusion characteristic of industrial societies moderates the one-sided steering of production and division of labour typical of pre-modern social orders. Third, and theoretically most troublesome, new forms of division of labour and emerging patterns of production may create their own validation as they bring about concordant preference structures; the latter are, after all, always socially shaped. Each of these assertions deserves brief elaboration.

A more efficient way of constructing the Egyptian pyramids, building the cathedral of Notre Dame, or sending machinery and people to the moon does not obviously add to the welfare of all, nor is it induced by the needs, wants and goals of all members of the societies involved. These projects were initiated by elites, whose priorities not only directed the allocation of resources but also shaped the development of technology and division of labour. Weak interests not only attract fewer resources for their satisfaction; they also fail to generate in the same measure technological and organizational innovation. The very development of the forces of production, then, is contingent on the alignment of power. True, not even the most powerful kings of the past had pain-killing medicines at their disposal just becuase they felt a need for them and exercised the greatest influence on productive innovation. But steady and concentrated attention to certain problems does make a difference in the advance of technology and the direction it takes, especially if other conditions facilitating such innovation are met – witness the dramatic changes in the technology of war as well as, perhaps, the unresolved problems of childbirth and, certainly, the belated advances in treating diarrhoea in the Third World.

The argument can be further elucidated by comparing modern societies of very different character. When the tables published by the World Bank (1979: 127, 1980: 111, 1981: 135) tell us that the gross national product of the German Democratic Republic exceeds that of the United Kingdom once population size is taken into account, anybody acquainted with the everyday life of common people in the two countries may first question the procedure of accounting used. Yet it is also reasonable to look for an explanation in the different priorities that steer the development and the deployment of the forces or production. One cannot eat steel plants or opportunities for life-long education, and assuring full employment can be very costly in other respects.

If the industrial organization in the state socialist countries of Eastern Europe shares nevertheless important features with shop-floor division of labour in the capitalist West, this does not prove that here we have the objectively most efficient methods of production. The explanation may well be that they are the most efficient for a given power constellation, which determines the weight of different gains and losses, and that the relative power of management and labour is not all that different in East and West. An analogous *raison du pouvoir* rather than the conditions of an objective productivity maximization would, in this perspective, be decisive.

The second point has been prepared by earlier discussion, especially in the immediately preceding chapter. Modern societies are characterized by a substantial diffusion of power when compared to almost all preceding social order of any complexity. Thus, there is also far less inequality in the determination of the direction of production, of technological development, and of the division of labour. Under any circumstance it is rare that changes in the division of labour are simply imposed by dominant interests; they usually are contested and even shaped by the anticipation of contest. The less unequal the power balance, the less onesidedly does the outcome reflect the interests and preference structures of dominant groups. When compared to slaves and serfs (and even when compared to the weakest groups in contemporary capitalist societies), modern industrial workers do have greater influence on the organization of their work and they participate more in the fruits of production. The intuitively persuasive judgement that the common people in modern society enjoy a vastly improved standard of living, then, is true in part because the modern productive apparatus – in capitalist as well as in state socialist countries – is less geared towards the satisfaction of narrowly confined privileged interests but is shaped in more (albeit far from completely) even fashion by the needs and wants of broad population segments.

It is true, beyond this consideration, that capitalism (and in different ways, state socialism too) has freed the allocation of human and material resources from restrictions based on a multiplicity of concerns other than those of production. This and the spur of competitive pressure have engendered continuous innovation in technology and the organization of production. While this permanent revolution has pushed productivity up, such productivity increases remain inherently linked to an uneven representation of interests. In relation to non-economic concerns and to the interests of the weaker groups, capitalist economic growth has often been a ruthless and even vicious process of change. Weighing its costs against the measurable income gains is impossible without making problematic and ultimately metaphysical assumptions about which interests are the expendable shells that have to be broken to make an omelette.

Finally, an assessment of gains and losses due to fundamental changes in the division of labour, and thus a comprehensive evaluation of productivity in different social formations, encounters extraordinary difficulties because of the variability of human needs and wants. On the one hand workers may come to accept – or not to mind intensely – even the most fragmented division of labour and the most exerting work discipline; on the other, capitalism has not only unleashed an unimagined flow of production, but has also generated previously unimagined wants. It was Durkheim who expressed the resulting indeterminacies by arguing that one could not reasonably think of the results of increasing division of labour as a continuous increase in happiness.

Durkheim conceived of the social and cultural shaping of needs and wants as homogeneous across social groups, though discontinuous from one epoch to another. 'Society', in his view, takes on different forms, but its imprint is compelling on all its members. Even though people's preference structures are ineluctably social in character and can never be understood in purely individual terms, it seems doubtful that the social and cultural shaping of needs and wants goes as far as Durkheim implied, that it ever eliminates the conflict of contradictory interests with unequal power. But it does complicate the picture far beyond a simple opposition of unchanging and stable interests; and it is also clear that these interests are never exhausted by material needs and the instrumental ways of meeting them. In this perspective it is quite plausible that we often find only limited periods of strong resistance to new forms of division of labour, after which not only resignation sets in but also a more lasting adaptation of standards and demands to the new conditions.

Overpowering facts create, to some extent, their own acceptance, and cultural hegemony can reshape needs and wants. Major changes in differentiation and division of labour can thus come close to establishing their own validation.[8]

HOW MUCH EXPLANATORY POWER TO POWER?

Power, then, must be an integral part of any analysis of the division of labour. Yet power seems rather unsuitable for the role as prime mover of historical change. Alignments of power are manifestly not constant givens. They are clearly influenced by factors not under the control of different power holders. Moreover, the exercise of power – even the most concentrated power – is manifestly not identical with social causation. Division of labour and the differentiation of social structure are clearly shaped also by factors other than the will of individuals and groups and the resources they can mobilize for their goals. What, then, is the place of power in the larger ensemble of factors that determine directly and indirectly division of labour and structural differentiation?

In the broadest sense, power is the human capacity to accomplish something – and to do so even against the opposition of others. The subjects exercising power may be individuals or groups and organizations. The latter are of particular importance for the analysis of social structures and their change. This turns the constitution of collective actors into a critical analytic issue, a subject that was discussed repeatedly in a variety of contexts. Here is the point where it appears crucial to retain, in contrast to many theories emphasizing the role of power, certain Durkheimian ideas about normative and cultural integration. Collective action does not come about simply because a set of people share certain interests, though common interests and the underlying structural relations are of the utmost importance. Collectivities capable of corporate action may be constituted partially through coercion as well as by providing benefits to the participating individuals; but despite the contentions of Olson (1965) and other rational choice theorists, the provision of individual advantage and the threat of individual suffering do not exhaust the 'logic of collective action'. They always presuppose to some extent what they seek to explain – the existence of coherent collective actors able to dispense punishment and reward. Effective corporate action of a plurality of persons also inevitably involves the development of lasting social attachments and a realignment of individual preference structures. This, in turn, can hardly be understood without reference to cultural presuppositions – to fundamental values, basic cognitive premises, and broad delineations of social identities and solidarities. These cultural bases which inevitably enter into the contruction and reconstruction of collective actors – of movements, organizations, and institutions – are themselves not unchanging; their change must ultimately be explained by human action. But to a large extent they are beyond the reach of intentional reordering and manipulation. This means that the very constitution of historical actors involves cultural elements that must be considered as givens in so far as the interests of contending groups in any particular situation are concerned. However, the commonalities thus utilized and reinforced rarely (if ever) turn all interacting individuals and groups into one consensual whole in which interests and goals are complementary and the significant values are shared. Against a fragmentary backdrop of partially shared understandings and normative orientations, divergent preference structures and discordant ideas of what is right provide the elements out of which potentially antagonistic collectivities and organizations are constructed. These may contend with each other, enter into alliances and even fuse into larger entities, or seek to subdue and destroy their opponents.[9]

The relative power of different collective actors derives from varying combinations of many different resources – from weapons' technology as well as from followers' loyalty; from property as well as effective organization of many participants; from the provision of the necessities of life as well as from offering and denying valued social affiliations; from knowledge of various kinds as well as from effective appeals to the attachments, passions and ideals of others. The basis of power is, as Weber put it, sociologically amorphous. Yet however amorphous power may be in its origins, its consequences have a quite definite social shape. It offers the chance to reach one's goals even against resistance. This generalized advantage is a strong incentive to seek out ways and means to stabilize, maintain and possibly enlarge a power position once it is attained.

One particular form of such stabilization attempts, and a particularly important one, is an organizational arrangement in which some are obliged to comply with the orders of others – Max Weber's *Herrschaft* or institutionalized domination. Institutionalized domination may still rest partially on the effective provision of goods and services as well as on the concordance of its authority claims with widely held values – on legitimation; but in its more elaborate forms, and especially if it can organize and monopolize the deployment of force, it tends to acquire a certain autonomy from the production and exchange of economic resources as well as from the web of social affiliations and the prescriptions of cultural tradition. It can then, in turn, exert a measure of influence on economic processes, social relations, and cultural outlook that varies with historical constellation, but that is significant even if it does not amount to unbounded hegemony.

The modern state fits that description, but it may also apply to power relations in the organization of production. As Robert Brenner (1976) has shown, the institution of serfdom did not simply yield to the extension of market exchange nor to the dynamics of population depletion. Lords sought to intensify their control over dependent peasants in the aftermath of the Black Death and the labour shortages it created. The ensuing struggles did not uniformly result in freeing agrarian labour. In Eastern Europe, serfdom was in fact imposed in the face of population depletion – conditions that in a simple supply-and-demand view should have had the opposite result. The domination system of serfdom had its own dynamic; it cannot be reduced to a mere function of supply and demand. We may add that cultural and religious ideas became relevant in the rural class struggles, but they did not earlier erode the relations between lord and serf on their own.

Power constellations, however constituted, are not the sole determinants of division of labour, structural differentiation, and social change. Environmental conditions obviously have an impact, the more so the closer even the most powerful individuals and groups are to the margins of physical survival. Population dynamics, too, are consequential even if increases in density do not at all regularly usher in advances in division of labour, as demonstrated by the relative stability of feudal Europe in the face of Malthusian ups and downs. Even the components of social, material, and ideational culture that are more clearly the product of collective human action have a life of their own that does not easily submit to intentional reordering. Moral and cognitive premises of social life do affect which social arrangements are viable, which innovations have an initial chance, and which patterns can become stabilized. We have seen, for instance, that the emergence of bureaucratization in its full-fledged form involved a reordering of moral and cognitive orientations which benefited from individualist and universalist cultural conceptions that had crystallized and matured long before. Most readers, finally, need all too little persuasion to consider technology a factor that is at least partially beyond the immediate control of powerful interests and that clearly makes its imprint on the division of labour.

What role, then, for power? Does it merely enact an organization of production and a division of labour that is largely determined by these other factors? That is the conventional view, especially if we add broad-based demand for the fruits of production as a further element. The results of our investigation argue for a different view.

Power constellations, of which the ability to pursue one's interests effectively in the market is an important though historically variable aspect, give prominence to some preference structures and leave others in a subordinate or even negligible position. *They thus shape the patterns of demand and incentive to which technological and organizational innovations respond.* Shifts in these power alignments entail corresponding shifts in the patterns of demand and incentive. However, the organization and the technology of production built up under earlier conditions inevitably constitute the baseline and the foundation for new developments. They are not malleable in the short run, responding instantly to new dominant interest constellations. Though it complicates the tracing of cause and effect, this historical persistence plainly does not eliminate the role of power.

The market's steering of production is commonly viewed as the antithesis to an ordering of productive and other social relations by power. But power is variously involved in a market economy.

1   As capitalism developed, power was required to 'free' the factors of production from social controls. The institution of serfdom rested on power, and it was broken by the exercise of power.

2   Even the model of competitive market exchange requires an institutional infrastructure guaranteed by coercion that protects, at a minimum, property and contract.

3   The most competitive market exchange does not eliminate, but simply reflects, the prior stratification of resources.

4   Markets approaching the model of perfect competition are rare, and monopolistic deviations represent power based on market position.

5   Since the unfettered play of market forces, competitive or not, strongly affects social interests with varied power resources, it tends to provoke multiple attempts at regulation and power-based 'interventions' in the market (Polanyi, 1944/57).

6   The boundaries of the market, the delineation of areas not simply subject to the rule of supply and demand, are matters of social contest. One example are the boundaries between family and labour markets, illustrated by the conflicts over child labour or over the labour force participation of women; similarly, most state activities are removed from market control, and the expanding scope of state action is clearly the product of powerful if conflicting interests.

Finally:

7   The business firm itself represents a major challenge to a vision of social relations ordered by the free play of the market. It is in fact a major instance of institutionalized domination, within which hired labour is subject to authority as far as the division and control of labour are concerned.[10]

The last two arguments point to a relatively direct impact of power on the ordering of social relations. Perfectly competitive or not, market functioning shapes only a fraction of social arrangements of production, not to mention the specialization of roles and organizations in other spheres of social life.

The impact of power and power interests on division of labour and structural differentiation is a complex matter, as one should expect given the abstract nature and broad empirical reach of the concepts of power and differentiation. Apodictic enumeration of major ideas will again serve to keep the review brief.

1   The interests of the powerful are typically served by the structural developments under consideration. As in other functionalist approaches this initial proposition identifies problems for explanation; it does not itself explain how this result comes about.

2   The interests of dominant groups are manifold and historically varied. Interests in the maintenance and possibly the expansion of power have a special place among them. We can assume them to have a particular prevalence among successful powerholders. But power interests do not exhaust the interests of the powerful, and I do not maintain that the sole or prime determinant of division of labour is the goal to maintain or increase power. This is an important factor, but only one among several.[11]

3   The interests of even the most powerful groups are not always effectively secured. The chances that they are secured are greatest if it is clear where one's advantage lies, as well as how it is to be attained, and if the cooperation of many actors is not required. These conditions are not rare, but they are far from generally given; especially the long-term effects of social change, which in turn may shape the distribution of power resources, are both hard to forsee and difficult to control. Thus powerful classes like the landed aristocracy in most agrarian societies and even the bourgeoisie in the capitalist countries of the West have lost power – in absolute or at least in relative terms – partly as a consequence of processes of division of labour that they themselves engendered or did not succeed in squashing. The development of parliamentary democracy is an obvious example.

4   Even the most powerful group can rarely just impose their designs on subordinate classes. Resistance and conflict are further reasons why the interests of the dominant groups are not always effectively secured. Since subordinate groups are likely to rely on different power resources, the transparency of the situation, and thus the scope for rational action as an explanatory factor, are further reduced. Yet the outcomes remain shaped by the exercise of power, however complex.

5   It is important not to conceive of power as a static given, even though the rational pursuit of self-interest puts a premium on the maintenance of power, and selective elimination of the negligent due to a struggle for power on the part of many groups increases the proportion of those who intelligently husband their power sources. New strategies, made possible by changing opportunities and innovative action (for instance, the partial bureaucratization of a patrimonial staff, or voluntary organization of members of a subordinate class) may critically enhance the power of a previously weaker group and change the balance of power significantly.

6   The interaction of different social forces with different power resources and antagonistic interests will often have results in the division of labour and in structural differentiation that are not just beyond the foresight and control of any one group but that are at odds with the intentions of all. This severely limits the importance of intentional action but, again, it does not negate the role of power in division of labour.

Adding these complexities to the direct and indirect impact of a variety of factors other than power that also shape division of labour may seem to leave only a limited and heavily qualified role for power in the development of division of labour, differentiation, and dedifferentiation. However, *power retains pride of place in the explanation of division of labour as far as the historical agency of individuals and groups is concerned*. In regard to human agency, whether it attains its goals or is obstructed or deflected by opposition as well as impersonal constraints and unforseen developments, other factors (such as environmental conditions or cultural traditions) enter the picture as elements in the constitution of collective actors and as variable resources of power; that is, they are in their effects mediated and reshaped by power constellations. Power, then, plays a most significant role as a *proximate* cause of division of labour, differentiation and dedifferentiation.

The study of division of labour and differentiation has in the past been closely associated with theories of evolution. Can the exploration of the role of power in structural differentiation contribute to a better understanding of very long-term structural change and its direction? The answer seems, at first, to be negative. Power comes into its own above all as a proximate cause of social differentiation, dedifferentiation and stagnation. In the very long run it seems that power itself may best be understood as a product of evolution (see Luhmann, 1979 and 1982; also Parsons, 1964, and Lenski, 1966). Yet our investigation suggests a number of considerations that may amount to a commentary of some consequence of theories of social evolution.

First, focusing on the specific processes through which division of labour and structural differentiation are changed may be a more promising strategy of analysis than directly searching for an explanation of general evolutionary trends towards greater complexity. Thus even if the role of power were altogether confined to that of a proximate cause in relatively short-term developments, an elucidation of actual mechanisms of change in division of labour and organizational complexity would provide evolutionary theories with a sorely needed processual detailing.

However, Durkheim's problem – how one can explain long-term evolutionary trends towards greater complexity in terms of improved satisfaction of needs and wants when human beings in the course of fundamental sociocultural transformations 'contact tastes and habits that they did not have, which is to say...change their nature' (Durkheim, 1893/1964: 240) – seems to apply with equal force to changes in the patterns of power. The value and the availability of different power resources, the formal structures of power, and the chances of different groups to obtain power are all profoundly affected by radical changes in the 'tastes and habits of people' as well as by changes in the division of labour and social structure. The conception of a *raison du pouvoir*, developed briefly in chapter 3, may provide a partial answer. Even if the opportunities of developing and exercising power have changed significantly over time due to transformations of people's preferences, as well as to changes in the division of labour and social organization, there seem to remain typically important similarities in the interests of changing dominant groups, and these should engender similar effects of social structural arrangements. It is true of most dominant groups that they do not have to suffer – and thus do not count as costs – many of the less desirable consequences of their actions. It is true of all dominant groups that they have a strong interest in maintaining their advantage. And it is true of many quite different dominant groups that their interests are best served by similar organizational forms – witness Weber's amply confirmed insistence that the new Soviet Russia would not be able to dispense with the bureaucratic machinery of rule. Similarly, it is at least a plausible hypothesis that the astounding stability and stagnation of many agrarian societies has one significant cause in the fact that the relations between lords and cultivators remained fundamentally unchanged and that they gave neither side strong incentives for innovation in the technology and organization of production.

These suggestions are not meant to hint at the possibility of a 'power theory of evolution'. However, any attempt at a theory of evolution would do well to consider power among the major relevant factors even in the longer run. Against this, it is not a valid objection that specialized power structures are not found in the simplest forms of human social life, and that therefore power must be considered a product rather than a cause of evolution. The same is true of economic organization as well as cultural tradition; it is true of any complex of social forces conceptualized initially in terms of the differentiated structure of the most complex societies. Furthermore, one must not confuse the search for causal conditions with the search for ultimate origins.

That constructing a theory of evolution makes sense is not an uncontested proposition. The trend towards greater complexity discerned by many analysts in the 'general evolution' of world history can be identified only with ambiguity and uncertainty. Given that history is full of reversals of possibly general trends towards greater complexity, of long periods of stagnation, of new starts which move into different areas of concern and display different directions and forms of differentiation, of countertrends that interact with uncertainly defined dominant developments, as well as of 'alternative routes' to similar levels of overall structural complexity, one may very well be sceptical of any theory of social evolution and take an agnostic position about the phenomenon. Focusing on the role of power in division of labour and social differentiation reinforces certain arguments of the sceptics. At any rate, it points towards significant indeterminacies even in long-term structural changes. If we saw reason to reject the view of industrial society as reflecting optimal, knowledge-based solutions to objective and inescapable problems, we argued by the same token for more degrees of freedom in the developmental possibilities of modern societies than technological and efficiency-based 'convergence' theories allow. This conclusion, as well as a number of other arguments – such as those about the historical persistence and short-term inflexibility of technology and social organization – suggest that comparative historical analyses in the mode of Max Weber will be more fruitful theoretically than the abstract questions pursued by classic and contemporary theorists of evolution.

ISSUES OF CRITIQUE AND EVALUATION

Is there a 'moral to the story' that demands separate consideration? Does it at all make sense to pursue questions of moral judgement when we deal with very broad and long-term historical changes? Niklas Luhmann (1982) has argued for a negative answer to these questions; and he is in good company. Both Hegel and Marx had little regard for moral pronouncements that claimed to judge historical change from an Archimedian point outside of history. However, the possibility of such a position transcending historical circumstance and relativity aside, reflection on matters of human value virtually forces itself on the analyst. It can be set aside, it can – and normally should be – differentiated from cognitive invertigation, but it seems hard to dismiss altogether. Evaluative reflection is meaningful beyond the question of whether it makes a difference: it carries its own meaning even if it had no instrumental significance. Moreover, it actually may make a difference. It most likely makes a difference by shaping our cognitive perspectives and overall intellectual outlook, and it deserves some attention for this reason alone.

It also may make a difference for the social changes and developments we have considered in this volume. With this I do not mean to claim that one can develop a specific moral blueprint for the future of division of labour and then hope to have it somehow implemented. But reflection on the standards for judging the human value of different social arrangements, especially if it is joined with analytic reflection on the modalities of structural change, may not be altogether without consequence. It is a correlate of the view that social structure is not given – by God, by nature, or by an inscrutable yet determinist logic of history – but is in the last analysis the outcome of aggregate human action and construction. What we have learned about the determinants of division of labour and social structure includes insights into a certain degree of variability of future developments, even though intentional action of any one collective actor has by itself a rather circumscribed explanatory power. Moreover, different conceptions of what is possible and what is right may have some – however limited – effect on the constitution of collective actors and the course of their actions. Yet developing appropriate value standards for judging broad developments of division of labour and social organization would far exceed the scope of this volume. Rather than mount an extended argument, I will simply indicate a few positions I am inclined to take. This is as much to warn the reader of moral preferences that may have informed and shaped my argument as it is, perhaps, to instigate similar reflections even if they lead to quite different results.

First is the principle of equality. The very language we use to describe and analyse power is imbued with egalitarian meanings and connotations. To say that serfdom as well as capitalist labour management rest on coercion (albeit in different ways) is to make an accurate statement, but one that at once implies critique. Similarly, to point out that a fully competitive market denies every participant power over the others is not only to indicate one feature of the model of perfect competition but to mobilize a moral approval that may be extended, beyond the confines of the model, to a less perfect reality. I do not mind the egalitarian presuppositions so deeply built into language and common sense that the power of the few over the many becomes, as Hume put it, the most surprising social phenomenon. Rather, embracing them, I wish to make them explicit. Thus the first standard for evaluation is simple yet far-reaching: a social arrangement is the more acceptable the more it can be seen as resting on the considered and uncoerced consent of all involved.[12]

It is compatible with this first standard to entertain ideas critical of prevailing needs, wants, outlooks and values. Such ideas are often associated with justifications for authoritarian impositions, but they are not themselves inherently authoritarian. They may be persuasive without the backing of power and deception. This by way of prefacing the second standard: even if alternative arrangements rest equally on consent, those giving people significantly less autonomy should be judged inferior to others that provide the participants with more freedom from personal and impersonal social control.

If neither the first nor this second rule seem to require much of a reordering of many people's preference structures, it is because both are close to the core of the prevailing ideological outlook – individualism. However, any two standards can come into conflict with each other and thus require difficult choices. This is true also of freedom and equality, though their incompatibility is often exaggerated by those who wish to contain the egalitarian demands of others. Moreover, both can conceivably come into conflict with the satisfaction of material needs and wants. If it has been shown repeatedly for several Western countries that autonomy and personal fulfilment at work rank highest as life goals among those who can take material success for granted, while material want-satisfaction is given higher priority by those with the least chances of success in either direction, we are probably confronted with adaptive distortions of preference structures that might well take on a different shape with a more egalitarian distribution of education and of career chances. At the collective level, the choice between fewer constraints and more material resources may be a difficult one. What can hardly be defended, however, is a choice made by those who do not have to endure the negative implications of their own preferences – even if they succeed in quieting dissent or inducing others to adjust their goals and hopes.

Even more complicated problems of choice are introduced by the third standard on the banner of the French Revolution – 'fraternity'. Association and solidarity with others as ends in themselves are part of any humane conception of the good society. Yet the ideal of fraternity is surrounded by a veritable crowd of open and difficult questions. First, solidarity with whom? Which delineations of community avoid both the love–hate antinomies of ingroup–outgroup patterns *and* the emptiness of all-inclusive identification? How are the relations among groups affected by their internal solidarity? How much tolerance for conflict does a society, or even the closest group, need? Choices must be made wherever 'trade-offs' emerge between community and equality, community and freedom, as well as community and material welfare. Finally, how much reasoned and discussed choice is compatible with deeply felt social attachment? Is the latter perhaps threatened by rational choice itself? Would it be more fulfilling if lived with as an unquestioned given?

I have no intention of answering these questions. Constructing a positive utopia is an undertaking made impossible by our knowledge of historical diversity, our ignorance about universal laws (perhaps) governing social life, and by our commitment to the first two standards of equality and freedom. Habermas's solution is appealing: the choices must be made by the participants. Judgement and critique focus on the way in which they were made, and the standards for evaluation derive from what people expect of each other in communication if they are not coerced and if they accept each other as equal persons, As to the substance of these issues, I would argue only that some forms of community and solidarity transcending radical individualist isolation are essential to any good society, that beyond certain thresholds the demands of liberty and equality should prevail over the claims of community, and that reasoned choice and commitment are preferable even if they lead to the loss of a sense of primordial affiliation.

Similar questions are raised by the necessity to achieve some integration of highly differentiated activities and to reach collective decisions. These problems are made more difficult by the vast scope and the high degree of division of labour in modern societies. Even if, as one may well argue, there was no necessity to the development that brought about the social world in which we live, there is no way of returning to simpler conditions. Issues of integration and governance are often invoked to justify authority and privilege. There is no doubt that complex trade-offs and difficult choices are involved here. I also have no doubt that these choices should be viewed in a very similar manner as just indicated for the choices raised by the ideal of community. I believe that radical democratization – not only confined to the political sphere but extended throughout social life – is a credible option that has substantial costs. I also believe that the simultaneous protection of freedom and equality may well come to be seen as outweighing these costs.

The experience of the most complex societies of the twentieth century is ambiguous. It gives reason to fear authoritarian and even totalitarian rule, but it also holds hope for a continuing equalization and deepening democratization of social life. The last two hundred years, though they were witness to the most destructive wars of human history and to an unprecedented victimization of defenceless people, have also seen the emergence of social structures that are less at odds with the standards of liberty, equality and fraternity than any complex social order of the past.

The different extant forms of industrial society, capitalist or socialist, have something in common that they will have to shed: they are social machines geared to the unending growth of material production. Turning away from material growth is not a short-term necessity. In the closely foreseeable future, in fact, expanding material production is a critical condition for reducing massive human misery. Yet there are powerful arguments that the growth of the last two hundred years cannot continue indefinitely without becoming self-destructive. The cultural and social–structural changes required by a turn away from continuous material growth are vast. They are at least as vast as those placed on the human agenda by the individualism and socialism that are the ideological children of the capitalist revolution.

Knowledge, technology and social organization follow in their changes an agenda that is socially determined. They do so slowly. That means old interests are better served than new ones. It also means that new departures may fail without prejudging the longer-term possibilities, though there is no guarantee that the creative potential of human societies will eventually match reasoned collective tasks. The hope is that persistent experimentation will bring us closer to a humane life in societies that can keep the peace with each other and with the world in which we exist.

Notes

1 POWER AND THE DIVISION OF LABOUR

1. At the beginning of his discussion of wages Adam Smith states (1976/1937: 65):

   The original state of things, in which the labourer enjoyed the whole produce of his own labour, could not last beyond the first introduction of the appropriation of land and the accumulation of stock. It was at an end, therefore, long before the most considerable improvements were made in the productive powers of labour, and it would be to no purpose to trace further what might have been its effect upon the recompence or wages of labour.

2. See chapter 2 for some further discussion of these issues.

2 THE RESULTS OF INCREASING DIVISION OF LABOUR

1. Stephen Marglin (1974) has given an account of division of labour and factory organization that is extremely sceptical of Smith's (and others') claims about efficiency increases due to industrial specialization. He, too, emphasizes the role played by power in the division of labour. I have learned much from his critique of Smith and his historical analysis, yet differ from his arguments about the productivity effects of division of labour and the role played by power interests, as the rest of this section and the reasoning in chapter 3 will show. Still, even though I conceive of the interrelations among division of labour, efficiency and power differently than Marglin does, we share very similar concerns and come to conclusions that are broadly compatible. The two lines of inquiry were developed independently. While Marglin turned critically away from and against neoclassical economics, my arguments (Rueschemeyer, 1974, 1977) turned critically away from

and against functionalist modernization theory of sociology. Though such a partial convergence of independently pursued inquiries does not amount to confirmation, it does constitute a distinct intellectual comfort.

2. This idea can be generalized. One might seek to distinguish all those human concerns whose vigorous pursuits interfere with each other – applying as a general principle the idea of which the legal treatment of 'conflict of interest' is a special case. The result would be a theoretical grid of potential and likely lines of structural differentiation. Talcott Parsons has attempted this in his conceptual framework of four basic functional problems that all social systems and subsystems have to cope with (see, e.g., Parsons, 1966). While intriguing, this attempt is tied to the problematic conception of human social life as organized in consensual social systems, and it lacks clear-cut translation rules which permit an unambiguous identification of the abstract issues – of 'adaptation', 'goal attainment', 'integration' and 'pattern maintenance' – in concrete reality.

3. Adam Smith may have left the analysis of productivity-enhancing effects of division of labour in such a rudimentary and incomplete state because he considered the discipline of competition to be of overriding importance. Yet unless we want to treat the changes in productive organizations (in analogy to biological evolution) as *random events*, which assume a functional form purely due to the effects of competitive survival and elimination, we do need an understanding of how different aspects of specialization affect productivity, whatever our estimate of the importance of competitive constraints.

4. In passing we should note the irony in the claim that competition safeguards the efficiency consequences of division of labour. There is after all a fundamental contradiction between the productivity claims made on behalf of competition and those made on behalf of division of labour and structural differentiation. The latter result in a pattern of ever-widening interdependence among specialized, non-competing units while the former requires many similar units that produce in parallel fashion the same or very similar goods and services. Advances in division of labour and the realization of economies of scale thus tend to limit competition and may in the extreme eliminate it. These issues are discussed in economics under the heading of the implications of 'increasing returns'; see Alfred Marshall (1890/1961), Allyn Young (1928), and George Stigler (1951).

5. For a thorough account of Marx's ideas and a reconstruction in terms of methodological individualism, which appeared too late to be incorporated here, see Elster (1985). The argument presented simplifies much more complex conceptual interrelations in the work of Marx,

though it is a close paraphrase of his argument in the *Economic and Philosophical Manuscripts* (1844/1964). As a short formulation it seems a far more adequate representation of his whole *oeuvre* than readings which see exploitation as fundamentally distinct from alienation and then view the latter as a romantic preoccupation of the young Marx replaced by the former in Marx's mature work. While the *word* 'alienation' plays no role in *Capital*, the *concept* is ever-present. This theoretical continuity in his work is evident beyond any doubt in the *Grundrisse* (1857/1971), in which Marx sketches arguments for *Capital*.

Exploitation followed for Marx from the very principles of political economy expounded by Smith and, especially, Ricardo, once capital becomes a socially distinct factor of production and assumes the dominant role in the organization of production. While in this view labour is the source of all economic value, the compensation of a worker for his labour is determined in the same way as the prices for all other commodities used in production: wages as well as other prices pay for the reproduction of the things and services used. That the reproduction cost of labour (the standard of living required for an adequate labour force across generations) is socially determined, does not affect the outcome of the argument: the surplus left after such payment of costs represents, by definition, exploitation if appropriated by someone other than the workers since it is labour that accounts for all economic value.

If the concept of exploitation in this sense is tied to the labour theory of value, its contours do not disappear completely if one moves away from this theory. At a minimum, the idea of exploitation entails a constellation of directly conflicting economic interests of two parties in an exchange relationship with sharp disparities of power.

6. It is the achievement of an excellent essay on alienation and anomie by Steven Lukes (1) to have shown that and how these questions are inextricably interrelated in the work of Marx and Durkheim, respectively; (2) to have demonstrated that this interrelatedness does not remove all of their ideas into a metaphysical realm insulated against arguments from empirical evidence; and (3) to have reclaimed the issues of evaluation for reasoned (if not primarily empirical nor predominantly cognitive) discourse. In regard to the last point, Lukes argues:

> Both sociological evidence and conceptual inquiry are relevant in the attempt to decide these matters, but in the end what is required is an ultimate and personal commitment (for which good, or bad, reasons may, none the less, be advanced). One may, of course, hold, as both Marx and Durkheim in different ways did, that one's values are, as it were, embedded in the facts, but this is itself a committed position (for which, again, good or bad, reasons may be advanced) (Lukes, 1967: 155).

7. The decision to focus on the *evaluation* of differentiated statuses (i.e.

on occupational prestige) was a self-conscious and deliberate decision about theoretical strategy which Talcott Parsons justified through his earlier critical investigation of the conceptual core of the theories of Marshall, Pareto, Durkheim and Weber (Parsons, 1937). Note that this strategy in the analysis of stratification explicitly leaves power in the status of an unexplained residual category:

It is convenient to conceptualize [the] element of discrepancy between the normatively defined 'ideal' ranking order and the actual state of affairs, in terms of the relation between ranking in value terms and 'power'. Power we may define as the realistic capacity of a system-unit to actualize its 'interests'. . . within the context of system-interaction and in this sense to exert influence on processes of the system.

This seems to give power a critical place in any analysis of actual stratification patterns; yet Parsons's analytic strategy is different:

Empirically the imperfections of integration of social systems. . . may be extremely important. However, the point of view from which we approach the analysis of stratification prescribes that analysis should focus on the common value-pattern aspect. Only through this can we gain stable points of reference for a technical theoretical analysis of the empirical influence of the other components of the system-process. This is essentially because on general theoretical grounds we can state that the 'focus' of the *structure* of a system of action lies in the common value-pattern aspect of its culture (Parsons, 1953: 95 and 97).

The consequences of his theoretical strategy are not remedied in Parsons's (1963) later work on 'power', since he then conceived power as a phenomenon that is *by definition* harnessed to the collective purposes and needs of a social system, a phenomenon quite different from what other theorists, from Marx and Weber or Mosca to the Parsons of 1953, had in mind when they spoke of power.

3 THE ROLE OF EFFICIENCY AND POWER IN EXPLANATIONS OF DIVISION OF LABOUR

1. On the role of functionalist reasoning in Marxist thought see Elster (1982) and the ensuing discussion in *Theory and Society*. The specific issues related to an efficiency explanation in conjunction with assumptions about competitive market pressure, a common pattern in all three traditions, will be discussed below. It might be noted that in the *Wealth of Nations* Adam Smith made a clear distinction between the increase on the productive power of labour due to specialization – the subject of his first chapter – and the 'Principle which gives Occasion to the

Division of labour', as he titled the second chapter. Smith saw division of labour ultimately grounded in the 'propensity to truck, barter and exchange' (1776/1937: 13), a propensity he viewed as characteristic of human nature and probably related to reason and speech. ('Whether this propensity be one of those original principles of human nature, of which no further account can be given; or whether, as seems more probable, it be the necessary consequence of the facilities of reason and speech, it belongs not to our present subject to enquire. It is common to all men, and to be found in no other race of animals. . .' – ibid.) Smith specifically insisted that division of labour 'is not originally the effect of any human wisdom, which foresees and intends that general opulence to which it gives occasion', contrasting it to the propensity to exchange, 'which has in view no such extensive utility' (ibid.). While this is of some interest to our discussion below of the functionalist logic of efficiency explanations of division of labour, it is not unreasonable to view this argument of Smith's as limited to the *origins* of division of labour and to see him grant a greater role to foresight and planning at various later stages of human history.

2. Even Emile Durkheim, who challenged major premises of the utilitarian analysis of division of labour, accepted without question the proposition that division of labour increases productivity. Since, as we shall see, he rejected the idea that division of labour advances *because* of these productivity effects, he had to develop awkward arguments designed to explain the higher level of consumption which corresponds to greater productivity. He invoked greater fatigue, refined needs corresponding to a greater use of intelligence in work, the fact that new products can activate latent wants, and the attraction of novelty as explanations.

3. Wilbert Moore (1968: 373) contends that the idea of selective adaptation has been neglected in recent sociological system theory and argues for its adoption:

In Darwinian evolutionary theory, structural differentiation derives from selective adaptation of organisms to their environment. Since environments differ both cross-sectionally and temporally, the idea of selective adaptation provides a way of accounting both for the observed diversity in structural forms and for continuing change. It is surprising that so little use has been made of this conceptual scheme in the theory of social systems, where it appears equally applicable.

This observation is roughly correct in regard to recent social theory; otherwise, it neglects the work of Bucher (1893/1901) and especially Max Weber (1922/68), who never loses sight of 'natural selection' as a force shaping the prevalent institutional patterns in different environments. As we will see below from Talcott Parsons's analysis, there are some good reasons why selective adaptation does not necessarily lead to determinate results.

4. For the best-known attempt to compose a catalogue of functional requisites see Aberle et al. (1950). An important set of unresolved issues, which I do not discuss in the text but which strengthens my sceptical conclusion, pertains to the necessary quality of the solution: how productive does an economy have to be for a society to 'get by', that is, maintain itself over generations? How much violence can be absorbed? How much lethargy and withdrawal is 'too much'?

5. To the four broad functional problems any social system has to deal with – in Parsons's abstract formulation: adaptation, goal attainment, integration and pattern maintenance – correspond four interrelated processes of evolutionary significance: adaptive upgrading, structural differentiation, integration, and a value generalization which can make meaningful and steer diverse activities and patterns by inclusive conceptions of what is desirable.

6. Durkheim did not pose these questions, even though they are suggested by what I called 'Durkheim's problem' – the issues raised by the historical variability of needs, wants and values and their structuring by social and cultural forces. He did not apply his insight to division within a society, probably because he was inclined – mistakenly, I submit – to conceive of needs and wants as being fairly uniformly determined by society and its *conscience collective* at any one time. Structured variation of needs and wants pertained for him to intercultural and interepochal differences rather than to divisions within a society. The strategy in social theory argued by Talcott Parsons since *The Structure of Social Action* (1937) (looking for shared goals and standards of evaluation emerging in systems involving a plurality of actors) has not succeeded in solving the basic problem. The most general thrust of Parsons's strategy is widely accepted. What has remained a bone of contention is that value consensus should be the main mechanism that provides for such an integration of preferences and evaluations. The critiques have been particularly insistent, as well as convincing, when value consensus is understood as spontaneous agreement rather than as the result (in significant part, at least) of indoctrination, deceit, manipulation and coercion. Another focus of criticism has been Parsons's inclination to think of such integration as characteristic of societies, rather than only of less inclusive 'pluralities of actors'. The integration theory of social systems has not been able to dispose of these critiques.

7. To cite but one dramatic example, in *The Transformation of American Law, 1780 to 1860* (1977) Morton Horwitz details the ways in which the English legal tradition was adapted to the emerging commercial and industrial capitalism in America. He shows how the law of property, contracts, negotiable instruments, liability and employment

(to name only a few areas) was transformed through judicial decision in such a manner as to favour entrepreneurial interests and in effect subsidize them at the expense of consumers, workers and farmers.

8. The position taken in the text is not particularly original. 'Money prices', argues Max Weber (1922/68: I, 108) who more than most social theorists sought to integrate economic analysis into his theoretical framework, 'are the product of conflicts of interest and of compromise; they thus result from power constellations'. The context for this remark is a discussion of the substantive conditions of formal rationality in a money economy. Weber considers three such conditions: (1) market struggle among at least relatively autonomous units; (2) capital accounting, the highest form of formal economic rationality, requires thorough market freedom; and (3) effective demand is always contingent on income distribution. In each of his brief commentaries on the three main propositions the role of power is highlighted. Our initial quote elaborates the first proposition. The second is rounded out by a critically important observation on the employment relationship: 'Strict capital accounting is further associated with the social phenomena of "shop discipline" and appropriation of the means of production, and that means: with the existence of a "system of domination" (*Herrschafts-sverhältnis*)' (ibid.). Weber, in other words, recognizes as much as Marx that division of labour in the workshop, under the domination of owners or managers, is constitutive of full-fledged capitalism – the closest approximation of formal economic rationality in human history. The third proposition points itself to the economic power inherent in the distribution of wealth. Weber concludes with the comment that formal economic rationality, the subject-matter of most economic analysis, is quite different from the various substantive rationalities that are informed by the ideals and interests of diverse groups: 'Formal and substantive rationality, no matter by what standard the latter is measured, are always in principle separate things, no matter that in many (and under certain very artificial assumptions even all) cases they may coincide empirically' (ibid.).

9. George C. Homans raised this objection when an earlier version of these ideas was presented to a colloquium at Harvard University in 1974. I am grateful for having been pressed to make my underlying arguments explicit.

10. See Durkheim (1893/1964: 280–2). As I have argued elsewhere (Rueschemeyer, 1982), while Durkheim's metatheoretical critique of utilitarian social theory as he saw it (not necessarily as it actually existed – see Camic, 1979) is still persuasive, his causal explanation of division of labour is questionable wherever it modifies the earlier body of thought. Ironically, it was his metatheoretical concerns critical of

utilitarian social theory that flawed his specific contributions to a causal explanation of social differentiation.

The explanation which Durkheim sought to modify argued that division of labour requires a large population in which – and this is the decisive factor – interaction is dense. Durkheim insisted that exchange and division of labour always presuppose an overarching moral community, which utilitarian analyses had neglected, and he rejected what classical economists had suggested as the link between increasing social density (expanding markets) and specialization – the efficiency gains that result from division of labour. Durkheim proposed instead, in a mistaken analogy to Darwin's theory which viewed the struggle for survival as the more intense the more similar the competing organisms are to each other, that increasing size and density would intensify competition to which specialization is an avoidance response. He overlooked the fact that Darwin spoke of a specialization of demands made on the resources in a given environment – of a specialization of consumption, as it were – while division of labour refers to the specialization of *production*. It is not at all clear why an increase in the consuming population or an expansion of markets should make competition among producers more intense and threaten their 'survival'; it seems more plausible to expect that under these conditions even marginal producers can still operate with a profit, that is, 'survive' more easily than with less demand and more circumscribed markets.

The relation between population density and changes in the division of labour is in fact rather complex. Increasing population density which preceded the Black Death in thirteenth-century Europe did not lead uniformly to notable advances in the division of labour. By contrast, the plague, which reduced the population drastically, may well have been a factor in subsequent advances of division of labour and technology. Gottfried (1983: 161) concludes from his study of *The Black Death*: 'Most survivors became richer. Western European peasants were, for the most part, freed from their customary bonds, and Europeans in general were spared the relentless pauperization that unbridled population growth caused in other areas of the Old World.'

4   DIVISION OF AUTHORITY, LEGITIMATION AND CONTROL

1. For simplicity's sake, I will often speak simply of the 'ruler', even though the discussion may deal with any incumbent of a supreme position of organized domination, be it in the economic or in the political sphere.
2. The special problems of 'professionalization' – the development of organizational forms for the vast expansion in the social use of knowledge

characteristic of modern political, economic and social life – are the subject of chapter 6.

3. Since Durkheim, the contrast between 'segmentation' and functional differentiation has had a firm place in the vocabulary of sociology. Segmented units do the same things in parallel fashion and as such do not engender interdependence; families in relation to each other, competing producers of a commodity, and nation-states are examples. Functionally differentiated units do different things in complementary fashion, and thus engender interdependence; families in relation to schools, different complementary occupations or various departments in a ministry are examples.

4. Perhaps shunning an exploration of 'what might have been', historians making this assumption run the risk of falling into a descriptive functionalism, which implies that the factual developments constitute reasonable responses to underlying problems as they arise. This seems a fair interpretation of Chandler's (1978) omission of any discussion of delegation of authority as a control dilemma in the development of nineteenth-century American business firms. In an earlier article (co-authored with L. Galambos) on the development of large business organizations in the United States, Chandler and Galambos (1970: 211) simply state: 'With diversification came decentralization of authority within the firm.' Though Payne (1978) very explicitly addresses the issue, the last sentence quoted in the text suggests a similar inclination to functionalist assumptions. Fohlen's (1978) discussion of French entrepreneurship tends to neglect the issue, even though he discusses earlier hypotheses of Landes (1949, 1951) and Sawyer (1951) about the contribution of the family firm pattern to a retardation of the French economy; the desire to retain family control was an important component especially of Landes's argument. The controversy surrounding this thesis primarily concerns the long-term stability of behaviour patterns of family firms and their effects on economic retardation. Less in question is the fact that for a long time problems of control restrained growth and division of authority in firms.

An unwillingness to risk changes in traditional relations and the structure of power, which outweighs productivity advantages, also seems the key to an explanation of economic inefficiencies in Latin American latifundia and urban enterprises; see Feder (1971: 87–8) and Barraclough (1973) on agriculture, and Cochran (1960: 529–30), more generally, on inclinations of Latin American entrepreneurs.

5. See Schwarz (1869), cited by Kocka (1978). Kocka also gives a vivid individual example of the consequences of failing to cope with such control problems:

With the 'railway king' Bethel Henry Strousberg (1823–84) we see clearly the difficulties of holding together a large diversified group of enterprises by individual personal management methods. This merchant, insurance agent, and journalist settled in Berlin in 1855 after a long stay in England. In the 1860s and early 70s he became the biggest, richest, and most spectacular railway-builder. He not only developed new methods of financing and founding lines but also remained in control of some of those that he built. In addition he bought and founded several industrial enterprises in mining, smelting, and heavy machinery, for supplying goods necessary for railway-building. In order to make himself 'independent' of suppliers, Strousberg tried to create a highly diversified concern. He founded or bought up the different constituents of the whole but did not understand how to integrate them. He failed to build up a controlling organization. Without this he lost the overall view, remained limited to intuitive, spontaneous decision, and lacked the necessary co-ordination. Partly for this reason, he went bankrupt in the depression of the early 1870s, wrote his autobiography in a Russian debtor's jail, and died in poverty (Kocka, 1978: 553).

6. Kocka (1978: 553–4), citing several other studies; see also Kocka (1971, 1969). For England, see Pollard (1965) as one of many authorities. Payne (1978) goes so far as to suggest that the remarkably high proportion of religious dissenters among the early English entrepreneurs can perhaps be explained by their more cohesive family and kinship ties.

7. The formula of 'divide-and-rule' implies a stronger emphasis on the ruler's conscious intent from the outset than is often justified. Of equal and perhaps greater significance are cases in which an already existing division is exploited as a fortuitous opportunity. Georg Simmel (1908/50: 154–62, 232–4) gave this constellation the name of 'tertius gaudens' – the laughing third party. I thank Jon Elster for pointing out that Simmel's idea applies to the present context.

8. Of the rich literature I cite only Weber (1922/68), Eisenstadt (1963) and Anderson (1974). The account given in the text is incomplete in regard to cultural resources such as universal legal norms (Roman law); the role of charismatic leadership is also only hinted at. What is crucial is the focus on the staff of domination, central to Weber's analysis.

9. Pollard (1965: 127) describes such status group formation in the case of the 'coal viewers', who developed out of agents for landowners into a quasi-professional body.

What emerges most clearly . . . is not only their family connection and the way in which their careers interlock in a limited number of large mining companies, but their awareness of each other, the creation of an applied science by piecemeal improvements quickly adopted and further improved by others, and an ethos which produced a ranking among them according to ability, originality, honesty and personal courage underground.

Though Pollard does not use the Weberian concept of 'status group', his account is full of such relevant materials (see, e.g., pp. 150–6). He shows, in particular, that such networks often encompassed both owners and managers (who often aspired to become owners).

Weber's concept of status group had a peculiar fate in modern sociology. It was assimilated into the notion of prestige and thus stripped of its organizational and structural content. Status or *ständische Lage* – a concept designed to capture certain generalizable features of such social forms as medieval and post-medieval estates – is inherently a relational concept with distinct social structural implications. Specific patterns of honour and deference, which define status groups, are not primarily a matter of attitudes, but express themselves in privileged association and social exclusion; they affect one's readiness to trust or to suspect, to be influenced by, or to turn a deaf ear to the opinion of others. Status groups – held together by a web of interrelations, by similar problems and by a shared position in society – tend to share a fairly similar style of life, an outlook and an ethos. Studying the emergence and change of status groups seems one of the strategic ways of gaining access to large-scale value change and the emergence of new institutional patterns, even in modern society. This assertion comes as a surprise only to those who take the old formula 'from status to contract' (Maine, 1861/1931) literally as a description of the essence of European modernity.

10. [A] system of domination may – as often occurs in practice – be so completely protected on the one hand by the obvious community of interest between the chief and his administrative staff (body-guards, Pretorians, 'red' or 'white' guards) as opposed to the subjects, on the other hand by the helplessness of the latter, that it can afford to drop even the pretence of a claim to legitimacy. But even then the mode of legitimation of the relation between chief and his staff may vary widely according to the type . . . of authority between them, and . . . this variation is highly significant for the structure of domination (Weber, 1922/68: I, 214).

11. If we momentarily broaden our view to include power struggles that also involve parties outside a given apparatus of power in addition to different groups within, we can see another major development of modern history in a similar light. The 'separation of powers' in government was the outcome of power struggles in which structural differentiation of the different branches of government was imposed from below. This clearly did not come about because of a drive towards greater efficiency in administration, adjudication and legislation, but rather because of attempts to limit the power of the crown.

The balance of power between the crown and other groups was also at stake in instances where a 'separation of powers' was imposed from above. Thus, when the Prussian kings took administrative tasks away from the *Regierungen* (organizational strongholds of the Junkers) and narrowed their function to judicial tasks, they moved in the direction of a structural differentiation of governmental functions, and at the same time gained important power advantages over their conservative opponents (see Rosenberg, 1958: esp. 55; Wagner, 1936).

12. As far as compliance is concerned, legitimation beliefs seem more important because they give moral blessing to other motives than because of their own motivating force. They make the difference between greed and the pursuit of earned reward, between cowardice and reasonable prudence, between blind personal attachment and praiseworthy loyalty. Purely ideal motives also play a direct role as an incentive to action; but they lead to martyrdom (which is rare) if the action is contrary to one's material interests, destructive of affectual ties with others and open to coercive reprisals.

13. The more complex but basically similar policies in contemporary Eastern Europe provide another example.

We may note in passing that the growing interdependence engendered by increased differentiation also poses significant power problems aside from legitimation issues. If such interdependence extends beyond a sphere of power, important resources may come under partial control of actual or potential opponents. Whether under these conditions those in charge will opt for self-sufficiency, and thus a limitation on certain advances of division of labour, depends – aside from problems of foresight and certain other factors – on their assessment of the likelihood of conflict and on the amount of control a likely enemy or coalition of enemies is seen as gaining.

5   THE ORGANIZATION OF WORK IN INDUSTRY

1. Work organization in the state socialist societies of Eastern Europe provides supplementary evidence on certain variant aspects of the industrial labour process. However, state socialist patterns of work organization are largely derivative, built on capitalist foundations and later modelled in significant measure after developments in capitalist economies. Furthermore, state socialist economies have had only a rather brief history; if the constellation of interests shaping division of labour on the shop floor were radically different from capitalism, their effects might be more visible in future years. (As we will see, changes in work organization in the capitalist West, too, are stretched out over long periods of time.) Finally, it is an understatement to say

that state socialist countries are less than well studied. Of course, comparative evidence from non-capitalist industrial societies could be of critical importance for tackling major questions about the organization of industrial work were it not for these problems. As things stand, differences among capitalist societies may prove as illuminating as contrasts (and similarities) between them and state socialist countries. Unfortunately, the comparative study of work organization is in a poor state even within the universe of capitalist countries.

2. In Marx's view, of course, the obstacles were the interests of the dominant classes, while in this account any crystallized social form fits the part, though social theory in the Durkheim tradition has applied it typically to pre-modern social formations, to peasant traditions or to the culture of a craft, rather than to entrepreneurially designed forms of organization. Noting the analogy between the two ideas amounts to more than idle play. It reminds us of the central role efficiency explanations play also in much of Marxian thought, though the Marxian amalgamations represent at least as strong modifications of the efficiency argument pure and simple as Durkheimian structural functionalism in sociology does.

3. Weber uses a very different language in his discussion of the relations between direct producers, managers and owners, the language of economic rationality; but the substance of his argument is on close inspection surprisingly similar. Competitive market pressures play the same role in both analyses. True, Weber does not directly focus his attention on the conflicts within 'the hidden abode of production', following in this neglect the lead of neoclasical economics; but he sees, in the pure case of a capitalist enterprise, workers as subject to a system of coercive commands which rests on the unequal distribution of capital assets and which remains in substance coercive even though the workers' submission is formally voluntary (Weber, 1922/68: I, 108 and 109–10).

His discussion why unfree labour is economically less rational has revealing implications for the work process of formally free labour: Unfree labour reduces, or in the extreme case eliminates, the workers' self-interest in work accomplishments, it cannot be rationally selected according to changing tasks and, due to its typically fixed character, it tends towards traditional fixations of work quotas.

Any attempt to exact performance from appropriated workers beyond that which has become traditionally established encounters traditional obstacles. These could only be overcome by the most ruthless methods, which are not without their danger from the point of view of the owner's self-interest, since they might undermine the traditionalistic bases of his authority (Weber 1922/68: I, 129).

The implication is, of course, that the formally free workers of the capitalist factory not only can be and are motivated by incentive pay and self-interest, not only can be and are selected on the market for changing tasks (and dismissed as tasks change again), but that it is possible to 'press performances out of them' which under typical conditions of unfree labour would require the 'most ruthless use of coercion' (to use a slightly different, but more precise rendering of Weber's German formulation).

Finally, while Weber employs throughout his discussion of the division and organization of labour primarily the aseptic language of 'formal rationality', informed by the reasoning of neoclassical economics, he occasionally punctuates this discourse with cutting reminders that this is a peculiar and not a comprehensively adequate conceptualization. Thus he speaks of the 'complete indifference of just the formally most perfect rationality of capital accounting toward all substantive postulates, whatever their character, an indifference which is absolute if the market is perfectly free' (Weber 1922/68: I, 108, translation slightly amended). Or again: 'Substantive and formal (in the sense of exact *calculation*) rationality inevitably diverge to a large extent. This fundamental and in the last analysis inescapable irrationality of the economy is one of the sources of any "social" problematic, above all of the problematic of socialism' (Weber 1922/68: I, 111, translation amended).

4. Weber was less certain of this outcome. Antagonistic class organization which pits workers against employers is in his view characteristic of capitalism, but collective action of workers as a class must not be taken for granted even in the long run since it is contingent on complex favourable conditions. Weber's description of these conditions does not differ very much from that of Marx, but his assessment of their chance to be realized does; see Weber (1922/68: I, 302–5).

5. Mancur Olson (1965) has argued that large numbers of people with common interests are kept from collective organization primarily by the operation of individual self-interest. A rational self-interested person, rather than making a commitment to the common cause, will opt to take a 'free ride' if participation entails individual costs while the benefits of collective action become available to all members of a certain category of people independent of their contribution. This means that individuals will contribute to a common cause only if they are coerced (as in the case of taxation or the draft) or if benefits are sufficiently individualized (as in the case of such membership benefits as insurance policies, journals, etc.). Small groups are exempted from the argument because here multiple goals, subtle yet powerful sanctions and more transparent cause–effect relations combine in complex ways

to make collective action more viable. For Olson the mistaken anticipations of Marx and others result in large part from not understanding this pervasive free-rider problem.

This is too simple an explanation. On the one hand, collective action of workers (and others as well) is not as pervasively hampered by self-interest as Olson assumes; on the other, precisely because it is a greater threat to the other side, working-class organization has been fought ruthlessly with all the means of economic and political power. Olson argues as if workers and other potential participants in collective action behaved in the manner of a profit-oriented corporation – an apparatus without emotions, attachments to people or value commitments. It is no accident that both Weber and Marx find one major source of collective class organization in the antagonism between classes – in conflicts which generate strong feelings and activate solidarities and moral commitments. This is not the place to develop a systematic critque as well as an alternative to Olson's theory of collective action. Suffice it to say that self-interested preferences for a 'free ride' do constitute a serious problem for all attempts at collective organization, but Olson turns self-interested behaviour into an unexamined premise of his analysis rather than specifying under which conditions we might expect it – or various more solidary alternatives instead.

6. As will be remembered from our brief discussion in chapter 1, Max Weber deemed the concept of power to be

sociologically amorphous. All conceivable qualities of a person and all conceivable combinations of circumstances may put him in a position to impose his will on a given situation. The sociological concept of domination must hence be more precise and can only mean the probability that a *command* will be obeyed (Weber, 1922/68 I, 53).

It is however clear from Weber's own use of the concept of power that he by no means intended to dismiss it with this characterization as 'sociologically amorphous'.

Technically, Weber's concept of domination does not 'imply either the existence of an administrative staff or, for that matter, of an organization. It is, however, uncommon to find it unrelated to at least one of these' (ibid.). Our use of 'organized domination' reflects this last comment; it does imply both an administrative staff and an organization with a clearly defined membership, a head and enforced regulations.

7. Burawoy (1979: 27). Burawoy separates his concept of consent loosely, yet polemically from the concept of legitimation, which he sees as a state of mind while consent is not only caused by, but is also expressed through, the organization of activities. Perhaps it is more useful to see the two concepts as closely related and complementary. It will be

remembered that in Max Weber's view differences in legitimation are primarily important because of the difference they make in the apparatus of power (chapter 4); the social impact of legitimating ideas is organizationally mediated. In the case of consent (of workers or, more generally, of subjects) organizational arrangements give rise to acceptance and, in effect, legitimation.

8. On curbing the foremen's arbitrary powers and the effects of announcing the five-dollar-a-day wage see Edwards (1979: 119, 121 and 126f.). Five dollars a day was an extraordinary wage; only a decade and a half earlier Frederick Taylor had offered the steelworker Schmidt $1.85 a day instead of $1.15, 'the same as all these cheap fellows are getting', provided Schmidt would 'do exactly as this man tells you tomorrow, from morning till night...And what's more, no back talk' (Frederick W. Taylor, 1911, quoted by Palmer, 1975: 38). David Montgomery (1979: 97) provides unemployment statistics in relation to strike activity from 1900 to 1925; 9 and 8.2 per cent were unemployed in 1912 and 1913, 14.7 and 15.6 per cent in 1914 and 1915, respectively (unemployed as percentages of non-farm employees).

9. See Barbara Garson (1975), Stanley Aronowitz (1973); Richard Edwards refers to Lordstown as an indication for his thesis that 'technical control' cannot any more function by itself as the major control system for labour in the core of the capitalist economy (Edwards, 1979: 129).

10. Charles Tilly (1981) gives brief overview of issues raised and results achieved by this work. A minimalist formulation of findings to date is simply that in Europe capital-intensive manufacturing was long preceded by small-scale rural industrialization surrounding merchant cities. A maximalist interpretation of the same results argues that this pervasive small-scale rural capitalism provided the capital bases for later large-scale industrialization and that, at the same time, it was associated with population growth which provided a massive labour supply and accounts in part for labour's weak bargaining position in the transitions to large-scale industry. Such maximalist interpretations in effect constitute

an alternative account of the transition from feudalism to capitalism: alternative to the classic Marxist account in which merchant capital, capital accumulated in urban manufacturing, and agrarian capital wrested from a dispossessed peasantry coalesced to provide the basis for large-scale production; alternative to the classic liberal account in which expanding trade and developing technology interacted to make large-scale production more efficient than other forms (Tilly, 1981: 8).

11. Thompson (1963: 308); a quote from A. Ure's *The Philosophy of Manufactures* (1835) on the following page details the customary wages of men by age and explains the 'motive to discontinue employing males

as far as can practically be done'. Sidney Pollard gives a quantitative sketch of early factory employment by sex and age:

When cotton power-loom weaving became predominant from 1820 on, women and children took over weaving also from men. By 1839, of 420,000 cotton factory workers 193,000 were aged under eighteen years; only 97,000 were adult males; and the rest were adult females. In other textiles the proportions were higher still: thus in 1844, when females represented about 56 per cent of the labor force in cotton mills, they formed around 70 per cent in woollen, silk, and flax mills (Pollard, 1978: 123).

12. Pollard (1978: 125) reports that 'a recent study of changes in the hours of labor since the eighteenth century had as one of its most striking findings the close correlation between short hours and high wages, and vice versa'. Thompson (1963: 312) argues:

Some economic historians appear to be unwilling (perhaps because of a concealed 'progressivism', which equates human progress with economic growth) to face the evident fact that technological innovation during the Industrial Revolution, until the railway age, did displace (except in the metal industries) adult skilled labor. Labor so displaced swelled the limitless supply of cheap labor.

13. Weber (1922/68: 138; translation amended). The stronger thesis of Marglin finds some support in Pollard's conclusions from the evidence. Remember that technical superiority of one form of production over another requires greater output with the same inputs. Longer hours and more intense work yielding greater output are no indication of technical superiority. Pollard sums complex evidence when he says:

In the earlier decades of industrialization (i.e., before 1850), the changeover to new processes had generally meant longer (and more regularly longer) hours, together with greater intensification of work, at roughly constant real wages. This crude method of achieving higher returns on capital, pursued by an unsophisticated entrepreneurial class, was bound to be self-defeating beyond a certain point (Pollard, 1978: 174).

One of the factors which seems to have defeated the method was greater effectiveness of union organization in Britain after 1850 (Pollard, 1978: 154). The discrepancy, implied in Pollard's judgement, between efficiency advances in terms of profitability and efficiency advances in terms of technical superiority, is at the heart of Marglin's case.

14. See, e.g., Palmer (1975), Friedman (1977), Montgomery (1979), Edwards (1979), Zimbalist (1979), Burawoy (1979 and 1981), Stark (1980), Littler and Salaman (1982), Sabel (1982).

15. See 'Trade unions', in *Encyclopedia of the Social Sciences*, vol. 15, New York: Macmillan, 1934; pp. 9 and 41. Population and especially union figures changed rapidly during the period. In the 1890s union

membership in the United States, not standardized for population size, was only a third of that in the far smaller population of Great Britain. In the first decade of this century absolute numbers reached parity, but the surge in membership just before and especially during World War One was stronger in Great Britain: in 1919 union membership in Great Britain had reached nearly eight million while in the United States it was just above four million (double the number of 1904 and nine times as many in 1897). In 1910 about 11 per cent of the non-agricultural labour force of the United States was union organized, with skilled workers more strongly represented in union membership. In mining and in the clothing industry the percentages were higher (27.3 per cent and 16.9 per cent respectively), but the crucial labour force category of 'metal, machinery, and ship building' was with 9 per cent just below the average (op. cit., p. 42).

16. In the following, I rely strongly on David Stark's (1980) re-analysis of the introduction of scientific management, which is based on a wealth of recent historical research.

17. I have only alluded to, rather than recounted, the findings of Montgomery on the comparative strength of craft organization in the United States at the time. Stark (1980) pursues the differences of interests between skilled and unskilled workers in the process of rationalization of work. Burawoy (1981) suggests that analogous developments in the British and American steel industries took a very different form because of a different distribution of market power and organizational strength.

18. Union membership in the United States increased from 7 per cent of the labour force (11 per cent of non-agricultural wage and salary workers) in 1930 to 16 (25) per cent in 1939/40 and to 22 (32) per cent in 1950. A union membership rate of 23 (28) per cent in the United States in 1970 compares with 44 (49) per cent in the United Kingdom, 30 (37) per cent in West Germany and 75 (87) per cent in Sweden. See Stephens (1979: 115–16). Since 1970 the proportion of union members in the American labour force has declined significantly.

19. Clearly our discussion here links up with theories of labour market segmentation in advanced capitalist economies. A recent contribution to this complex literature, which is not taken up here, is Gordon, Edwards and Reich (1982).

6 THE POLITICAL ECONOMY OF PROFESSIONALIZATION

1. Their major concern in *The German Ideology* was to develop the contrast between their own conceptions of historical change and those of the

idealist Young Hegelians, 'our erstwhile philosophical conscience', as
Marx later put it. A reader who is more interested in Marx's views
on their own terms than in this severing of an umbilical cord which
had lost its function will have to engage in the – inevitably risky –
enterprise of reading the text against its grain. The historical allusions
of the text give interesting support for such a reading. In the following
passage, for instance, Marx and Engels combine their debunking of
an absolute idealism with a diagnosis of a complex power situation that
is not at all simplistic:

> in an age and in a country where royal power, aristocracy and bourgeoisie
> are contending for mastery and where, therefore, mastery is shared, the
> doctrine of the separation of powers proves to be the dominant idea and
> is expressed as an 'eternal law' (op. cit.: 173).

Another important passage assigns to ideas – if used in class struggle
– a rather consequential (and probably too weighty) role. At issue is
'the phenomenon that increasingly abstract ideas hold sway, i.e. ideas
which increasingly take the form of universality'. Marx and Engels
explain this by the process of class struggle in modernity which itself
is shaped by the ideas used:

> each new class which puts itself in the place of one ruling before it, is
> compelled, merely in order to carry through its aim, to represent its interest
> as the common interest of all the members of society, that is, expressed
> in ideal form: it has to give its ideas the form of universality . . . Every new
> class, therefore, achieves its hegemony only on a broader basis than that
> of the class ruling previously, whereas the opposition of the non-ruling class
> against the new ruling class later develops all the more sharply and pro-
> foundly. Both these things determine the fact that the struggle to be waged
> against this new ruling class, in its turn, aims at a more decided and radical
> negation of the previous conditions of society than would all previous classes
> which sought to rule (op. cit.: 174).

2. Marx neglected the modern professions and their particular institutional
forms, but he did not miss the paramount role which systematic and
professionalized knowledge began to play in the modern political
economy. Thus he treats science as a productive force, as for instance
in this passage which formulates the starting point of Braverman's
exploration of the 'separation of conception from execution' in modern
industrial work (see chapter 5):

> The knowledge, the judgment, and the will, which, though in ever so small
> a degree are practised by the independent peasant or handicraftsman, in
> the same way as the savage makes the whole art of war consist in the exercise
> of his personal cunning – these faculties are now required only for the
> workshop as a whole. Intelligence in production expands in one direction,

because it vanishes in many others. What is lost by the detail labourers, is concentrated in the capital that employs them. It is a result of the division of labour in manufactures, that the labourer is brought face to face with the intellectual potencies of the material process of production, as the property of another, and as a ruling power. This separation begins in simple co-operation, where the capitalist represents to the single workman, the oneness and the will of the associated labour. It is developed in manufacture which cuts down the labourer into a detail labourer. It is completed in modern industry, which makes science a productive force distinct from labour and presses it into the service of capital (1867/1959: 361).

3. In these disputes functionalist interpretations are criticized from a variety of positions that emphasize conflict, historical variability, and what might be called 'the politics of knowledge'. (See Goode, Merton and Huntington, 1956; Goode, 1957 and 1969; Merton, 1960; and Parsons, 1968; vs. Freidson, 1970a and b, 1977, 1983; Johnson, 1972 and 1977; and Rueschemeyer, 1964, 1973 chapter 1, 1983).

4. The reciprocities of a more personalized relationship with the experts may appear to many upper middle class members as a desirable substitute, an egalitarian equivalent of feudal patterns, one might say. This does avoid complex control machinery and provides some insurance against neglect and abuse, but for obvious reasons it cannot be available to many clients.

5. Of course, the conditions listed above as favourable for collective organization vary from one expert group to another and also across different countries and historical periods. American lawyers, for example, were and are a much more heterogeneous group than physicians in twentieth-century North America or lawyers in Germany; and this is reflected in the lesser strength and influence of their professional organizations (see Rueschemeyer, 1973).

6. The knowledge base of the professions had been virtually left unanalysed by functionalist studies of the professions (Parsons, 1939, 1968; Merton, 1960; Goode, 1957, 1969). That the knowledge of experts must not be taken for granted (beyond simple specifications such as that it must be sy tematic) and that it is itself not independent of the interests and actions of the professional group are arguments that have gained more and more influence in the sociological debate over the role of the professions. They were introduced most forcefully by Freidson (1970a). A current assessment of the discussion is found in Rueschemeyer (1983), while an earlier essay of the author (Rueschemeyer, 1964) pointed to differences in the composition of the knowledge of different professions and the problems this raises for functionalist interpretations. Some passages in the present discussion are taken from Rueschemeyer (1983) with minor modifications.

7. The tensions and contradictions involved in this pattern are well illustrated by Protestant theology in much of nineteenth-century Germany. Within the university critical historical studies of the bible as well as other lines of analysis and argument subversive of traditional religion flourished, while university-trained ministers would lose their employment, which was controlled by the state, if they preached what they had learned in their university studies.

8. In the United States, outlays for research and development grew from three-tenths of 1 per cent of the gross national product in 1940 to 1 per cent in 1952 and to 3 per cent in 1964 (OECD, 1968: 30; Ben David, 1971: 173).

9. See Ben-David (1971). His *analysis* argues that a more decentralized and competitive pattern is more conducive to the advancement of science. Yet his *evidence* for England and the United States does not bear this out. He acknowledges the successes of British science but treats them, not quite convincingly, as due to the advantages of a 'junior partner' who is able to borrow from the leader. This borrowing is easier in pure than applied science, he argues, because the latter has to take varied local conditions into account. Hence, in his argument, the weakness of applied research in England.

10. Ben-David (1971, chapters 2 and 3) gives an interesting account of the forces that curbed scientific growth in traditional societies including ancient Greece. A significant element among them was the vested interest various 'professional' groups had in their established practices and mysteries.

11. However, it is important for our argument here to note that at the core of the functionalist model there is the power of knowledge experts, even though this often takes second place to an idealizing emphasis on the professions' service orientation. In his remarkable essay on 'The theoretical limits of professionalization', Goode (1969) makes it very clear that occupations that are not potentially dangerous to the interests of their clients have no prospects for full professional status, no matter how intense their devotion to service.

12. An autonomously organized bar with high status in society at large played in seventeenth-century England a crucial role in limitation of government (Eusden, 1958).

13. 'The new professional men brought one scale of values – the gentleman's – to bear upon the other – the trademan's – and produced a specialized variety of business morality which came to be known as "professional ethics" or "etiquette".' Thus the somewhat dismissive formulation of W. J. Reader (1966: 158–9). M. S. Larson, whose account I have largely followed in the paragraph above, puts it this way:

at the core of the professional project, we find the fusion of antithetical ideological structures and a potential for permanent tension between 'civilizing function' and market-orientation, between 'protection of society' and the securing of a market, between intrinsic and extrinsic values of work (1977: 63).

14. These broader sociocultural consequences of professionalization have recently received more attention; see Daheim (1973), Bledstein (1976) and Larson (1977).

15. For a somewhat different but not incompatible analysis of the sources of such moral indifference among the German elites see Baum (1981). The particular formulation about membership in a bureaucratic organization and membership in an autonomous profession as contrasting basis of legitimation for claims to speak and act in the public interests is indebted to a discussion with Bernard Silberman.

16. See Ginzberg (1983: 481) for a typical example from the field of radiology. Similar processes are found in all professions. Johnstone and Hopson (1967, chapter 4) discuss specialization in the law along these lines.

17. In an earlier comparison of the health systems of Britain and the United States Stevens took a position that acknowledged the impact of historical differences but anticipated a convergence of institutional structure due to the universalistic character of medicine and health problems: '. . . it is probable that eventually, whatever the original differences, the demands of scientific medicine will bring the organizational structures of medical services closer together' (Stevens, 1966: 354–5).

18. Only a few contrasts can occupy us here. See Rueschemeyer (1964 and 1978) and Dingwall and Lewis (1983) for more extended comparisons.

19. See Horwitz (1977) and Rueschemeyer (1973: 160–6). This 'golden age' of American law was at the same time a period of very weak professional organization (Pound, 1953); therefore we speak here only of the autonomy and power of the legal elite.

20. Extreme forms of the tendencies described are found in the large cities of the United States. See Carlin (1962, 1966), Ladinsky (1963), Smigel (1964), Rueschemeyer (1973), and most recently Heinz and Laumann (1982).

21. Lenin (1917/74). See also Wright (1978) for a contrasting discussion of Weber and Lenin, which in my opinion gives to much credit to the latter's position.

22. We saw in chapter 4 that the early groups of managers in English industrial firms had professional orientations in common, which made trust and delegation of authority easier. The professional ethos, together

with class culture and personal ties, prepared the emergence of the culture of bureaucratic loyalty and commitment. Larson suggests a similar interpretation of Chandler's portrait (1962) of the emergence of the multidivisional firm, in which the problem of trust is largely taken for granted:

> it is legitimate... to assume that the decentralization and delegation of authority inherent in the multidivisional structure compelled the monopolistic corporations to rely on professionalism as a preexisting means of limiting the potential abuse of discretion (Larson, 1977: 199).

The 'professional' orientation that thus complements the institutional patterns of bureaucratic control may not be grounded in one particular professional community but may represent a generalized characteristic of knowledge-bearing occupations or even of highly educated people. A liberal college education is appreciated by many American employers not so much for any specific skills as for the self-discipline and a generalized outlook on work and society that tend to be associated with educational success.

23. The issue of state autonomy has been the subject of a long debate between instrumentalist and structuralist neo-Marxist views. The latter insist that the very maintenance of the capitalist system requires a degree of autonomy for the state apparatus that is not compatible with the position of those who see the capitalist state directly as an instrument of dominant interests. There are occasions where even dominant particular interests have to be restrained lest they undercut the functioning of the system. See Jessop (1982) and Carnoy (1984) for two excellent overviews of this complex debate. The structuralists give us little by way of explaining what determines state action and keeps it in line with system requirements. In a less functionalist vein, one may ask specific questions about the conditions that variously affect the autonomy of state organizations under different circumstances; see Evans, Rueschemeyer and Skocpol (1985).

24. See Stepan (1973 and 1978) on the military forces in Latin America, and Weir and Skocpol (1985) on the role of the British Treasury in blocking 'Keynesian' responses to the Great Depression.

25. To the extent that it is, as in the case of many engineers and technicians in product development, the exemption from bureaucratic controls will be weakened. The same qualification applies to the other dimensions of leverage.

7   ON DEDIFFERENTIATION

1. This is true even though important theoretical tenets, in different traditions of social thought, warn and warned the analyst against

the fallacy of extending contemporary master trends both into the future and into the past. Quite aside from the fact that Marx's vision of the future society anticipated a radical, if not very plausible, reduction of specialization and institutional complexity, the dialectical models of change alive in most varieties of Marxism and neo-Marxism are at odds with any assumption of simple unilinearity and irreversibility of sociocultural change. Neo-evolutionary theories of a non-Marxist variety typically set themselves apart from older evolutionary arguments by disavowing unilinearity, irreversibility and inevitability of evolution (see, e.g., Bellah, 1964, and Eisenstadt, 1964b). There is no need to discuss here whether the attribution of these ideas to authors such as Herbert Spencer is correct or not (see Rueschemeyer, 1985). Pitirim Sorokin warned as early as 1933 in strong and colourful language against the 'attractive "weeds" so abundantly yielded by the theories of limitless extension of causal relations and the half-poisonous exhilarating "hashish" of the theories of Evolution and Progress with their unbounded trends' (1933: 19).

Not only sociologists work with biases that favour differentiation, and not only theoretical or ideological inclinations militate against a careful analysis of devolutionary processes. As Charles Tilly observes:

> History abounds in devolutionary processes, yet the historical record itself conceals them. The very association of documentary production with centripetal movements slants the record to some extent against devolution. Just as the development of large-scale organization and central controls tends to accelerate the production of written records, particularization and shrinkage tend to choke it off (1970: 465).

2. For a systematic theoretical argument on technical innovation and a critical review of earlier theories see Jon Elster (1983).
3. Corporate control of the urban production process by the guilds was, of course, not the only cause of the spread of domestic industry; lower labour costs in the countryside were probably a more important factor. Similarly, competition from rural industry was far from the only cause of the guild system's problems and eventual demise; increasing polarization between poor and well-to-do artisans and increasing dependence of craftsmen on merchants were more important, especially in export production centres. Yet the two causal strands identified do seem a significant part of a very complex, and still very much debated, historical picture.
4. Lukes (1973) discusses the complex intellectual structure of the bundle of ideas brought together under this heading – their historical concatenations, their analytic and normative divergencies and associations. Lukes treats individualism as a set of philosophic, political, religious or social scientific ideas. The present argument focuses on social values

and norms, which may to a large extent remain ideals but which do form a significant part of the normative order of virtually all modern and political system.

5. Weber developed this more in his political writings than in *Economy and Society*, though there are brief statements to the same effect in that unfinished work, (See Weber, 1922/68: 219–20, but especially his 'Parliament and government in a reconstructed Germany,' reprinted in Weber, 1968: 1381–1469. See also Bendix, 1960: 438–57, and Wright, 1978.)

Talcott Parsons elaborates in an introductory essay on Weber's analysis of rational–legal domination in ways that are directly pertinent to the broader issues discussed above. Writing from an intense concern with the fall of Germany into Nazi barbarism, he saw precisely in the functionally specific and formal features of Western political institutions a source of instability (Parsons, 1947: 64, 68–70, 80).

6. The latter types of association were characteristic of German political culture before and after World War One (see, e.g., Roth, 1963), and similar patterns were much discussed in the Netherlands after World War Two (see Lijphart, 1968), to cite only two examples.

7. Thus Talcott Parsons discusses it as a process running counter to or retreating from 'progressive' forms of social evolution. Consider the developments he treats as instances of dedifferentiation: fundamentalist reactions to the strains and tensions inherent in modern social life, the insistence on an ethic of absolute values in the face of complex cause –effect interdependencies and uncertain knowledge (Max Weber's *Gesinnungsethik*), ideologies and religious movements that refuse to accept a differentiation between government and the sources of legitimation (Parson's examples are the Puritan Calvinist movement and the modern Communist parties), and the movements that endanger the autonomy of the 'cognitive complex' of free inquiry by insisting that value commitments be fused with any intellextual exploration. For this list of instances I am indebted to Tiryakian (1983) who refers especially to Parsons (1969 and 1978).

8 CODA

1. That several such treatises were recently published confirms that the problems are real. In contrast to the turn of the century when every major social theorist produced his own 'system' without much historical reflection, current works of this kind tend to build critically on the record of social theory since the beginning of the nineteenth century and on the issues that emerged as central in that by now highly

reflexive intellectual history. See for instance Habermas (1981) and Alexander (1982–3); one can also consider a set of recent works of Giddens (1976, 1979, 1981, 1984) as a similar undertaking. An important systematic discussion that draws less on review of past intellectual developments is Runciman (1983).

2. This is certainly true of authors as different as Engels, Spencer and Parsons. One might point to a passage in the introduction to Engels's *Origin of the Family, Private Property and the State* (1884/1972) that seems to suggest a similar fundamental distinction between the production and reproduction of the material conditions of social life on the one hand and the 'production of human beings' on the other. However, the point of his work was precisely to integrate the analysis of both.

3. While nineteenth-century authors speculated from certain indications about prehistoric patterns of matriarchy (Bachofen, 1861/1948; Morgan, 1877; Engels, 1884/1972), observation of contemporary simple societies has not identified a single such case, and anthropologists are more than sceptical about the earlier speculations. There is disagreement about the existence of societies with true sexual equality. Rosaldo and Lamphere (1974, Introduction: 3) argue that 'all contemporary societies are to some extent male-dominated, and although the degree and expression of female subordination vary greatly, sexual asymmetry is presently a universal fact of human social life'. Sanday (1981) points out that this universal sexual asymmetry argument depends on issues of definition. She concludes a brief review of different positions with this comment: 'One [author] uses equality in the sense of *sameness*, and the other uses equality in the sense of *interdependence* and *balance*' (1981: 170). The former definition comes in her view close to identifying the universality of role differentiation by sex with the universality of sexual inequality: 'There is no society I know of in which the sexes give equal energy to exactly the same activities and decisions. Nor are there many societies in which both sexes have the same access to the same resources' (1981: 169). If the latter definition is chosen, sexual equality is not uncommon. Sanday lists one-third of her sample of 139 societies from the Human Relations Area File in the category of sexual equality (1981: Table 8.2, 168). Neither side to the controversy considers biological factors as causes of overriding importance. 'Biological factors', argue Rosaldo and Lamphere (1974: 7), 'may make certain sociocultural arrangements highly likely, but with changes in technology, population size, ideas, and aspirations our social order can change.'

4. A consideration of this sort offers a rationale for the approach taken by Sanday (1981), who abandoned a more exclusively materialistic framework held earlier (Sanday, 1973). Also related is the observation that women often have a *de facto* power and influence that exceed

publicly recognized authority and culturally legitimated rights (Rosaldo and Lamphere, 1974, Introduction: 3; Rosaldo, 1974: 21).

5. Carnoy (1984), Gold, Lo and Wright (1975), and Jessop (1982) give excellent overviews of the neo-Marxist debates on the state during the 1960s and 1970s. Nordlinger (1981) seeks to accommodate the conception of state autonomy in the pluralist paradigm of political analysis. Held et al. (1983) offer an overview of current work on the state in the form of a reader, and Poggi (1978) provides an original introduction to the sociology of the state. Evans, Rueschemeyer and Skocpol (1985) focus on comparative historical research on the state while drawing on the recent theoretical debates.

6. No serious student of socioeconomic development would today maintain that development and underdevelopment can be understood without taking the transnational dimension into account. At the same time, dependency and world system theories have not escaped trenchant criticisms. See Frank (1969), Cardozo and Faletto (1979), Wallerstein (1974a, 1974b, 1980). Palma (1978), and O'Brien (1975) are instructive critical surveys. Lall (1975) presents an interesting critique of the *dependencia* position. An important critique of Sweezy, Frank and Wallerstein from a Marxist position is Brenner (1977).

7. Albert O. Hirschman argued in 1945:

> power elements and disequilibria are potentially inherent in such 'harmless' trade relations as have always taken place, e.g., between big and small, rich and poor, industrial and agricultural countries – relations that could be fully in accord with the principles taught by the theory of international trade (1945: 40; see also 1978: 46).

In other words, power asymmetries can result from foreign trade even if market exchange is free and monopolistic advantages are absent; an example is the case in which a small or poor country has most of its foreign trade concentrated in the exchange with a rich or large country in whose foreign trade this particular exchange represents only a small fraction.

8. This raises complex questions about the mechanisms involved in such developments. It also raises again the philosophical questions which we already encountered in the discussion of alienation and anomie (chapter 2).

Carl Schmitt's suggestive formula of the 'normative Kraft des Faktischen', Heider's and Festinger's formulations of balance theory and cognitive dissonance theory, and more specific, as well as more specifically sociological hypotheses about communication patterns, group and reference group formation, socialization, and legitimacy beliefs affecting relative deprivation and relative satisfaction – these are a few examples of theoretical ideas helpful in identifying the conditions under which people's values, interests and aspirations will or will not adapt to the actual conditions of their lives. On a more general plane, both Durkheim (1893/1964) and Simmel (1890) have focused on changes in the moral order of society and in the orientations of individuals following – and at least potentially fitting and validating – processes of differentiation and division of labour. Conditions under which people maintain or develop values, interests and aspirations at variance with their actual life chances and at odds with dominant ideas and interests are, of course, equally important to identify. Eisenstadt (1964a) argues that all institutionalizations of a social order exclude or disadvantage certain groups and persistent interests, and he derives from this an important perspective for the analysis of inherent strains and immanent tendencies towards change. Jürgen Habermas has developed the concept of the ideal speech situation as a philosophical yardstick for assessing normatively to what extent a given social arrangement approximates an order that truly rests on consent (1981).

9. Talcott Parsons, taking off from the same broad conception of power as the capacity to achieve collective ends, as well as from similar Durkheimian ideas about the constitution of human collectivities, has developed a complex reconceptualization of power of an impressive coherence and elegance (Parsons, 1963). I mention it here primarily to point out two ways in which it differs radically from the conception used here.

In Parsons's conceptualization, power is embedded in a systemic view of society. It serves to specify and to attain collective goals that are in line with the functioning of society as a systemic whole. No such assumption is made here. In fact, the view advanced here makes a diametrically opposed assumption – that it is not particularly fruitful to conceive of societies as systems capable of corporate action, that in spite of certain partial commonalities such as some of the cultural premises of collectivity formation just mentioned (which incidentally are often not confined within the boundaries of one society), they tend to be deeply divided in the fundamental elements of social action and association – in interests, values and definitions of reality. At the same time the ideas derived from Durkheim's insights into the specific character of social phenomena are retained here for the understanding of any collective action. Collectivity formations and re-formations are, however, seen as far more partial and conflictual than in Parsons's conception.

Building on the notion that power ultimately involves the capacity to 'get things done', Parsons insists that power is best understood in 'non-zero-sum' terms – that is, by considering especially the conditions under which a power centre can extend its reach and capacity without diminishing the power of other units. While this analytic focus fits well into the overall thrust of his theoretical argument, one must not lose sight of the fact that even in non-zero–sum 'games' there may still be – and are likely to be – relative winners and losers. Neither a modern state nor a business corporation in an oligopolistic market can afford to neglect such losses and gains, even if they are only relative. The conception of power employed here takes absolute increases in trans-formative capacity fully into account, but it retains a sharp focus on the resulting alignments of relative power.

10. Marglin (1973: 17–18) points out that the perfectly competitive model has no place for the business firm and the hierarchical ordering of work. Two important surveys of recent economic thinking on the firm are Marris and Mueller (1980) and Williamson (1981).

That the capitalist reality has been very different from a model free of coercion was, as we have seen, pressed home by Marx and recognized by Weber. It was also acknowledged by Spencer, who envisioned as the eventual outcome of 'industrial evolution' workers cooperatives 'where there are no antagonistic interests'.

We have seen that, in common with political regulations and ecclesiastical regulation, the regulation of labour becomes less coercive as society assumes a higher type. Here we reach a form in which the coerciveness has diminished to the smallest degree consistent with combined action. Each member is his own master inspite of the work he does; and it is subject only to such rules, established by majority of the members, as are needful for maintaining order. The transition from the compulsory cooperation of militancy to the voluntary cooperation of industrialism is completed. Under present arrangements it is incomplete. A wage-earner, while he voluntarily agrees to give so many hours work for so much pay, does not, during performance of his work, act in a purely voluntary way; he is coerced by the consciousness that discharge will follow if he idles, and is sometimes more manifestly coerced by an overlooker' (Spencer, 1876/1975: III, 562–3).

11. This is a major difference between the arguments presented here and the thesis of Steven Marglin (1973). Marglin takes off from the question: Is hierarchical authority mandated by efficiency and thus inevitable? He then sets out to show that specialization under the control of an entrepreneur and the aggregation of jobs in factories served entrepreneurial power interests (as well as their economic gain) and were not required to advance technological efficiency. I agree that power interests are important, but so are other interests of the powerful, and these are also likely to be more efficiently served.

Marglin retains the concept of technological efficiency, defined objectively as more output for the same inputs, and he distinguishes it from economic efficiency. Yet identifying concretely different inputs as 'the same', more or less requires a principle of equivalency, which neoclassical economics finds in the equilibrium prices of a fully competitive system. Marglin subjects this solution to justified criticism but does not provide an alternative. In the argument presented here, principles of equivalency are given in the variable and imperfectly aggregated preference structures of people among which the preference structures of the more powerful individuals and groups acquire a strategic importance.

12. I realize that the qualifications 'considered' and 'uncoerced' raise complex questions about genuine consensus and consent-based criteria of justice, but will not discuss them here. See Rawls (1971) and Habermas (1976 and 1981).

Bibliography

Abegglen, James C. 1958: *The Japanese Factory: aspects of its social organization*. Glencoe, Illinois: Free Press.

Aberle, David F., Cohen, Albert K., Davis, A. K., Levy, Marion J. and Sutton. Francis X. 1950: The functional requisites of a society. *Ethics*, 9, 100–11.

Alexander, Jeffrey C. 1982–3: *Theoretical Logic in Sociology*, 4 vols. Berkeley: University of California Press.

Anderson, Perry 1974: *Lineages of the Absolute State*. New York: Schocken.

Arnold, H. L. and Faurote, L. F. 1915: *Ford Methods and the Ford Shops*. New York: Engineering Magazine Company.

Aronowitz, Stanley 1973: *False Promises: the shaping of American working class consciousness*. New York: McGraw-Hill.

Austin, John 1832/1954: *The Province of Jurisprudence Determined*. New York: Noonday Press; first published in 1832.

Bachofen, Johann Jakob 1861/1948: *Das Mutterrecht*. In Meuli, K. (ed.), *Johann Jakob Bachofens gesammelte Werke*, vols 2 and 3. Basel: Schwabe; first published in 1861.

Bachrach, Peter and Baratz, Morton.S. 1970: *Power and Poverty*. New York: Oxford University Press.

Barber, Bernard 1957: *Social Stratification*. New York: Harcourt, Brace.

Barraclough, Solon L. (ed.) 1973: *Agrarian Structure in Latin America*. Lexington, Mass.: Lexington.

Barry, D. D. and Berman, H. J. 1968: The Soviet legal profession. *Harvard Law Review*, 82, 1–42.

Baum, Rainer C. 1981: *The Holocaust and the German Elite: genocide and national suicide in Germany, 1871–1945*. Totowa, N.J.: Rowman and Littlefield.

Baynes, N. H. 1943: The decline of the Roman power in Western Europe: some modern explanations. *Journal of Roman Studies*, 33, 29–35.

Beck, Carl 1963: Bureaucracy and political development in Eastern Europe. In LaPalombara, J. (ed.), *Bureaucracy and Political Development*. Princeton: Princeton University Press, 268–300.

Bell, Daniel 1973: *The Coming of Post-Industrial Society*. New York: Basic Books.

Bellah, Robert N. 1964: Religious evolution. *American Sociological Review*, 29, 358–374.

Ben-David, Joseph 1971: *The Scientist's Role in Society: a comparative study*. Englewood Cliffs, N.J.: Prentice-Hall.

Bendix, Reinhard 1956: *Work and Authority in Industry: ideologies of management in the course of industrialization*. New York: Wiley.

  1960: *Max Weber: an intellectual portrait*. Garden City, N.Y.: Doubleday; 2nd edn. Berkeley: University of California Press, 1977.

Benedict, Ruth 1934: *Patterns of Culture*. Boston: Houghton Mifflin.

Berle, Adolf A., Jr. and Means, Gardiner C. 1932: *The Modern Corporation and Private Property*. New York: Commerce Clearing House.

Berman, Harold J. 1983: *Law and Revolution: the formation of the Western legal tradition*. Cambridge, Mass.: Harvard University Press.

Blauner, Robert 1964: *Alienation and Freedom: the factory worker and his industry*. Chicago: University of Chicago Press.

Bledstein, B. J. 1976: *The Culture of Professionalism*. New York: Norton.

Bott, Elizabeth 1957: *Family and Social Network: roles, norms, and external relationships in ordinary urban families*. New York: Free Press.

Bourdieu, Pierre 1976: Le champ scientifique. *Les Actes de la Recherche Scientifique en Sciences Sociales*, 3, 88–104.

Braverman, Harry 1974: *Labor and Monopoly Capital: the degradation of work in the twentieth century*. New York: Monthly Review Press.

Brenner, Robert 1976: Agrarian class structure and economic development in pre-industrial Europe. *Past and Present*, 70, 30–75.

  1977: The origins of capitalist development: a critique of neo-Smithian Marxism. *New Left Review*, no. 107, 25–92.

Bucher, Karl 1893/1901: *Industrial Evolution*. New York: Holt; first German publication 1893.

Bucher, R. and Strauss, Anselm L.: Professions in process. *American Journal of Sociology*, 66, 325–34.

Burawoy, Michael 1978: Toward a Marxist theory of the labor process: Braverman and beyond. *Politics and Society*, 8, 247–312.

  1979: *Manufacturing Consent: changes in the labor process under monopoly capitalism*. Chicago: University of Chicago Press.

  1981: Terrains of contest: factory and state under capitalism and socialism. *Socialist Review*, 11, 83–124.

Burin, Frederic S. 1952: Bureaucracy and National Socialism: a reconsideration of Weberian theory. In Merton, R. K. et al. (eds), *Reader in Bureaucracy*. Glencoe, Ill.: Free Press, 33–47.

Camic, Charles 1979. The utilitarians revisited. *American Journal of Sociology*, 85, 516–50.

Cardozo, Fernando H. and Faletto, E. 1979: *Dependency and Development in Latin America*. Berkeley: University of California Press.

Carlin, Jerome E. 1962: *Lawyers on Their Own: a study of individual practitioners in Chicago*. New Brunswick, N.J.: Rutgers University Press.

1966: *Lawyers' Ethics: a survey of the New York City bar*. New York: Russell Sage.

Carnoy, Martin 1984: *The State and Political Theory*. Princeton: Princeton University Press.

Chandler, Alfred D. Jr. 1962: *Strategy and Structure*. Cambridge, Mass.: MIT Press.

1978: The United States: evolution of enterprise. In: Mathias, P. and Postan, M. M. (eds), *The Industrial Economies: capital, labour, and enterprise*, vol. 7, part 2 of *The Cambridge Economic History of Europe*. Cambridge: Cambridge University Press, 70–133.

Chandler, Alfred D. and Galambos, Louis 1970: The development of large-scale enterprise in modern America. *Journal of Economic History*, 30, 201–17.

Childe, V. Gordon 1953: *Man Makes Himself*. New York: Mentor.

Chinoy, Ely 1955: *Automobile Workers and the American Dream*. New York: Doubleday.

Cochran, Thomas C. 1960: Cultural factors in economic growth. *Journal of Economic History*, 20, 513–30.

Daheim, Hansjuergen 1973: Professionalisierung: Begriff und einige latente Makrofunktionen. In Albrecht, G., Daheim, H. and Sack, F. (eds), *Soziologie: René Koenig zum 65. Geburtstag*. Opladen: Westdeutscher Verlag, 232–49.

Dahrendorf, Ralf 1959: *Class and Class Conflict in Industrial Society*. Stanford, Cal.: Stanford University Press.

Davis, Kingsley and Moore, Wilbert E. 1945: Some principles of stratification. *American Sociological Review*, 10, 242–9.

Derber, Charles 1982: Toward a new theory of professionals as workers: advanced capitalism and postindustrial labor. In Derber, C. (ed.), *Professionals as Workers: mental labor in advanced capitalism*, Boston: C. K. Hall and Co., 193–208.

Deutsch, Karl W. 1961: Social mobilization and political development. *American Political Science Review*, 55, 493–511.

Diamond, Stanley 1971: The rule of law versus the order of custom. In Wolff, R. P. (ed.), *The Rule of Law*. New York: Simon and Schuster, 115–44.

Dingwall, Robert 1983: Introduction. In Dingwall, R. and Lewis, Ph. (eds), *The Sociology of the Professions*, London: Macmillan, 1–13.

Dingwall, Robert and Lewis, Philip (eds) 1983: *The Sociology of the Professions: lawyers, doctors and others*. London: Macmillan.

Dore, Ronald, P. 1973: *British Factory, Japanese Factory: the origins of national diversity in industrial relations.* Berkeley: University of California Press.

Dray, W. H. 1967: Philosophy of history. In Edwards, P. (ed.), *Encyclopedia of Philosophy,* New York: Macmillan and Free Press, vol. 6, 247–54.

Durkheim, Emile 1893/1964: *The Division of Labor.* New York: Free Press; first French publication 1893.

Edwards, Richard 1979: *Contested Terrain: the transformation of the workplace in the twentieth century.* New York: Basic Books/Harper Torch Books.

Eisenstadt, S. N. 1963: *The Political System of Empires.* New York: Free Press.

    1964a: Institutionalization and change. *American Sociological Review,* 29, 235–47.

.   1964b: Social change, differentiation and evolution. *American Sociological Review,* 29, 375–86.

    1968: Introduction. In Eisenstadt, S. N. (ed.), *Max Weber on Charisma and Institution-Building.* Chicago: University of Chicago Press, v–lvi.

Elster, Jon 1982: Marxism, functionalism and game theory. *Theory and Society,* 11, 453–82.

    1983: *Explaining Technical Change: a case study in the philosophy of science,* Cambridge and New York: Cambridge University Press.

    1985: *Making Sense of Marx.* Cambridge and New York: Cambridge University Press.

Engels, Frederick 1884/1972: *Origin of the Family, private property and the state.* New York: International Publishers; first German publication 1884.

Eusden, J. D. 1958: *Puritans, Lawyers and Politics in Early Seventeenth Century England.* New Haven: Yale University Press.

Evans, Peter B. 1975: Multiple hierarchies and organizational control. *Administrative Science Quarterly,* 20, 250–8.

Evans, Peter, Dietrich Rueschemeyer and Theda Scopol (eds) 1985: *Bringing the State Back In.* New York and Cambridge: Cambridge University Press.

Fainsod, Merle 1963: Bureaucracy and modernization: the Russian and Soviet case. In Lapalombara, J. (ed.), *Bureaucracy and Political Development.* Princeton: Princeton University Press, 233–67.

Feder, Ernest 1971: *The Rape of the Peasantry: Latin America's landholding system.* Garden City, N.J.: Anchor.

Fohlen, Claude 1978: Entrepreneurship and management in France in the nineteenth century. In Mathias, P. and Postan, M. M. (eds), *The Industrial Economies: capital, labour, and enterprise,* vol. 7, part 1 of *The Cambridge Economic History of Europe.* Cambridge: Cambridge University Press.

Fox, Alan 1974: *Beyond Contract: work, power and trust relations.* London: Faber and Faber.

Frank, Andre G. 1969: *Latin America: underdevelopment or revolution?* New York: Monthly Review Press.

Freidson, Eliot 1970a: *Profession of Medicine: a study of the sociology of applied knowledge.* New York: Dodd, Mead and Co.

1970b: *Professional Dominance: the structure of medical care.* Chicago: Aldine-Atherton.

1977: The futures of professionalization. In Stacey, M., Reid, M. E., Dingwall, R. and Heath, C. (eds), *Health and the Division of Labour.* London: Croom Helm, 14–38.

1983: The theory of the professions: state of the art. In Dingwall, R. and Lewis, P. (eds), *The Sociology of the Professions*, London: Macmillan, 19–37.

Friedman, Andrew L. 1977: *Industry and Labour: class struggle at work and monopoly capitalism.* London: Macmillan.

Friedmann, Georges 1961: *The Anatomy of Work.* New York: Free Press.

Fuller, Lon L. 1969: *The Morality of Law.* Rev. edn. New Haven: Yale University Press.

1971: Human interaction and the law. In Wolff, R. P. (ed.), *The Rule of Law*, New York: Simon and Schuster, 171–217.

Gallie, W. B. 1955–56: Essentially contested concepts. *Proceedings of the Aristotelian Society*, 56, 167–98.

Garnsey, Elizabeth 1981: The rediscovery of the division of labor. *Theory and Society*, 10, 337–58.

Garson, Barbara 1975: *All the Livelong Day.* New York: Doubleday.

Giddens, Anthony 1976: *New Rules of Sociological Method.* London: Hutchinson.

1979: *Central Problems in Social Theory.* London: Macmillan.

1981: *A Contemporary Critique of Historical Materialism.* London: Macmillan.

1984: *The Constitution of Society.* Cambridge: Polity Press.

Ginzberg, Eli 1983: Allied health resources. In Mechanic, D. (ed.), *Handbook of Health, Health Care, and the Health Professions*, New York: Free Press, 479–94.

Gold, David A., Lo, Clarence Y. H. and Wright, Erik Olin 1975: Recent developments in Marxist theories of the capitalist state. *Monthly Review*, 27, 29–43.

Goode, William J. 1957: Community within a community: the professions. *American Sociological Review*, 22, 194–200.

1967: The protection of the inept. *American Sociological Review*, 32, 5–19.

1969: The theoretical limits of professionalization. In Etzioni, A. (ed.), *The Semi-Professions and Their Organization*, New York: Free Press, 266–313.

Goode, William J., Merton, Robert K. and Huntington, M. J. 1956: *The Professions in Modern Society.* New York: Russel Sage Foundation (mimeo).

Gordon, David M., Edwards, Richard and Reich, Michael 1982: *Segmented Work, Divided Workers: the historical transformation of labor in the United States*. Cambridge and New York: Cambridge University Press.

Gottfried, Robert S. 1983: *The Black Death: natural and human disaster in medieval Europe*. New York: Free Press,

Greenwood, Ernest 1957: Attributes of a profession. *Social Work*, 2, 44–55.

Gumplowicz, Ludwig 1885/1963: *Outlines of Sociology*. New York: Paine-Whitman; first German publication 1885.

Habermas, Jürgen 1976: *Communication and the Evolution of Society*. Boston: Beacon Press.

  1981: *Theorie des kommunikativen Handelns*, 2 vols. Frankfurt: Suhrkamp; English translation of vol. 1: *The Theory of Communicative Action: reason and the rationalization of society*. Boston: Beacon Press, 1984.

Haug, Marie 1975: The deprofessionalization of everyone? *Sociological Focus*, 8, 197–213.

Heinz, John P. and Laumann, Edward O. 1982: *Chicago Laywers: the social structure of the bar*. New York and Chicago: Russell Sage Foundation and American Bar Foundation.

Held, David et al. (eds) 1983: *States and Societies*. Oxford: Basil Blackwell; New York: New York University Press.

Hill, Stephen 1981: *Competition and Control at Work*. London: Heinemann.

Hirschman, Albert O. 1945: *National Power and the Structure of Foreign Trade*. Berkeley: University of California Press.

  1978: Beyond asymmetry: critical notes on myself as a young man and on some other old friends. *International Organization*, 32, 45–50.

Horwitz, Morton J. 1977: *The Transformation of American Law, 1780–1860*. Cambridge, Mass.: Harvard University Press.

Huntington, Samuel P. 1968: *Political Order in Changing Societies*. New Haven: Yale University Press.

Jessop, Bob 1982: *The Capitalist State: Marxist theories and methods*. Oxford: Martin Robertson.

Johnson, Terence J. 1972: *Professions and Power*. London: Macmillan.

  1977: The professions in the class structure. In Scase, R. (ed.), *Industrial Society: class, cleavage and control*. London: Allen and Unwin, 93–110.

Johnstone, Quintin and Hopson, D. Jr. 1967: *Lawyers and their Work: an analysis of the legal profession in the United States and in England*. Indianapolis: Bobbs-Merrill.

Jones, A. H. M. 1955: The decline and fall of the Roman Empire. *History*. 40, 209–26.

  1964: *The Later Roman Empire*. Oxford: Basil Blackwell.

Kaelble, Hartmut 1978: Soziale Mobilitaet in Deutschland, 1900–1960. In Kaelble, H. et al. (eds), *Probleme der Modernisierung in Deutschland*. Opladen: Westdeutscher Verlag, 235–327.

Kocka, Jürgen 1969: *Unvernehmensverwaltung und Angestelltenschaft am Beispiel Siemens, 1844–1914: Zum Verhaeltnis von Kapitalismus und Buerokratie in der deutschen Industrialisierung*. Stuttgart: Klett.

— 1971: Family and bureaucracy in German industrial management, 1850–1914. *Business History Review*, 45, 133–54.

— 1978: Entrepreneurs and managers in German industrialization. In Mathias, P. and Postan, M. M. (eds), *The Industrial Economies: capital, labour, and enterprise*, vol. 7, part 1 of *The Cambridge Economic History of Europe*. Cambridge: Cambridge University Press, 492–589.

— 1980: *White Collar Workers in America 1890–1940: a social-political history in international perspective*. London and Beverly Hills: Sage Publications.

Kornhauser, Arthur 1965: *Mental Health of the Industrial Worker*. New York: Wiley.

Kuhn, Thomas S. 1970: *The Structure of Scientific Revolutions*, 2nd edn. Chicago: Chicago University Press.

Ladinsky, J. 1963: Careers of lawyers, law practice, and legal institutions. *American Sociological Review*, 28, 47–54.

Lall, Sanjaya 1975: Is 'dependence' a useful concept in analysing underdevelopment? *World Development*, 3, 799–810.

Landes, David S. 1949: French entrepreneurship and industrial growth in the nineteenth century. *Journal of Economic History*, 9, 45–61.

— 1951: French business and the businessman: a social and cultural analysis. In Earle, E. M. (ed.), *Modern France*. Princeton: Princeton University Press, 334–53.

Larson, Magali Sarfatti 1977: *The Rise of Professionalism: a sociological analysis*. Berkeley: University of California Press.

— 1980: Proletarianization and educated labor. *Theory and Society*, 9, 131–75.

Layton, Edwin 1971: *The Revolt of the Engineers*. Cleveland: Press of Case Western Reserve University.

Leis, Nancy B. 1974: Women in groups: Ijaw women's associations. In Rosaldo, M. Z. and Lamphere, L. (eds), *Woman, Culture and Society*. Stanford: Stanford University Press, 223–42.

Lenin, V. I. 1917/74: *State and Revolution*. New York: International Publishers.

Lenski, Gerhard E. 1966: *Power and Privilege*. New York: McGraw-Hill.

Lenski, Gerhard and Lenski, Jean 1974: *Human Societies: an introduction to macrosociology*. New York: McGraw-Hill.

Lijphart, Arend 1968: *The Politics of Accommodation: pluralism and democracy in the Netherlands*. Berkeley: University of California Press.

Lindsay, A. D. 1932: Individualism. In Seligman, E. R. A. and Johnson, A. (eds), *Encyclopaedia of the Social Sciences*, New York: Macmillan, vol. 7, 674–80.

Littler, Craig R. and Salaman, Graeme 1982: Bravermania and beyond: recent theories of the labour process. *Sociology*, 16, 251–69.

Luhmann, Niklas 1979: *Trust and Power*. New York: Wiley.

—— 1982: *The Differentiation of Society*. New York: Columbia University Press.

Lukes, Steven 1967: Alienation and anomie. In Laslett, Peter and Runciman W. G. (eds), *Philosophy, Politics and Society*, 3rd series. Oxford: Basil Blackwell, 134–56.

—— 1973: *Individualism*. New York: Harper and Row.

—— 1974: *Power: a radical view*. London: Macmillan.

Maine, Henry Sumner 1861/1931: *Ancient Law*. Oxford: Oxford University Press; first published in 1861.

Mann, Michael 1973: *Consciousness and Action among the Western Working Class*. London: Macmillan.

Marglin, Stephen A. 1974: What do bosses do? The origins and functions of hierarchy in capitalist production. *Review of Radical Political Economics*, Summer. Quoted here from the reprint in Gorz, A. (ed.), 1978. *The Division of Labour*. Hassocks, Sussex: Harvester Press, 13–54.

Marris, Robin and Mueller, Dennis C. 1981: The corporation, competition, and the invisible hand. *Journal of Economic Literature*, 18, 32–63.

Marsh, Robert M. and Mannari, Hiroshi 1976: *Modernization and the Japanese Factory*. Princeton: Princeton University Press.

Marshall, Alfred 1890/1961: *Principles of Economics*, 2 vols. New York and London: Macmillan; first published 1890.

Marshall, T. H. 1950: *Citizenship and Social Class, and Other Essays*. Cambridge: Cambridge University Press.

Marx, Karl 1843/1964: On the Jewish question. In Marx, Karl, *Early Writings* (ed. by T. B. Bottomore). New York: McGraw-Hill; first published in 1843.

—— 1844/1964: Economic philosophical manuscripts. In Marx, Karl, *Early Writings* (ed. by T. B. Bottomore). New York: McGraw-Hill.

—— 1847/n.d.: *The Poverty of Philosophy*. New York: International Publishers; first published in 1847.

—— 1857/1971: *The Grundrisse* (ed. by David McLellan). New York: Harper and Row.

—— 1867/1959: *Capital*, vol. I. Moscow: Foreign Languages Publishing House; first published 1867.

Marx, Karl and Engels, Frederick 1845–6/1978: The German ideology, part 1. In Tucker, R. C. (ed.), *The Marx–Engels Reader*, 2nd edn. New York: Norton, 146–200; written in 1845–6; first published in Moscow in 1932.

Matsushima, Shizuo 1966: Labour–management relations in Japan. In Halmos, P. (ed.), *Japanese Social Studies, Sociological Review*, monograph 10, 69–81.

Maurice, Marc, François Sellier and Jean-Jacques Silvestre 1979: La production de la hiérarchie dans l'entreprise: recherche d'une effet sociétal. *Revue Française de Sociologie*, 20, 331–80.

Mayo, Elton 1945: *The Social Problems of an Industrial Civilization*. Boston, Mass.: Division of Research, Graduate School of Business Administration, Harvard University.

McKinlay, John B. 1982: Toward the proletarianization of physicians. In Derber, C. (ed.), *Professionals as Workers: mental labor in advanced capitalism*. Boston: G. K. Hall and Co., 37–62.

Mechanic, David 1983: Physicians. In Mechanic, D. (ed.), *Handbook of Health, Health Care, and the Health Professions*. New York: Free Press, 479–94.

Meek, Ronald L. 1977: *Smith, Marx and After: ten essays in the development of economic thought*. London: Chapman and Hall.

Merton, Robert K. 1960: *Some Thoughts on the Professions in American Society*. Providence: Brown University Papers, 37.

Michels, Robert 1908/49: *Political Parties*. Glencoe, Ill.: Free Press; first German publication 1908.

Montgomery, David 1979: *Worker's Control in America: studies in the history of work*. Cambridge and New York: Cambridge University Press.

Moore, Wilbert E. 1968: Social change. In Sills, D. L. (ed.), *International Encyclopedia of the Social Sciences*, vol. 14. New York: Macmillan and Free Press.

Morgan, Lewis Henry 1877: *Ancient Society*. New York: Holt.

Myrdal, Gunnar 1930/61: *The Political Element in the Development of Economic Theory*. Cambridge, Mass.: Harvard University Press; first Swedish publication 1930.

Nordlinger, Eric A. 1981: *On the Autonomy of the Democratic State*. Cambridge, Mass.: Harvard University Press.

North, Douglass C. 1979: A framework for analyzing the state in economic history. *Explorations in Economic History*, 16, 249–59.

O'Brien, Philip J. 1975: A critique of Latin American theories of dependency. In Oxaal, I., Barnett, T. and Booth, D. (eds), *Beyond the Sociology of Development*. London: Routledge and Kegan Paul.

OECD 1968: *Reviews of National Science Policy, United States*. Paris: OECD.

Olson, Mancur 1965: *The Logic of Collective Action: public goods and the theory of groups*. Cambridge, Mass.: Harvard University Press.

Oppenheimer, Martin 1973: The proletarianization of the professional. In Halmos, P (ed.), *Professionalization and Social Change. Sociological Review*, monograph 20.

Palma, Gabriel 1978: Dependency: a formal theory of underdevelopment or a method for the analysis of concrete situations of underdevelopment? *World Development*, 6, 881–924.

Palmer, Bryan 1975: Class, conception and conflict: the thrust for efficiency, managerial views of labor and the working class rebellion, 1903–1922. *Review of Radical Political Economics*, 7, 31–49.

Parsons, Talcott 1937: *The Structure of Social Action*. New York: McGraw-Hill.

1939: The professions and social structure. *Social Forces*, 17, 457–67.

1940: An analytical approach to the theory of stratification. *American Journal of Sociology*, 45, 841–62.

1947: Introduction. In Weber, Max, *The Theory of Social and Economic Organization*. New York: Oxford University Press, 1–86.

1951: *The Social System*. Glencoe, Ill.: Free Press.

1953: A revised analytical approach to the theory of social stratification. In Bendix, R. and Lipset, S. M. (eds), *Class, Status, and Power*. Glencoe, Ill.: Free Press, 92–128.

1963: On the concept of political power. *Proceedings of the American Philosophical Society*, 107; reprinted in Bendix, R. and Lipset, S. M. (eds), *Class, Status, and Power*, 2nd edn. New York: Free Press 1966, 240–65.

1964: Evolutionary universals in society. *American Sociological Review*, 29, 339–57.

1966: *Societies: evolutionary and comparative perspectives*. Englewood Cliffs, N.J.: Prentice-Hall.

1968: Professions. In Sills, D. (ed.), *International Encyclopedia of the Social Sciences*, vol. 12. New York: Macmillan and Free Press, 536–47.

1969: *Politics and Social Structure*. New York: Free Press.

1971: *The System of Modern Societies*. Englewood Cliffs, N.J.: Prentice-Hall.

1978: The university 'bundle': a study of the balance between differentiation and integration. In Parsons, Talcott, *Action Theory and the Human Condition*. New York: Free Press.

Patterson, Orlando 1982: *Slavery and Social Death: a comparative study*. Cambridge, Mass.: Harvard University Press.

Payne, Peter, L. 1978: Industrial entrepreneurship and management in Great Britain. In Mathias, P. and Postan, M. M. (eds), *The Industrial Economies: capital, labour and interprise*, vol. 7, part 1 of *The Cambridge Economic History of Europe*. Cambridge: Cambridge University Press, 180–230.

Poggi, Gianfranco 1978: *The Development of the Modern State: a sociological introduction*. Stanford: Stanford University Press.

Polanyi, Karl 1944/57: *The Great Transformation*. Boston: Beacon Press; first published in 1944.

Pollard, Sidney 1965: *The Genesis of Modern Management: a study of the industrial revolution in Great Britain*. London: E. Arnold, and Cambridge, Mass.: Harvard University Press.

1978: Labour in Britain. In Mathias, P. and Postan, M. M. (eds), *The Industrial Economies: capital, labour, and enterprise*, vol. 7, part 1 of *The Cambridge Economic History of Europe*. Cambridge: Cambridge University Press, 97–179.

Portwood, Derek and Fielding, Alan 1981: Privilege and the professions. *Sociological Review*, 29, 749–73.

Pound, Roscoe 1953: *The Lawyer from Antiquity to Modern Times*. St Paul, Minn.: West Publishing Co.

Rawls, John 1971: *A Theory of Justice*. Cambridge, Mass.: Harvard University Press.

Reader, W. J. 1966: *Professional Men: the rise of the professional classes in nineteenth century England*. London: Weidenfeld & Nicolson.

Rosaldo, Michelle Zimbalist 1974: Woman, culture and society: a theoretical overview. In Zimbalist, M. Z. and Lamphere, L. (eds), *Woman, Culture, and Society*. Stanford: Stanford University Press, 17–42.

Rosaldo, Michelle Zimbalist and Lamphere, Louise (eds) 1974: *Woman, Culture, and Society*. Stanford: Stanford University Press.

Rosenberg, Hans 1958: *Bureaucracy, Aristocracy and Autocracy*. Cambridge, Mass.: Harvard University Press.

Roth, Guenther H. 1963: *The Social Democrats of Imperial Germany*. Totowa, N.J.: Bedminster.

Rueschemeyer, Dietrich 1964: Doctors and laywers: a comment on the theory of the professions. *Canadian Review of Sociology and Anthropology*, 1, 17–30.

1969: Partielle Modernisierung. In Zapf, W. (ed.), *Theorien des sozialen Wandels*, Koeln: Kiepenheuer and Witsch, 382–396; expanded English version in Loubser, J. J. et al. (eds), 1976: *Explorations in General Theory in the Social Sciences: essays in honor of Talcott Parsons*. New York: Free Press, 756–772.

1973: *Lawyers and Their Society: a comparative study of the legal profession in Germany and in the United States*. Cambridge, Mass.: Harvard University Press.

1974: Reflections on structural differentiation. *Zeitschrift fuer Soziologie*, 83, 1–25.

1977: Structural differentiation, efficiency, and power. *American Journal of Sociology*, 83, 1–25.

1978: The legal profession in comparative perspective. In Johnson, H. M. (ed.), *The Social system and Legal Process*. San Francisco: Jossey Bass, 97–127.

1982: On Durkheim's explanation of division of labor. *American Journal of Sociology*, 88, 579–89.

1983: Professional autonomy and the social control of experts. In

Dingwall, R. and Lewis, P. (eds), *The Sociology of the Professions*. London: Macmillan, 38–58.

1985: Spencer and Durkheim über Arbeitsteilung und Differenzierung: Kontinuität oder Bruch? In Luhmann, N. (ed.), *Soziale Differenzierung: Zur Geschichte einer Idee*. Opladen: Westdeutscher Verlag, 163–80.

Rueschemeyer, Marilyn 1982: The work collective: response and adaptation in the structure of work in the German Democratic Republic. *Dialectical Anthropology*, 7, 155–63.

Rueschemeyer, Marilyn and Scharf, Bradley forthcoming: Labor unions in the German Democratic Republic. In Pravda, A. and Ruble, B. (eds), *Trade Unions in Communist States*. London and Boston: Allen and Unwin.

Runciman, W. G. 1983: *A Treatise on Social Theory*, vol. 1: *The Methodology of Social Theory*. Cambridge: Cambridge University Press.

Sabel, Charles F. 1982: *Work and Politics: the division of labor in industry*. Cambridge: Cambridge University Press.

Sabel, Charles F. and Stark, David 1982: Planning, politics, and shop floor power: hidden forms of bargaining in Soviet-imposed state-socialist societies. *Politics and Society*, 11, 439–75.

Sacks, Karen 1974: Engels revisited: women, the organization of production, and private property. In Rosaldo, M. Z. and Lamphere, L. (eds), *Woman, Culture and Society*. Stanford: Stanford University Press, 207–22.

Sanday, Peggy Reeves 1973: Toward a theory of the status of women. *American Anthropologist*, 75, 1682–1700.

1974: Female status in the public domain. In Rosaldo, M. Z. and Lamphere, L. (eds), *Woman, Culture, and Society*. Stanford: Stanford University Press, 189–206.

1981: *Female Power and Male Dominance: on the origins of sexual inequality*. Cambridge and New York: Cambridge University Press.

Sawyer, John E. 1951: Strains in the social structure of modern France. In Earle, E. M. (ed.), *Modern France*. Princeton: Princeton University Press, 293–312.

Schattschneider, E. E. 1960: *The Semi-Sovereign People: a realist's view of democracy in America*. New York: Holt, Rinehart and Winston.

Schwarz, O. 1869: Die Betriebsformen der modernen Grossindustrie. *Zeitschrift fuer die gesamte Staatswissenschaft*, 25, 595.

Shils, Edward A. 1965: Charisma, order and status. *American Sociological Review*, 30, 199–213.

Silberman, Bernard 1982: State bureaucratization: a comparative analysis. Manuscript. Chicago: Department of Political Science, University of Chicago.

Shryock, Richard Harrison 1948–9: American indifference to basic science during the nineteenth century. *Archives Internationales d'Histoire des Sciences*, no. 28, 3–18; reprinted in Barber, B. and Wirsch, W. (eds), 1962: *The Sociology of Science*. New York: Free Press, 98–110.

Simmel, Georg 1908/50: *The Sociology of Georg Simmel*, (ed. by Kurt Wolff). Glencoe, Ill.: Free Press; relevant sections appeared first in *Soziologie: Untersuchungen über die Formen der Vergesellschaftung*. Leipzig: Duncker and Humblot, 1908.

　　1890: *Ueber soziale Differenzierung: Soziologische und psychologische Untersuchungen*. Leipzig: Duncker and Humblot.

Simon, Herbert A. 1962: The architecture of complexity. *Proceedings of the American Philosophical Society*, 106, 467–82.

Smelser, Neil J. 1959: *Social Change in the Industrial Revolution*. Chicago: University of Chicago Press.

　　1963: Mechanisms of change and adjustments to change. In Hoselitz, B. F. and Moore, W. E. (eds), *Industrialization and Society*. The Hague: UNESCO and Mouton, 32–54.

Smigel, Erwin O. 1964: *The Wall Street Lawyer*. New York: Free Press.

Smith, Adam 1776/1937: *An Inquiry into the Nature and Causes of the Wealth of Nations* (Cannan edition). New York: Random House Modern Library.

Smith, Michael R. 1972: Modernization and bureaucratic rationality: the Prussian case. Unpubl. Master's thesis, Brown University.

Sorokin, Pitirim A. 1933: The principle of limits applied to problems of causal or functional relationship between societal variables and of the direction of social processes. In *Social Process*. Papers presented at the 26th Annual Meeting of the American Sociological Society. Chicago: American Sociological Society.

Spencer, Herbert 1876–97/1975: *The Principles of Sociology*, 3 vols. Westport, Conn.: Greenwood Press; first published 1876–97.

Stacey, Margaret 1981: The division of labour revisited, or overcoming the two Adams. In Abrams, P., Deem, R., Finch, J. and Rock, P. (eds), *Practice and Progress: British sociology 1950–1980*, London: Allen and Unwin, 172–90.

Stark, David 1980: Class struggle and the transformation of the labor process: a relational approach. *Theory and Society*, 9, 89–130.

Stepan, Alfred 1973: The new professionalism of internal warfare and military role expansion. In Stepan, A (ed.), *Authoritarian Brazil: origins, policies and future*. New Haven: Yale University Press.

　　1978: *The State and Society: Peru in comparative perspective*. Princeton: Princeton University Press.

Stephens, Evelyne Huber and Stephens, John D. 1982: The labor movement, political power, and workers' participation in Western Europe. *Political Power and Social Theory*, 3, 215–49.

Stephens, John D. 1979: *The Transition from Capitalism to Socialism*. London: Macmillan.

Stevens, Rosemary 1966: *Medical practice in Modern England: the impact of specialization and state medicine*. New Haven and London: Yale University Press.

1971: *American Medicine and the Public Interest*. New Haven and London: Yale University Press.

1983: Comparisons in health care: Britain as contrast to the United States. In Mechanic, D. (ed.), *Handbook of Health, Health Care, and the Health Professions*. New York: Free Press, 281–304.

Stigler, George J. 1951: The division of labor is limited by the extent of the market. *Journal of Political Economy*, 59, 185–93.

Stinchcombe, Arthur L. 1965: Social structure and organizations. In March, J. (ed.), *Handbook of Organizations*. Chicago: Rand McNally, 142–93.

1968: *Constructing Social Theories*. New York: Harcourt, Brace and World.

Stone, Deborah A. 1980: *The Limits of Professional Power: national health care in the Federal Republic of Germany*. Chicago: University of Chicago Press.

Taylor, Frederick W. 1911: *The Principles of Scientific Management*. New York: Harper.

Thompson, E. P. 1963: *The Making of the English Working Class*. London: Gollancz.

Tilly, Charles 1970: Clio and Minerva. In McKinney, J. C. and Tiryakian, E. A. (eds), *Theoretical Sociology: perspectives and developments*. New York: Appleton-Century-Crofts, 433–66.

1981: Flows of capital and forms of industry in Europe, 1500–1900. Working paper 237 of the Center for Research on Social Organization, University of Michigan.

Tiryakian, Edward A. 1983: On the theoretical significance of dedifferentiation. Unpublished manuscript, Duke University.

Tocqueville, Alexis de (1835–40/1966); *Democracy in America*, 3 vols. New Rochelle, N.Y.: Arlington House; first French publication in 1835 and 1840.

Treiman, Donald J. 1977: *Occupational Prestige in Comparative Perspective*. New York: Academic Press.

Veblen, Thorstein 1899/1934: *The Theory of the Leisure Class*. New York: Modern Library; first published in 1899.

Wagner, Albrecht 1936: *Der Kampf der Justiz gegen die Verwaltung in Preussen*. Hamburg: Hanseatische Verlagsanstalt.

Walker, Charles R. and Guest, Robert H. 1952: *The Man on the Assembly Line*. Cambridge. Mass.: Harvard University Press.

Wallerstein, Immanuel, 1974a. *The Modern World System: capitalist agriculture and the origins of the European world-economy in the sixteenth century*. New York: Academic Press.

 1974b: The rise and future demise of the world capitalist system: concepts for comparative analysis. *Comparative Studies in Society and History*, 16, 389–415.

 1980: *The Modern World System: mercantilism and the consolidation of the European world-economy, 1600–1750*. New York: Academic Press.

Weber, Max 1919/58: Politics as a vocation. In Gerth, H. H. and Mills, C. W. M. (eds), *From Max Weber: essays in sociology*. New York and Oxford University Press, Galaxy Books, 77–128.

 1922/68: *Economy and Society*, 2 vols. New York: Bedminster Press; second printing Berkeley: University of California Press, 1978; translation of *Wirtschaft und Gesellschaft*, 4th edn. Tübingen: J. C. B. Mohr (Paul Siebeck), 1956; first published 1922.

Weir, Margaret and Skocpol, Theda 1985: State structures and the possibilities for 'Keynesian' responses to the Great Depression in Sweden, Britain, and the United States. In Evans, P., Rueschemeyer, D. and Skocpol, T. (eds), *Bringing the State Back In*. New York and Cambridge: Cambridge University Press.

Williamson, Oliver E. 1981: The modern corporation: origins, evolution, attributes. *Journal of Economic Literature*, 19, 1537–68.

Work in America 1973, Report of a Special Task Force to the Secretary of Health, Education and Welfare. Cambridge, Mass.: MIT Press.

World Bank 1979, 1980 and 1981: *World Development Report*. New York: Oxford University Press.

Wright, Eric O. 1978: *Class, Crisis, and the State*. London: New Left Books.

Young, Allyn A. 1928: Increasing returns and economic progress. *Economic Journal*, 38, 527–42.

Zeitlin, Maurice 1974: Corporate ownership and control: the large corporations and the capitalist class. *American Journal of Sociology*, 79, 1073–119.

Zimbalist, Andrew (ed.) 1979: *Case Studies on the Labor Process*. New York: Monthly Review Press.

Index

adaptive capacity, *see* efficiency
agglomeration of functions, 3,
    161
    see also dedifferentiation
alienation, 16, 21–30, 52, 157
aristocratization, 146–7, 148
assembly line, 28, 79–80
associations
    of men and women, 175
    in modern societies, 34
    of professions, 111, 119, 121
    see also collective organization;
    unions
autarky, 211n3
authority
    division of, 54–70
    imposition of, 20
    and professions, 106–7
    specialized roles of, 18
    undermining of, 68, 145–6,
        157, 159
    see also domination, organized
autonomy, 26, 196
    bureaucracy, 63–4, 64–6, 94
    of craftsmen, 71, 81, 90
    and individualism, 154–7
    of knowledge, 105–6, 117
    of organizations, 135, 160, 162
    of professions, 109–10,
        114–17, 120–3, 126, 127,
        130–1, 132, 135, 139

of specialized positions, 68
of the state, 93, 103
of workers, 28
see also discretion

bargaining power
    of professions, 106–7
    of workers and employers, 10,
        95, 96, 100
    see also collective organization;
        market position
Bellah, Robert, 154
Ben-David, Joseph, 113, 220n9
Bendix, Reinhard, 26–7
Benedict, Ruth, 174
Bentham, Jeremy, 177
Berman, Harold J., 106
blockages of differentiation, 13,
    52, 56–7, 141
    see also stagnation;
        dedifferentiation
Braverman, Harry, 80, 88, 92
Brazil, 159
breakthrough
    in bureaucratization, 55, 60,
        64, 67–8
    in evolution, 42–3
Brenner, Robert, 8, 188
Britain
    Health policy, 129–30, 221n17
    large enterprises, 61